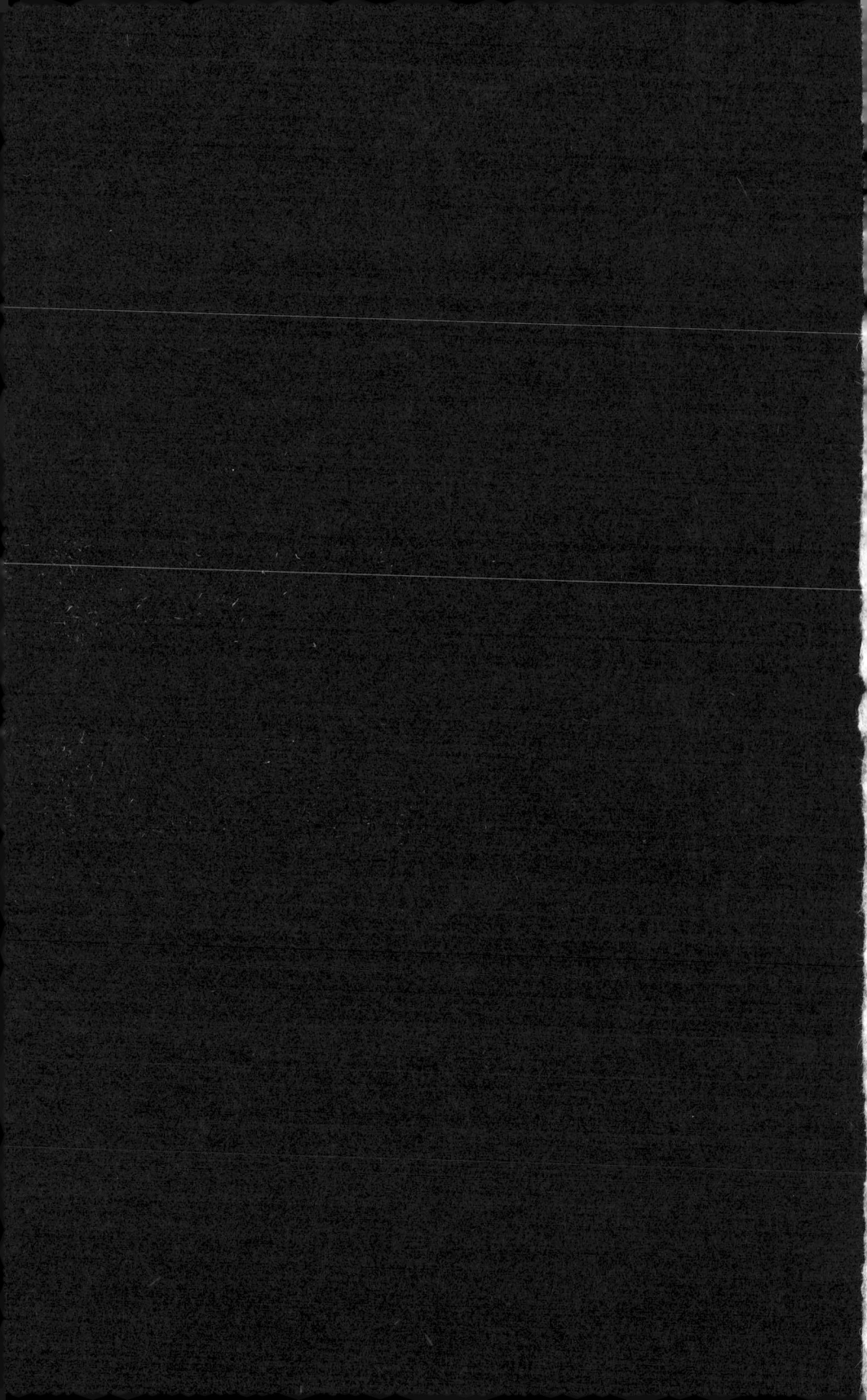

JUDAISM ONLINE

JUDAISM ONLINE

CONFRONTING SPIRITUALITY
ON THE INTERNET

SUSAN M. ZAKAR
DOVID Y. B. KAUFMANN

𝒥𝒜

JASON ARONSON INC.
NORTHVALE, NEW JERSEY
JERUSALEM

This book was set in 11 pt. Times Roman by Alpha Graphics of Pittsfield, New Hampshire, and printed and bound by Book-mart Press, Inc. of North Bergen, New Jersey.

10 9 8 7 6 5 4 3 2 1

Library of Congress Cataloging-in-Publication Data

Zakar, Susan M.
    Judaism online : confronting spirituality on the Internet / by
Susan M. Zakar and Dovid Y. B. Kaufmann.
        p.   cm.
    ISBN 0-7657-9984-7
    1. Proselytes and proselyting, Jewish—Converts from Christianity—
Biography.   2. Jewish way of life.   I. Kaufmann, Dovid Y. B.,
1951–   .   II. Title.
BM729.P7K34   1998
296.7'14'092
[B]—DC21   97–25747

Manufactured in the United States of America. Jason Aronson Inc. offers books and cassettes. For information and catalog write to Jason Aronson Inc., 230 Livingston Street, Northvale, New Jersey 07647.

The journey to find Truth is seldom accomplished alone.
With much love I dedicate this book to my husband, Joe,
whose love and support paved the road before me;
and to my children, David and Julie,
who have traveled it together with me.
— S.Z.

To my family
— D.K.

Contents

Acknowledgments

I would like to express a very special thank you to my husband, Joe, and my children, David and Julie, for all their love, support and patience during the many months it took to bring this book to light; to my teacher, rabbi, and friend, Binyomin Field, for spending many tireless hours teaching me what it means to be *truly* Jewish, by word and personal example, and for encouraging me to write about my journey; and finally, to David Kaufmann—my mentor, friend, motivator, and co-author— who has so often helped me to find within Torah the answer to life's questions.

Susan Zakar

I would like to thank my family for their support and patience; my friends and colleagues both on and off the Internet for sharpening my thinking and deepending my understanding; and, of course, Sue Zakar, for trusting me as a lamplighter.

David Kaufmann

Both of us would like to thank Arthur Kurzweil, Managing Editor Pamela Roth, Production Editor Kenneth J. Silver, and the rest of the staff of Jason Aronson Inc. for their support, guidance, and faith in this project.

Prologue

DK: Despite the publicity and promotion, the Internet remains a strange phenomenon. It has reinvented epistolary forms of communication; it operates on almost purely democratic principles; it has created the foundation for a global network, the "world village." One can remain completely anonymous on the Internet, which means there are few external controls over scams, fraud, lies, and hate-mongering. One must read—and respond—carefully, critically, and with discrimination, for not everything written makes sense or everything asserted is true. On the other hand, the anonymity also creates an atmosphere of trust, openness, inquiry, and learning. Corresponding on the Internet, whether by e-mail or in a discussion group (called "newsgroups"), is a way of testing ourselves, looking in the mirror of other's ideas and opinions, without the embarrassment of being seen. Not only can we interact with people we've never met and may never meet, but we can also have an influence far beyond our physical environment. The Lubavitcher Rebbe has talked about a Jew being a "lamplighter," going out into the darkness to kindle the spark of Godliness, the connection with Torah and the Jewish people; surely the Internet provides an unprecedented opportunity to do just that—to spread the wellsprings of Judaism.

In the spring of 1993, I was a regular participant in the Jewish discussion group soc.culture.jewish (scj, for short) for a number of months. I had made some friends, gotten into heated debates, and, I hoped, shed some light on issues important to the Jewish community. I approached the discussions as a participant and a teacher; I looked for opportunities to learn something new, to find out what others thought (whether their ideas were correct or valid, I wanted to know the what and why of their thinking). I also looked for opportunities to teach, to help other Jews in their search for truth, which means a life committed to observance of the *mitzvos* (commandments) and study of Torah.

I remember well the message that Sue Zakar posted. You'll read about it later on, so for now I'll simply say that my response probably read like a homework assignment. I answered her question, though many others—some on the same topic—I ignored, leaving them for someone else to answer. As with all else in life, the reason, ultimately, must be attributed to *hashgocha pratis*, Divine Providence. Over the ensuing months, as Sue Zakar recognized and began to deal with a serious problem, she turned to many whom she'd "met" on the Internet. During the last stage of her journey (which began with fundamentalist Christianity and ended with observant Judaism), I was able to answer a few questions and provide some guidance and support.

From the beginning, I thought her story ought to be told, that a book—whether novel, memoir, or something else—had to be written. Urged by her network of friends to share her experiences, to help others who have gone or are now going along the "long shorter path," she asked if I would help give structure to the story, to make a narrative of the plot of her life.

The result you will read. I think this book is unusual for not only what it says, but how it says it: Written by e-mail, it incorporates a number of genres. It's an autobiographical memoir; it's a series of essays on Jewish life and observance; it's a discussion in letters. Naturally, in discussing the changes, experiences, and decisions of a life as "well-traveled" as Sue Zakar's has been, there will be moments of controversy and uneasiness—most especially, perhaps, for the reader who encounters them, at least in this form, for the first time. Throughout, while we have been honest and critical about ideas, lifestyles, and viewpoints, we have also strived to respect individuals. *Ahavas Yisroel*, love for your fellow Jew, includes the idea that the inherent goodness in most people is concealed only by bad philosophies, errors of judgment, or wrong actions.

Most of all, you will read of one person's courageous struggle for truth, for Torah, for the covenant between the Jewish people and God. I invite you to share in this story. Its final joy and triumph foreshadows Isaiah's prophecy regarding the time of *Moshiach* when "the whole world will be filled with knowledge of Godliness as the waters cover the ocean bed."

SZ: Looking back on our lives is like grabbing a handful of sand. A quick glance and we see nothing out of the ordinary, nothing so valuable or worthwhile. But look closely. It is not an undifferentiated mass of dust, but thousands of tiny gems, of every color and shape, tiny jewels, bits of gold. And if God is so concerned with even the smallest grains of sand, then how much more so the days of our lives, each one in its own way a jewel, a gleaming diamond.

So I have been privileged—blessed is a better word—to write this book, to examine, with the help of a trusted friend, all those grains of sand, the events in my life, and to put them in order and perspective, to see the hand of God in the order of things.

As you will discover in the story that follows, David Kaufmann and I met over the Internet when he reached out to offer guidance and support in a particularly difficult period of my life. When I was torn by emotional conflicts, his was a voice of reason in the ether. In many ways, he became a teacher to me as I traveled the last leg of my journey to find truth.

My path had taken me from fundamentalist Christianity to Conservative and Reform Judaism, to long stints of almost ignoring God, to, in the end, observant Judaism. Along the way I kept a journal, recorded odd thoughts, and gathered e-mail. So many grains of sand. I needed to sort them out. It seemed natural to turn to David Kaufmann to do that. We had already been corresponding for almost a year and a half. He knew a lot about my journey. But, most of all, he was consistently and persistently devoted to looking at life through the lens of Torah. Therein, I knew that I too would find truth and meaning.

So we "talked." In reality, our conversation transpired only over e-mail. We never actually met during this time. But in my mind we were in the same room, sitting with a coffee table between us, me telling David about my path through life, showing him pages in my journal and copies of old e-mail. And David would listen; he would question and comment, give me perspective, and sometimes correct my thinking.

Like all conversations, ours took twists and turns, sometimes straying and returning; sometimes eliciting my tears; sometimes unearthing buried emotions and hidden or long-forgotten thoughts.

Deciding to make our conversation public was not easy. It was hard to part with the privacy of my deepest thoughts. Yet I also realized that it was important that they be shared, for the sake of others who are making similar spiritual journeys. I wanted, in whatever way I could, to tell them that they are not alone. I also wanted those who never had to make the journey to understand how very real and important it is.

1
Beginnings and False Starts

DK: You've finally brought closure to your story. It's been a long and, for me, interesting series of events.

SZ: A lot has changed in the over two years we've been corresponding on the Internet. Still, it's hard to make sense of it all. There's a lot about me you still don't know. Things that happened years ago when I was just a kid in school. I don't understand why I ended up on some of the paths I did. I feel rather ashamed for having walked down some of them. At the same time, I sense that I have to come to terms with my past, to learn from it, to give it some meaning. It's an overwhelming task to try to face alone. I know it's a big favor to ask, but. . . .

DK: . . . But can we talk about it? Of course. I've been suggesting that for a while. Besides, I'm very interested in endings, especially happy ones, and to get there you usually have to start at the beginning.

SZ: The beginning seems like a very long time ago. I was raised in a mid-sized town in Washington State. We were a typical American middle-class family with two kids and a dog. My older brother and I attended the local public schools. My parents were wonderful people who stressed values like promptness and honesty and clean living. My father was a self-starter, for the most part self-employed. My mother was a homemaker and kept the books for my father's business. I don't think we lacked for any material thing.

Our family didn't practice any particular religion. We observed the usual gamut of Christian holidays, but in a secular fashion.

As I grew older, I began to think about religion—about God—more and more. There was something magical about it. I think I still saw God as an old man living in some cloudy heaven surrounded by angels, but I thought it must be nice to have some kindly figure "up there" to whom to turn when I needed help.

Maybe it was because of the image I had of God that, as I approached puberty, I began to think I'd made a mistake. I was fascinated by all things scientific—my parents must have spent a fortune buying me all those magnets and optics and experiment kits. I figured that if science had all the answers, we didn't really need God. I lost interest in religion.

I soon realized that science didn't have all the answers, and became anxious over a world that seemed to be crumbling around me. I wondered if there would be a future, or if we'd all be blown away in a nuclear war. As I entered high school, the questions became more intense. I slowly returned to some kind of faith in God; maybe I needed hope, maybe I just wanted to believe in something.

During high school I began to keep a journal of my writing. At first it was just poetry that betrayed the awkwardness of my youthful mind as well as the confusion, hope, and fear that I was beginning to feel:

> See the people in the shadows,
> They walk in the dark,
> They walk in the valley of the shadow of doubt.
> There is no trust here,
> And fear is the master over men.
> Hear the people in the dark,
> Have pity for them.
> Their cries reach no one but Death.
> The people walk in the darkness,
> But their eyes are accustomed to night.
> So they see all the bad and shun all the good,

And they trust nobody but themselves.
See the people in the shadows,
They walk in the dark.
They walk in the valley of the shadow of doubt.
Fear for these people.
They have not seen the light above them,
Which shines like a diamond afire,
And lights the ways of all those,
Who look up without fear of falling.
But the light is high,
And only those with the courage to climb to its horizon,
Are honorable enough to walk in its dawn.
And the light is upon the mountaintop,
And the mountain is called faith.

In many of my poems, I seemed to connect a lack of faith, a lack of connection to God, with evil. It was almost instinctive. I had a vision, but no real way to approach it.

During my last year of high school, I took a comparative philosophies course. We examined religious philosophies from humanism and atheism to Buddhism, Judaism, and various forms of Christianity. At the end of the course we were asked to write a paper describing which philosophy best fit us, and why. I wrote on Judaism. I felt good about a belief in one God. I felt good about a faith that said that what a person *does* is important. I began to try to learn as much about Judaism as I could. Not having the courage to approach a rabbi or anyone else to talk about my feelings, I tried to learn on my own. I remember going to the library and getting a siddur. I memorized the whole *Amidah* in English. (The *Amidah* is the central prayer of the service, said standing and recited to oneself.) I read whatever Jewish books I could get my hands on. I decided that I would convert, but was very shy about approaching a rabbi. I wrote a note exhorting myself to call him. I never did.

I knew, too, that I needed to tell my parents that I wanted to convert. They were not enthusiastic, but they consented to allow me to do so if I agreed to postpone any decision on the matter for one year.

That was the year I went off to college in Bellingham, Washington. I didn't know many people there, save for a Jewish friend named Steve who had arrived a couple of years before. He was active in student government and got me involved in it, too. Steve knew that I was drawn to Judaism, but we didn't talk about it much. He wasn't very religious.

Like many students who leave home for the college campus, I became quite lonely. My family, my loving support system, was no longer there. Suddenly, cosmic questions took on deep import. The lack of religious or spiritual direction became an acute pain.

I spoke of it in my journal:

Fear, despair, loneliness. Acids packaged in a bottle marked "WHY" and dumped undiluted into my empty soul; there to burn and pain, and poison. I would have screamed to the world in my torture, but I was isolated, so I thought, in my misery.

Who could I turn to? I couldn't even understand what I felt. How could anyone else?

I had lost faith in myself. I felt alone, believing that others had the answers that I could not find. A fragment of a poem expressed the pain:

Help me! Help me! Someone please! Show me a firm place to stand, a faith, a belief! Lest I remain forever within this Hell, A God-forsaken, soul-breaking limbo!

I was driven to find some kind of truth, and was ready to walk down any path to find it.

DK: I'll tell you a hasidic story about paths and trails. A traveler, wanting to go to the king's palace, came to a road with two paths heading into a forest. A young boy stood nearby, so the traveler asked which road led to the palace. "They both do," answered the boy. "But which is shorter?" asked the traveler. Pointing to one, the boy said, "This is the short-longer way, and that," pointing to the other, "is the long-shorter way." The traveler decided to take the shorter path—that is, the short-longer way. Indeed, the road seemed easy to travel, smooth and straight. In almost no time, he saw the palace before him. But the road made one last turn and led straight into an impassable barrier of thorns and brambles. Try as he might, the traveler couldn't get through. He had no choice but to go back. The boy was standing there waiting for him. The traveler had no choice but to take the long-shorter way. Naturally, it took a long time to get to the palace, but the road successfully traversed all the rivers, fallen trees, and so on, and led—after a long journey—directly to the palace.

SZ: If the palace is truth, then I think I've lived the story. Like the traveler, I turned to the short-longer way first.

Perhaps it was not even truth that I sought: I was desperate for an answer—almost any answer to my emotional emptiness. I turned toward a friend I'd met in student government, a Christian named Tom.

Tom took my concerns seriously. He asked if my "hang-up" was about God. I admitted that it was. He told me he could give me an answer. I trusted him; after all, he was my friend. He was taking the time to care and listen. Tom explained the fundamental beliefs of Christianity and said I had to accept and believe them, too. I was in no position to protest. If this was the shortest path to the palace, I was ready to run upon it. It felt good to have answers. Judaism was laid aside, a forgotten hope replaced by promises of happiness and salvation.

I began to socialize in Christian circles, becoming more and more deeply involved—first in student groups, then in a local Christian coffeehouse scene, where I encountered "Charismatic Christians." I became a part of it, believing myself to be "born again" and "filled with the spirit." Through the next year of college and during my summers at home, I lived as a very committed fundamentalist Christian. I proselytized on street corners, on campus, and on trips organized by the local church to "spread the Gospel." I went to prayer meetings and church services, and said "Amen!" to many a stirring sermon. My journal began to swell with prayers and praises to my newfound "savior." I accepted the fundamentalists' belief about the only path to heaven and that anything short of that was a sure path to eternal damnation. Yet. . . .

I was reluctant to acknowledge, even to myself, the not-so-occasional misgivings that began to haunt me. In those circles, questions were a sign of doubt—a lack of faith in a belief system where faith was paramount. I had turned to Christianity in search of an answer to my loneliness and emotional distress. As I began to see beyond those emotions, my soul pulled me back toward the Judaism I had cast aside.

There, still reverberating deep inside my soul, were the words of the *Shema* [the declaration that God is One], the knowledge that when all is said and done, one does not equal three. I questioned.

I had blinked. I had let my eyes open for a fraction of a second, and had seen that the path to the palace was blocked by an impenetrable hedge of thorns. I could close my eyes again, but what I had seen was undeniable. I began a long and difficult struggle trying to sort out what was true from what only seemed true; what I believed from what I wanted to believe.

I was confused, crying out to God, acknowledging in some meager way that I was not hearing Him. I needed to find God again—I as an individual, not as part of a group, nor as a voice in a chorus.

Yet I fought it. I tried to be a good Christian. I went to church. I prayed and sang hymns. At one level, I was still "convinced" that Christianity was true—all those Bible studies and sermons and prayer meetings had done a good job. At a deeper level, the *Shema* was churning its message inside me.

The connections I had felt with Judaism were still there. Somehow, as hard as I tried, and prayed for, and worked to convince myself, I could not ultimately reconcile the words of the *Shema* with the Christian concept of Trinity. I found myself questioning, and wondering about the Judaism that I had cast aside.

Emotional and theological issues were all mixed up. I had no skills to deal with theological issues. I didn't know who to turn to, who to talk to. I wanted so badly to find a neutral party; a religious crisis hotline, if you will. I began to sink into serious despair, feeling the conflict like a war:

> How the battle rages,
> Two sides in biting conflict.
> And I a soldier in this war,
> Deafened by the stomping feet
> Which are mine alone.
> Frightened by the agonizing cries
> Which do not escape from me.
> This war is beyond comprehension.
> True, I have every assurance that we shall win
> Peace with honor in the end.
> But now I am worn,
> Torn.

I do not know that I want to fight any more.
I do not desire defection either.
Perhaps what I really want is just to ignore the war and die.
They would think me insane,
And perhaps I am.
They would say to fight for the Good Commander.
They say the joys of winning the battle are great
Compared to the momentary pain.
And perhaps it is true,
But somehow the noise of battle,
And the pain,
And fear,
Make it easy to forget.

I was trying to defend what others had convinced me of on the one hand, and what I kept comprehending as true on the other. To remain a Christian meant battling, as it were, my own soul. To leave Christianity meant defection, and everyone knows what happens when a soldier defects: There is no return.

DK: Yes, the conditionals are quite striking, but only in contrast with the assertiveness of the parts where you recognize the truth: "I a soldier . . . deafened . . . frightened" . . . "I am worn, torn." What's also interesting is the deliberate denial of your feelings and awareness, and how feeble that denial is: "I do not know that I want to fight"—yes, you did know. "I do not desire defection, either"—yes, you did desire defection. And then those two "perhaps," which are really just concessions to the "have been assured"—the passive acceptance of *sheker* [falsehood].

The poem shows that you knew what you did not want to acknowledge. Security in one area required self-denial in another.

I know that what you were going through was emotional and intellectual torture. I also know that you realized that you were postponing the "surgery" and just making it more difficult. Fear of the operation, so to speak, overwhelmed the reality of the pain. When we know that something will change—that we must change, leave behind forever what had once been meaningful or useful or fun, but now we see as false or useless or childish—we tend to delay, find an excuse, confuse ourselves.

It's part of the experience of transition. In many ways, it's the most difficult. Once the decision is made, obstacles become challenges and previous objections become trivial irritations.

SZ: I wasn't yet ready to make any decisions, though one event triggered an emotional turnaround that would eventually signal just such a decision.

In the fall of 1973, during my senior year at college, I attended an ice-cream social sponsored by a campus Christian organization. I was aware that it was Yom Kippur, but knew that it shouldn't affect me. After all, I was Christian, not Jewish.

Someone came in and announced that Israel had been attacked. I did not expect the reaction I had to the news. Suddenly, I was no longer hungry or in a mood to socialize. Suddenly, I felt more out of place than I ever had in my life. At the next opportune moment I excused myself and went home. The next day I wrote this poem:

> The Land calls
>   with a voice I cannot ignore.
> The Land calls, the beautiful Land
>   seen without eyes,
> And the call
>   heard without ears.
> The Land, the Land
>   calls, it shouts.
> It cries a glorious cry.
>
> And the trees of the Land
>   I love them
> And each leaf upon them
>   I love.
>
> I know the sap of those trees,
>   for it flows also in me.
> The trees, I cry because of the trees.
>   And I weep for their barrenness.
> I long to water them, tend them.
> I hate those who would harm the trees,
>   would chop them down.
> Upon their injury my sap also flows out.

> When their branches are bare,
>> how shall my leaves bud—they shall not
> The grief is as poison.
>
> The Land, the trees, the call:
>> I must go to my own.

Looking back now, I realize that this was it, the event, *sine qua non,* that marked the turning point in my life. I think that, from here on, it was inevitable that someday I would be a Jew.

As I look back now at what drew me into Christianity, I see that I never questioned sources or authority or tradition or texts. I never really questioned anything. I just accepted and "believed," because that is what I was "supposed" to do. I didn't stop to ask whether it made sense. The fact that it didn't, or couldn't, was probably the source of the deeper confusion that surfaced later.

DK: Along the same lines, I might also ask, given several years' hindsight, how much the natural instability of college helped or hindered your spiritual observations.

SZ: College life—or maybe just my age—made me vulnerable. At home, kids still have the social and religious constraints of the family and community to keep things in balance. At college, these disappear; for many, there are no real external checks and balances.

DK: That's an important point, because *mitzvos*—the commandments—are, in a sense, external checks and balances. Torah recognizes what secular culture denies: that our internal checks and balances—morality—can only reflect our external checks and balances —the demands to which we willingly submit. Of course, ideally, once we willingly submit our will to His will, the *mitzvos* become internalized.

SZ: I had no such demands, no particular responsibilities, no strong ties to be broken, no definite goals. Like many of my peers, I was just drifting in the wind. As a result, it was easy to be pulled into just about anything.

DK: Or into nothing.

It doesn't have to be this way. There's a famous hasidic story about Rabbi Meir of Premlishan. In the middle of winter, he'd go over treacherous ground, icy mountain slopes, to get to the region's *mikvah*. A couple of scoffers made light of the achievement and tried the same route. After very little progress, a lot of bruises, and a broken bone or two, they managed to get back to the village. When they asked Rabbi Meir how he managed the dangerous journey without injury, he replied, "When one is tied Above, one doesn't fall below."

If the college students, or any of us, are tied, really tied, to family, community—to the Jewish people and to God—we won't fall. (Of course, we must remember that only *mitzvos* truly bind us to the Jewish people and to God.)

SZ: But I didn't—couldn't—have all those ties. I had family; I respected my parents. That's all I had.

DK: One last question before we get back to your history. What would you say now to a nineteen-year-old Sue? To a non-Jew beginning the search?

SZ: This I would tell them both: First, the search is important. Coming to terms with God and truth is one of our most important tasks as human beings—and the most important part of the search is the questions.

DK: Maybe the most important—and the reason for our humanity.

SZ: I'd also say that if something makes you afraid to question, then run from it like the plague. *Emes* [truth] shines in the light of questions, and *sheker* [falsehood] is destroyed by them.

Second, don't confuse emotional relief with truth, or warm fuzzies with a religious revelation. Use your senses and your God-given intellect to look critically at any philosophy before committing yourself to it.

Finally, don't look for easy answers; look for answers that are true.

But—and I say this with a twinge of regret—we can't go back and take other roads. We can only learn from the roads we have already taken.

DK: I can understand regret. But basic to *teshuvah*, I think, is that the closeness—*devekus*, in Hebrew—to God transforms even regret. We could not be who we are, we could not perform the *mitzvos* we do, without that which we have regretted.

SZ: From that time on, my journal was no longer filled with Christian prayers and praises. It began to reflect my sense that changes were underway. I wrote:

> I'm about to walk away from Christianity. For what? For this: God and His people.
>
> I find it very difficult to consider myself a gentile—really! Everything, within me that is, looks outward as a Jew. I cannot explain, suffice it to say it is so. The Jewish people are my brothers and sisters and Israel, Israel is my home and I am tied to it and love it and pray for it and yearn to walk upon it, to even die there.
>
> Yet, I would never dare to declare myself to be Jewish. If I am, I have no evidence except my heartbeat, my soul. But I could never degrade Judaism so much as to claim it falsely. So I cannot claim it, only feel it. Now will I convert? Risk eternity in Hell? For Israel, for the Jewish people, for the Lord God who chose them? I just don't quite know.

DK: The second-to-last paragraph eloquently expresses the test of a convert: whither thou goest. I'm sure you've spoken for many converts. Conversion—being Jewish—is about an unconditional commitment, self-sacrifice.

But then, why the hesitation, the retreat in the last paragraph?

SZ: I had gone a great distance down the short-longer path. I could not traverse back its length in one instant. For another five or six months I would have to fight off the mental and emotional ties that anchored me to Christianity. Still, I had turned . . . at some level I understood where I belonged.

The other thing that strikes me about this journal entry, given later events, was the statement that "I could never degrade Judaism so much as to claim it falsely." Little did I know. . . .

DK: Yes, we'll get to that.

SZ: It was a time of intense feelings. The journal was filled with my thoughts:

The Lord planted a seed in Zion.
Then the seed grew to a mighty tree.
Its roots extended deep into the past
And as it grew, the nations
Chopped that great tree down,
But its roots they could not remove.
When it fell, the tree scattered its seed.
The young saplings grew all over the earth.
But there was not on them even a single leaf
Which did not turn to the place of its birth.
As time passed some of the leaves forgot about the root,
And turned from it to face the sun.
Soon some trees became like the forest all around
and had forgotten their noble birth.
One day a leaf turned from the sun toward Zion,
Not knowing just why it did so.
There the leaf saw a living root,
Which sprouted leaves of the leaf's own.
The leaf could not rest,
It was by one thought possessed:
I must, I shall go to my root, my home.

DK: There doesn't seem to be much internal fighting in that entry. The decision, it seems to me, has already been made. That's a statement of fact, of something definitely determined. The only question is how and when.

SZ: Yes, but it was a very difficult time. In one long journal entry I talked about feeling like I wanted to die, but realizing that that wasn't an option. The entry concludes with these words:

I don't understand any of this. I give up. Let life have me, it seems I am able to have no part of it. I can only cry out to God if God is God now. And all eloquence I lay aside. My prayer is simple: Father, help! Amen.

The answer to that prayer came quickly. The next day I wrote down a new prayer. It began with the *Shema*, and ended with these words:

Today is November 24. For some time now I've been playing games. I am not a Christian. I don't believe in the Trinity. I believe that God is One. That He IS. But I am stuck. Many people would be hurt if I told them what I've told You. But pretending is a lot like a lie. It isn't good to lie or hurt people. Forgive me for my mistakes, God. Sustain me 'til I enter as a child of Israel. Amen.

DK: It didn't take long for you to accept the realization that you weren't a Christian—less than two months, from the Yom Kippur War in early October until your journal entry in late November. Of course, I'm sure that seemed like a long time to you. Now came the time to act on the decision, to begin again your search for Judaism—after several years' hiatus. How did that proceed?

SZ: Since I was just about to leave college, I knew that there would be an opportune time to make that final "break" with the least disruption and embarrassment.

I finished up my college studies that December and went back to live at home with my family. I got a job as a bank teller. On the outside I was a stable and well-adjusted young woman. Inside, the struggle continued. I talked about being ". . . tired of the cycles. Belief, disappointment, doubt, resignation, hope, faith, reinforcement, belief . . . cycles."

DK: The exhaustion is understandable. You had come to an emotionally traumatic realization. You didn't wallow in your fatigue, though, did you?

SZ: Wallow, no—but I still had to spend some time coming to terms with the changes that were occurring. Mostly, I wrote in my journal. I realized that I had to "move on," that I had to make some important decisions. I wasn't really sure *how* yet.

DK: Maybe we should look at one of the journal entries from that time.

SZ: Okay. Here is one from February 1974. I was twenty-one years old, and had been back at home for a couple of months.

I am undecided yet as to which course I should take in life. It seems that I am still very young and the world is a very unfamiliar place. The world is the place of my residence, though, and of God's choosing, not of my own. So, as I live here, it is best that I live to His laws.

DK: I rather like the diffidence of the second sentence: "It seems that I am still very young." There's a kind of wistful sagacity in that, as if you're suddenly aware that you're young, but maybe you're not. It's a far different entry from most of your earlier ones, though: There's no *sturm und drang*, no turmoil, no inner rage or demand; there's only a contented resignation.

Also significant, I think, is that you recognized the importance—and the concept—of Divine law, that the relationship with God is expressed and confirmed through actions that accord with Divinely prescribed behavior: *mitzvos*. (Of course, you didn't know what that meant yet.)

However, I suspect that not all the entries were so peaceful or accepting, although I doubt they had the urgency or strife anymore, either.

SZ: No, but when I wrote about religion and spirituality, I still slipped into and out of certainty and doubt. For instance, I wrote:

Faith, God, belief, such big words, such big meaning and great depth in them. I fear I have all but abandoned completely the Christian faith. I am not certain now what faith I am, but this:
God is One. He is good.
His character is one of justice, compassion, love, mercy, truth, righteousness and Holiness.

DK: It's not so much that you were afraid that you had abandoned Christianity, but that you didn't know how or with what to replace it. It's the fear that comes from realizing that one phase or idea or relationship has died—or was simply wrong—but the next one hasn't arrived. Why is it late? Where is it? we ask ourselves. It's like being unbalanced, isn't it? The negative is clear, but the positive, which you *know* has to be around someplace, can't yet be found. To coin a phrase, it's the juggling transition.

The idea is expressed in Psalms as "Turn from evil and do good." Having done one doesn't automatically qualify as doing the other. So you'd turned, so to speak, but hadn't yet done.

SZ: I had finally come back to the crossroads of the short-longer path and the long-shorter path. I think I stood there at the intersection for a while, just trying to get my bearings. I was less concerned with where I'd been than with where I still needed to go. I recorded this passage in the journal:

> There is within me a desire to follow God in faith, in the true faith. I can ask only that He guide me to it, or back to it. I know that God is great over all and able to do it in my life.
> May my heart perceive His love.
> May my hand do righteousness unto Him.
> May my eyes be opened to His truth.
> May my lips and spirit ever praise Him.
>
> Blessed is the Lord God.
> Blessed is the King of Israel.
> Blessed is He forever.
> Amen.

SZ: Despite the fact that I was finished with Christianity, my outlook on religion was still strongly influenced by it. I still saw religion in a faith-based, nonphysical way. The vocabulary makes it obvious: belief, faith, questioning, conflict, love, conscience, and so on. I had encountered the Oneness of God, but not yet His instruction.

DK: It seems to me that you had changed at least this much: You were now struggling to be a psalmist or a prophet, which for many is a first step toward becoming—or living like—a Jew. Still, you didn't recognize what Torah was, what it demanded; that without Torah—without a set of rules and guidelines—there can be no relationship. The Ten Commandments, for instance, contain not only "I am the Lord your God" and "Do not murder," but also "Observe the Sabbath." The prophets and King David lived first and foremost according to Torah—meaning *all* of Jewish law. A relationship is in the details, the petty minutiae of daily life. Checking a closet corner for *chometz* before Pesach does more for one's relationship with God than a chorus of hallelujahs or "feeling Jewish" in the heart.

It's what we do that counts; action is the main thing. That action is defined by *halacha*, Jewish law that implements Torah.

You know, after the *Shema*, the declaration of the Oneness of God (Hear, O Israel, the Lord Who is our God, the Lord is One), comes an acknowledgment of His kingship, His authority. The *Shema* continues with a set of commandments—first about commitment (the love for God should be with all one's emotional attributes, will, and essence), then concerning action—how we should speak, what we should learn, and what we need to do to remind ourselves of and participate in the relationship (for example, *tefillin, mezuzah*).

I guess that the rest of your story is how you encountered, accepted, and began to obey God's instructions, His will—the Torah.

SZ: I went to the synagogue on a couple of Friday nights at about this time.

DK: Now that you were investigating Judaism again, how did your parents react?

SZ: I never really discussed it with my parents. I didn't see much point in it. Perhaps in the back of my mind I felt that they had passed on their chance to teach me about God when I was a child. They seemed to be willing to give me "space" to grow and become who I needed to become. Remember, I already had their permission to convert. I had waited far beyond that year's moratorium. I never felt it necessary to ask again.

In general, I settled into an uneventful life. On one of my visits to the synagogue, I met a woman who was to become a close friend. Paula was Catholic. Her grandmother had been Jewish, and Paula felt an affinity for Judaism. As far as I know, it never went further than that.

As for me, the intense battle inside had subsided. Christianity was behind me. I knew the direction in which to head. I was much happier. I didn't feel that everything had to have an instant fix. I was willing to go a little slower, let things happen at their own pace.

There were no cataclysmic events, nothing that really stands out except that I was becoming more and more aware of anything or anybody Jewish.

DK: Most transitions are like that, I think. A gradual emergence, a growing awareness—often in many areas. What I find interesting here is how you were attracted to "anything or anybody" Jewish. It sounds like you naturally gravitated that way.

SZ: I think that there was almost a mystique about it, an idealization of Judaism in my mind. Of course, I really knew very little. What I knew was sort of an aggregate of what I'd read in books, what I'd seen on a couple of visits to the synagogue, the impressions that I'd gotten from Steve and a few other Jewish friends, and what I remembered from the talk the cantor gave back in high school.

The opportunity to grow further came at the beginning of the summer, when a World's Fair exhibition took place in my hometown. There were exhibits from around the world, including a large one presented by the [former] Soviet Union where I liked to spend time because it gave me a chance to practice my Russian. The synagogue was sponsoring a "Free Soviet Jews" exhibit a block or two away from the Fair gates. I stopped by to talk with the folks who were running the exhibit and took an interest in it, even volunteering to help out if they wanted me. They did.

The exhibit was housed in what used to be a small movie theater. There were the usual pictures and stories, and we occasionally had lectures. Mostly we just talked about the plight of those Jews who were victims of an anti-Semitic and oppressive government, and the need to speak out and demand that our government take a more active role in gaining their freedom, their right to emigrate to Israel. We met a good number of Fair visitors there, as well as folks from the synagogue who dropped in to check on things. Sometimes the Soviets from the Exposition would stop by to tell us that it was insensitive and impolite to have such a place so near the Exposition, where the virtues of cooperation were being extolled. Needless to say, we didn't agree—or go away!

The Fair committee had arranged for chaplains from the community to serve the visitors. One of the chaplains was Leo, the cantor from the synagogue, who had spoken several years before to my high-school class. Leo was about in his sixties at the time. He was a man who spoke with a sincerity that left no doubt that the words were born of personal experience. He recognized me from the Soviet Jews exhibit, and we began to talk. I told him that I remembered his talk to our class and that I was interested in Judaism. He very much encouraged (what I think he perceived as) my curiosity, and invited me to come visit the synagogue. I eagerly accepted, not mentioning that I had been there before.

DK: He must have seen something special in you. I don't think that kind of encouragement is very common.

SZ: I don't know about me, but he was certainly a very special person. This meeting, this invitation, was a very significant event, which I recorded in my journal. I wrote that I was again considering conversion to Judaism, but that

> . . . In many ways, I am a shy person and quite afraid to jump into the midst of this people on my own. Yet I trust God, and it seems that God is answering that trust. Last night the Cantor himself invited me to come to services at Temple. I will go. . . .

DK: I wonder if you recognized the echo of Ruth in your last sentence. Interestingly, Abraham, the first Jew, the father of all converts and the paradigm for all the Jewish people, including converts—because he embodies *mesiras nefesh* (self-sacrifice)—is introduced in the Torah with the same idea: Go. The first Torah portion dedicated to Abraham begins with God's command, *Lech l'cha*—Go. (By the way, this literally means, "go to yourself," which, in terms of Chassidus, indicates the importance and nature of *mesiras nefesh*, self-sacrifice, a going to the essence of the self, one's Divine soul.)

This idea of "going" applies to every Jew, since it's the essence of being a *baal teshuvah*—someone who returns, who goes back to his source.

SZ: We have but to turn and open our eyes. . . . Once confronted with that source, we are awakened to the need to return. It is a powerful drive, almost a revelation. I felt it then, and I noted it in my journal:

> Now I want to come home to where I've always sensed I belonged: Under the shadow of the wings of the God of Israel, caressed in the arms of our Lord. May God in His lovingkindness make it so.

SZ: The cantor, Leo, helped me adjust, both at the synagogue and when-ever we encountered each other at the fair or exhibit. A survivor of labor camps, Leo had a lot of stories to tell. He told how he and his wife were married with a ketubah written on a scrap of paper they found in the forest. He told how his prewar vocation of being a con-cert whistler got him out from under the thumb of camp guards. He told me, and asked me never to forget, that one should always strive to learn, to learn everything, because one never knows what little piece of knowledge or learned skill may one day save a life or bring free-dom. I have not forgotten.

DK: You shouldn't. It's true. This reminds me of something. The rab-bis tell us, *Ma'aseh avos, siman l'bonim* (the deeds of the fathers are a sign for the children); they also point out that the Aggadah—the stories and parables in the Talmud—contain deep theological and eso-teric truths. It seems to me, as you speak of the cantor, that you're confirming the power of storytelling. Maybe truth is in the stories, or at least in how we read them.

SZ: . . . Or how they are told to us.

Besides being a source of inspiration, Leo was the one to whom I turned when I had questions about the service. He encouraged me to come to services on *Shabbos* morning as well as on Friday night. After the first time, I understood why. The services were very different. Fri-day night was just like a Reform service, mostly English, a lot of re-sponsive readings, and singing with the accompaniment of an organ. *Shabbos* morning was more traditional. Instead of being in the big main sanctuary (a large semicircular room with seats arranged on a ramp like a lecture hall or theater), we met in a much smaller alcove just off to the side. *Shabbos* mornings were a lot closer to an Ortho-dox service.

Most of the service was in Hebrew. I managed to follow along with the help of some kind folks who mentioned page numbers. I read the English translation and sort of hummed along when they sang.

DK: How did you feel? After all, this was a far different form of wor-ship than you had previously experienced. I'm sure there was some strangeness, some disorientation, as well as some exhilaration, right?

SZ: I think what made me feel most uncomfortable at first was not knowing what to expect—what was acceptable. Was it okay for me, as a woman, to be there? Where should I sit? I felt conspicuous.

Once I got past that, I felt disoriented. Trying to follow the service without getting lost was a challenge. I found that I used the songs as markers for where we were.

DK: That's the reaction of a lot of people. They go from feeling conspicuous to feeling disoriented. But then they like it; they begin to appreciate why Jews have worshipped this way for thousands of years. It's a shame that so many Jews today don't know how to or want to pray. On the other hand, I have a lot of respect and admiration for those who make the effort.

SZ: The "strangeness," as you put it, I just accepted as what Judaism "is." I appreciated the difference. And the exhilaration was more from a feeling of "I finally made it here—this is what I wanted." It was the relief of having made the connection, just *being* there, being in a synagogue, being with Jews. I felt like an orphan who had just found a family to adopt me.

DK: The comfort of coming home.

SZ: It seemed like it. It seemed like home.

After the morning service there was always a kiddush. It was herring, challah, schnapps [liquor], wine, and cake or cookies. We'd talk for a while, and the rabbi would usually say something, teach a little. The first few times I went, I really didn't know what to make of everything, but this group, being so small, seemed to take me in. They were really very nice people. I still felt a little awkward, and it took a while to develop a taste for that herring, but I did feel welcome, even more so than at the evening services, where there were so many more people. It is just harder, logistically, to get situated in larger groups.

So, all these initial experiences were shaping my view of what Judaism was, what Jewish worship entailed, what Jewish community meant. I really had no counterpoint to the right or the left, since this was the city's only synagogue.

I began to attend the services on Friday night and *Shabbos* mornings almost every week. I enjoyed the experience immensely. There was so much to learn, so much to absorb.

I didn't talk much with the rabbi at this point. I was a little frightened by him. He seemed overpowering, severe in some way. It was an initial impression; as I got to know him the image softened considerably. I preferred to turn to the cantor with questions in the beginning: "What was that song about?" "What was this prayer for?" Simple questions. Judaism began to take form and substance; it was no longer just a projection of what I read or heard.

After several weeks of attending services and helping out at the Soviet Jewry exhibit, I was feeling more sure than ever that this was the direction I wanted to take. I felt no conflict within, no wrestling with conscience. I decided to ask about conversion.

First I broached the subject with the cantor. He took me very seriously, and told me that I had to talk to the rabbi about such matters, that he could not help me out. It was not the answer that I wanted. I didn't know how to ask; I was afraid to ask.

Then something odd happened. I guess it could have just been a coincidence, but the timing was incredible, so much so that I recorded it in my journal. I found a note lying on my dresser, a note that I had written four years earlier exhorting myself to overcome my trepidation, to call a rabbi about converting to Judaism. It was written before my involvement in Christianity—just a scrap of paper that should have been long gone—but there it was, staring me in the face at exactly the time I was dealing with the problem.

This time I called.

2
First Steps

DK: So what happened when you finally got to see the rabbi?

SZ: I was extremely nervous. What would I say? How would I say it? And the rabbi still, by his very title, seemed bigger than life to me. I wrote about my feelings in the journal:

Again I approach the paper with only the desire to write, without knowing what I want to write about. Lately I've been typing up all my writings. Now I almost feel like this is the last chapter. I doubt it will be the last, but certainly it is part of a new one. There is something new ahead of me: Conversion to Judaism. I am certain now about this, yet at the same time, I am very afraid. Many times I ask, "Why am I afraid?" but I can never answer that question. Yet, what is even more puzzling is "Why become a Jew?" Maybe I am really afraid because of that question, because I can't answer it. The answer is there, but it seems so deep inside me that the attempt to express it only fails. Anyway, I want to try. First there is God. I love God, the One God of the whole universe, the God of Israel. I want to do what is right in His eyes. I want my love towards Him to be expressed in the reality of my life. Secondly, there is community. I cannot live alone. I want to live my life in the midst of a people whom I can love and feel a part of. And so the Jews are such a people to me. There is also a rich and wise past from which to draw strength for living in the present. So here are two reasons for converting, and though only two, I must ask: If God, and People, are not enough reasons to commit my life to the Jewish People, then no number of reasons besides, shall ever be enough. But these two reasons are enough. That is why I will convert. A new chapter is about to begin.

DK: I think you expressed the reasons very well. By the way, do you remember the story of Elijah hiding in the cave? If you recall, God was not in the strong wind, the earthquake, or the fire. God was in the still, small voice. That, I think, is the answer "so deep inside" it can't be expressed.

Beyond that, the prerequisite for conversion is a desire to attach one's self to God and the Jewish people. What you wrote in your journal is not just reason enough, it's the only true reason for conversion. (You also gave, unknowingly, a very good reason for the *mitzvos*: "I want my love towards Him to be expressed in the reality of my life." It's the little things—the daily acts—that make feelings real.)

I think if you compare this passage to some of your earlier journal entries, you'll find a recognition of the need for action here that didn't exist before.

Did that passage help you come to terms with your fears? Did they become more identifiable? This wasn't your first new experience, or even your first new religious experience. Yet you describe it quite differently than you describe the others. Maybe fear came from recognizing that true spirituality, closeness to God—true *teshuvah*—requires change. That's reality, and that's scary.

SZ: I wrote the passage, in part, to help me come to terms with the fears I had. Precisely because this was not my first new religious experience, I was a little unsure of myself—"Am I making another mistake?" I was also apprehensive about meeting with the rabbi, and had concerns about how my family would react.

Yet there was another kind of fear working *with* me: the fear that I would miss this second chance to become who I knew, in my heart, I wanted to be.

In the end, despite my trepidation, I took a seat in the rabbi's office and told him that I wanted to convert to Judaism. The meeting was very brief. He simply told me that the matter would have to wait until after the High Holidays. No encouragement, no discouragement, just "wait." So what could I do? I waited. And I counted the days:

> . . . Last Monday I asked the Rabbi about converting, when that would be possible. He responded that it would be after High Holy Days. That means about the beginning of October we can consider it more. It seems like a long time from now, but in fact it's only seven weeks, forty-nine days. Not so long really. I can wait, and use the time to study, to learn. . . .

I've often mused at the count of seven weeks, seven sevens. It seems so prophetic—almost like approaching Shavuos.

DK: That was more "prophetic" than you realize. On Shavuos, when the Jewish people received the Torah, everyone converted! Maimonides explains it in his *Mishneh Torah*. Essentially, everyone went to the *mikvah*, and so on, because entering the covenant—accepting the yoke of God's kingship and commandments—was a conversion, a change of status and nature. That day, the Jews became a people.

There's also a reason for why seven weeks passed between Passover, when the Jews became free, and Shavuos, when they became a people. According to Jewish mysticism, Godliness manifests itself in ten emanations (*sefiros*, in Hebrew), each expressing a different aspect of Godliness. The first three are intellectual attributes (wisdom, understanding, and knowledge—*chochmah*, *binah*, and *daas*); the last seven are emotional attributes or character traits, such as kindness, severity, harmony, and the like. Each attribute contains within it all seven, so there's kindness of kindness, severity of kindness (like a parent disciplining a child), and so forth. (That adds up to forty-nine, of course.)

The Talmud explains that the Jewish people in Egypt had sunk to the forty-ninth level of impurity or evil. In order to receive the Torah, to enter a covenant with God, they had to purify or refine each aspect. Each day between Passover and Shavuos—when we count the *omer*—also serves to elevate us one level.

So, you see, your journey paralleled that of not only many converts, but, in fact, the whole Jewish people.

SZ: But of course I didn't know about Shavuos at that point. I didn't know about a lot of things, including whether I really knew what I was getting into. Was I so sure about converting? What were my *real* motives?

Suddenly I find myself questioning: What am I doing converting to Judaism? Am I running toward a faith, a heartfelt belief, or am I simply running away from Christianity? Do I really know what I am doing, or am I in an emotional state of near insanity? And when I question, I am forced to answer—

First, I am not running away from Christianity, but purposing myself toward Judaism. The real question that is confronted is "Who is my God?" The Lord is my God. He is one and alone. Yet, believing in one God is one thing, becoming Jewish is another. I can believe in one God and still be gentile. Why go to all that effort to convert? A need for a law, for a moral guideline, a standard of behavior, social and political conduct: A good and honest lifestyle—Torah and tradition, wisdom of God and wisdom of experience. I have never encountered a legal and moral code, an ethic higher than they are in Judaism. But even these I could follow without converting.

DK: So what did you do during those seven weeks? Did you do any more reading, talk to anyone else? Or did you just wait patiently?

SZ: I tried to find books to read, and I kept going to services. It was a waiting game. I was a little disappointed that the rabbi didn't share my sense of urgency. I wanted to move quickly. There really wasn't anyone else to talk to, not in an official sense, anyway. With only one rabbi in town, it never occurred to me to ask anyone else.

DK: The sense of urgency is understandable—and not uncommon.

SZ: I began to think more about religious issues, and already was seeing myself as Jewish. I wrote a prayer in my journal—I'll share it with you—that talks about "we" and "they"—Jews and non-Jews. Perhaps it seems *chutzpadik* to consider myself a Jew at that point, but apparently I believed that accepting One God and Torah and caring about *am Yisroel* were enough to make me Jewish. Still, I like the entry. There was still a youthful cynicism about most of humanity, yet hopefulness was hidden within:

Lord,

It isn't necessary to look hard to find many things wrong in the world: Injustice, hate, malice, bigotry, dishonesty, dishonor, and so much more. It's all around us, it's difficult to escape from it. Even idolatry is becoming more prevalent. And people are forgetting You. Ignoring You. Denying You. They ridicule our faith in You, yet they despair for lack of any faith. They berate Your Law, but their standards (if indeed they have any) are nowhere near Yours in their sense of what is good. Truly we can see that the ways of the masses which surround us are not Your ways. They are not the ways we should follow. And, yet, sometimes we are drawn toward them, even into them. We stray from the paths and precepts of Your Torah and walk the ways of the peoples around us. We seek to make peace with the world by becoming like it. But we acknowledge to You that we are wrong. If we turn away from Your Torah, turn away from Your direction in our lives, we are not at peace with ourselves. And, if not at peace with ourselves, we can neither be at peace with the world, nor teach the world Your peace. Grant us forgiveness, O Lord, that in turning back from our straying ways, we may by Your mercy walk the paths of righteousness. Lord, be merciful and grant us strength to persevere in justice and truth. Restore us by Your love, that we may wholly devote our love, our lives to You.

Amen.

DK: Yes, you still had your cynicism. (I think that cynicism is often a by-product or manifestation of idealism.) You also had obviously begun to learn a little bit: There's the Maccabean stand of the few against the many. And the *Shulchan Aruch* begins with instructions how to answer those who mock *halacha*, recognizing that sarcasm is often used as a weapon against faith.

So the seven weeks were almost over. When the High Holidays came, what did you do? How did you feel?

SZ: Well, that selection was written just before Rosh Hashanah. I was beginning to look at issues of right and wrong, and to establish that Torah did not follow upon social mores. That was an important step. Also, the Jewish liturgy was beginning to show; the prayer is written with the communal plural "we."

DK: I noticed.

SZ: I don't remember much about the holidays themselves, nor did I write about them in the journal. I don't know why. Perhaps because I didn't understand the meaning of the days. Perhaps because, with the differences in liturgy, it was too confusing to be meaningful.

I met with the rabbi after Yom Kippur. He, of course, recognized me by then, but didn't know much about me. We talked a little about my background. He asked why I wanted to be Jewish, and said that there wasn't any real reason to convert—it was just asking for trouble. I knew that he was supposed to discourage me as part of the process, so I wasn't surprised or upset by the response. He did make it clear that Christianity and Judaism were incompatible, that one could not believe in both. I assured him that I had burned that bridge. He asked about my family. I told him that they had given their permission some time ago, and he seemed satisfied.

Finally, he talked about how to proceed. He said that I should join the confirmation class to study. I was a little surprised at how short a time our meeting lasted. It was probably only about fifteen or twenty minutes. He had a much different demeanor than the cantor—much more businesslike, and, for me, more difficult to relate to. In the year and a half that followed, I never went to him for advice or counsel, or, for that matter, for halachic questions. I think I saw him as the "CEO" of the synagogue, and sometimes teacher. I respected him, but the element of personal trust was absent.

3
Conservative

DK: Other than attending the confirmation class once a week, what type of learning did the rabbi have you do? What activities, other than attending synagogue?

SZ: Not much, in fact.

The confirmation classes—for children past bar and bat mitzvah—met on Sunday mornings for about an hour and were largely academic—about history and holidays.

There was also an adult Hebrew class. It covered the basics of how to read, with some conversational element. It took me far enough that I could work out word sounds, learn a little vocabulary, and follow the parts of the liturgy that I already knew. It was a start, a taste of what might be hidden in the pages of the siddur.

DK: That's about what most Jewish children get out of four or five years of afternoon Hebrew school.

SZ: That's true. Academically, I was able to get to that level in a matter of months because I was interested and already had done a lot of reading. What I was missing was the family experience, what it means to live Jewishly. It isn't something one can learn in a classroom, and those classes were really all there was. I didn't meet with the rabbi or anyone else regularly for individual study. I didn't have a support family. I never spent *Shabbos* or any Yom Tov with anyone. As I said, there was no experiential learning.

DK: I'd like to emphasize the importance of experiential learning. Something comes alive for us, has meaning, when we experience it. It's the difference between the spectator and the participant. The fan in the stands, no matter how involved, can have no more than a vicarious understanding, a counterfeit thrill, an imitation experience. To feel "the real thing," one has to do it—go through the process. The fan's passion and the audience's catharsis only prove how vitally we need to live *in media res*—in the middle of things, how desperately we need to experience the process of doing, even artificially.

In *Tanya*, the Alter Rebbe explains the three levels of knowledge— Wisdom, Understanding, and Knowledge (*Chochmah, Binah,* and *Daas*). Briefly, *Chochmah* (Wisdom) is the initial spark of awareness; *Binah* (Understanding) is the development and differentiation of awareness into specifics and particulars; *Daas* (Knowledge) internalizes the intellectual and personalizes it, so that the intellect affects and is connected to what moves us: our emotions, the feelings of love and fear and their variations.

If we look in the Torah, we see knowledge—*daas*—used in this sense of recognition and internalization, of experience: Adam *knew* Eve; *know* before Whom you stand; Job's "I didn't *know*." In fact, that's what we say when reality hasn't penetrated, when the truth, the totality of a situation, hasn't become part of us: "I didn't know," i.e., didn't have *daas*.

The need to experience goes beyond "Try it, you'll like it." Without experience, there's no existence: One must do to live; one must do Jewishly to live Jewishly.

It sounds like your conversion process—like so much of Jewish education today—lacked *daas*.

The rabbis explain the three types of laws in Judaism: *Mishpatim* (statutes), which are rational the civil and criminal codes, laws that "civilize" and that are fairly universal ("Don't steal," for example).

Most people know these in one form or another, though not necessarily the Jewish form. The next type is called *eidus* (testimonies), which are also rational, but idiosyncratic to the Jewish people: the calendar, history, and holidays. It's Passover as the Fourth of July as it were. Then there are *chukim* (decrees), which are suprarational: Laws like *kashrus* and those of ritual purity exist simply because "God said so." These are the ones the nations and scoffers make fun of; yet these most clearly define the Jewish *daas*.

SZ: Perhaps that explains why *kashrus* and observing *Shabbos* were presented as good, as "Jewish," but were not seen as imperative, as an incontestable demand of God. Most folks I knew didn't bother with them when they became too inconvenient.

DK: Exactly! If they "didn't bother," it's because they didn't understand their importance; they didn't have the *daas*. They didn't know. It's the "had I known" phenomenon.

Torah tells us, though, that all the laws have value because they have the same source. In other words, we should not accept the *mishpatim* because they make sense, or observe the *eidus* because they give us an identity, but we should fulfill those *mitzvos* as we fulfill the *chukim*—because God said so. The truth of Torah doesn't depend on my understanding. Rather, through knowing—the *daas*—of Torah, I come to understand the truth of Torah.

It's not just the ABCs of Judaism—the facts, figures, how-to's, and reasons. We're talking about people not getting the experiential education. That means, by the way, as with all education, making mistakes and learning from them.

We should also remember that good people do the wrong thing. If we judge actions—which is all we can judge—the criterion has to be *halacha*. It must be *halacha* because, whether the act belongs to the category of *mishpatim*, *eidus*, or *chukim*, whether law is explicitly stated in the Torah or implicitly derived by talmudic hermeneutics, the action is prescribed or proscribed because "God said so."

SZ: One subject that was not taught during my conversion was that of *taharas mishpacha*, family purity. I don't know if it wasn't addressed because I was still single, or because the community had no *mikvah* anyway. Whatever the reason, I never had any idea of its existence.

DK: It also may not have been addressed because it was deemed unimportant, something about which we "know better"—which is ironic, considering the meaning of the phrase.

Where are we now? Any journal entries?

SZ: Let me take you to mid-October 1974. I had been going to services at the synagogue for about three months, and reading whatever Jewish books the local bookstores kept on their shelves. There is an extensive entry in my journal in which I record my impressions of Jewish worship. It is as instructive for what it doesn't say as for what it does.

DK: It is extensive, but I think it's worth looking at in detail. Let's go through it section by section.

SZ: Okay, here's the first part:

> It seems that it's time to sit down and write again, perhaps it should have been written earlier. Time seems to move on so fast—it's hard to keep up with it. My situation is changing. I am in an apartment now, and so not as tied materially to my parents. Also I'm attending services at Temple quite regularly. (Maybe too regularly—I sometimes get kidded about it.) It's a good time to record some of my impressions of Jewish worship.
>
> First, from a religious perspective, there is a traditional sameness to the liturgy which varies little except for the sermon which the Rabbi gives. That, however, is not unusual. From my experience (be it Baptist, Pentecostal, or Jewish) it is, in fact, unavoidable. Liturgy, ordered liturgy, is fundamental to responsible worship. Even if it is not planned by sages, it seems to eventually emerge.

DK: That's a cogent observation. The rabbis long ago recognized the dynamic tension within prayer. In *Pirkei Avos*, for example, we are warned not to make prayer something mechanical. Yet the same rabbis insisted on an established order of prayer, a daily habitual routine. The hasidic movement gained adherents—and opponents—because it emphasized the recitation of prayer with sincerity and enthusiasm.

Over the years, I've frequently encountered questions like, "Why can't I just pray when I feel like it? Why do I have to use someone else's words?" Indeed, having an "ordered liturgy," to use your term, seems to inhibit the spontaneity of prayer. Yet this assumes that all prayer should be spontaneous. Certainly our sages encourage and value such immediate, passionate responses—the instinctive turning to God with gratitude or for comfort. But, as the Hebrew word *tefillah* indicates, prayer is also a time for self-judgment, for reaffirming and redefining the relationship—individual and communal—with God.

And relationships are defined by ritual: acts repeated but invested with variations of emotional nuances. The repetition of the act— whether it's the ritual "good morning" to the boss, the ritual bedtime story, the ritual taking out of the garbage—creates, through its consistency, a solidity and security from which meaning—relational communication—can emerge. Just think how many different "messages" we generate depending on the emotional investment behind the act: One can say "I love you," "I'm angry," "I'm responsible," through the "mundane." In fact, we become aware of, transmit, and experience the inner reality, the spiritual center, only through ritual. We define ourselves and declare and convey our values through how, and with what, we ritualize our lives.

Prayer is the ritual that unites us with God. That may be why it's written in *HaYom Yom* that the beginning of descent is a lack of effort (*avodah*) in prayer.

SZ: We should talk more about that, about what it means to put effort into prayer. In fact, the journal picks up on this subject as it continues:

Well, that observation aside, the Jewish prayer book has some of the most beautiful prayers that I have ever read. What is difficult for me is to "spiritually embrace them." They are almost a challenge, a goal to attain. I want to pray them as my prayers, not read them as someone else's prayers. But this demands not only concentration in the praying, but a living which is in accord with those prayers. Mercy, forgiveness, kindness, peace, help, love, justice—the things I pray for I must live for. That fact will and does make those prayers, however often prayed, a challenge and beauty all my life. The whole aspect of prayer is an especially important one to me. Liturgically, the same written prayers are recited each week (be they in Hebrew or English). Yet, they are like the water brought out of an ever-filling well. Their depth grows with the praying, and each time the heart speaks with new meaning and fervor, even though the mouth may utter the same words. The prayers are demanding. They cannot be simply read—they must be prayed with a heart and mind focused on God. For me, it is one of the most difficult aspects of prayer, for it is so easy for my mind to wander, my heart to stray. I am convinced that I must become more disciplined. . . .

DK: Insightful and beautifully said. In the words of the Rebbe Rashab, "Prayer requires *daas*." That's what you mean when you say, "each time the heart speaks with new meaning and fervor, even though the mouth may utter the same words. The prayers are demanding. They cannot be simply read—they must be prayed with a heart and mind focused on God."

SZ: Is time the key to significance and effort in prayer?

DK: I'm not sure. There's a hasidic story that speaks to the question. At the wedding of the granddaughter of the Alter Rebbe and the grandson of Rabbi Levi Yitzchok of Berditchev—two of the most famous and important early leaders of Chassidism—many dignitaries and Chassidim gathered for the festivities. Naturally, there was much discussion about the goings-on in Lubavitch and Berditchev. Once the Alter Rebbe asked, "What's going on at the *mechutan*'s?" (A *mechutan* is a relative by marriage, i.e., the two fathers-in-law are *mechutanim*.) He was told that Rabbi Levi Yitzchok had already finished the morning prayers. The Alter Rebbe responded, "He runs a hand over his eyes and his soul is ready to soar. But I cannot even begin to pray without several hours of preparation." Later, the question was reversed; Rabbi Levi Yitzchok asked about Rabbi Schneur Zalman (the Alter Rebbe) and was told that he had not yet begun the morning prayers. Rabbi Levi Yitzchok's response? "Whenever he arrives in heaven, he is accepted with open arms. But if I wish to enter the gates of prayer, I must come at the set time, when they are open for all."

SZ: It would seem, then, that prayer is a very individual process. We each need to find our own way.

DK: Yet it occurs within a communal context. The prayers were written in the first person plural for a reason.

SZ: Let's see; the journal moves from "prayer" to "song":

The songs in the liturgy are themselves an experience. Sung in the Hebrew tongue, they carry on their melodies an expression of feelings, of
passions, of Jewish life which I am sure would be impossible to express
in any other way. I love the songs, and even with my limited knowledge
of Hebrew, am learning some of them. Often, the melodies—if not the
words—remain in my mind for the whole week until I again am able to
greet them on the Sabbath.

DK: Song and music have been integral parts of Jewish worship from
the Song at the Sea to King David, to the Temple service, and on.
There was a time, though, when prayer and music were not associated. One of the "innovations" of Chassidism was to bring song back
into the services. The hasidic *niggun*, the often wordless melody that
expresses the yearning, joy, and sorrow of the soul, has become an
integral part of Jewish life. Song has again become a vital expression
of Jewish ideals, and not just in the synagogue. *Tehillim* (psalms) and
verses from elsewhere in Tanach serve as the basis for melodies that
rival popular music for liveliness. But oh, the difference in the message!

SZ: The journal continues:

Now, concerning Hebrew. What can I say? Of course God will understand any language we pray in. To me it (Hebrew) is a major root in the
tree of Judaism, or perhaps like the sap of the tree. It is a binding agent,
a force of unification . . . for all Jews in the world. For that reason I am
even sad to see that it's not being learned, and learned well, by all Jews,
for it would enable them to communicate with, to sing with, and to pray
with their brothers and sisters anywhere in the world. And further it would
enable them to fully appreciate the content, import and beauty of the Bible,
and the wisdom of the great scholars and rabbis.

DK: Here, you touch on an issue that has concerned Jewish educators
for many years. So often children are taught only to read Hebrew,
which simply means to decipher the *aleph-beis* into sounds. The
average time spent learning Hebrew in the afternoon Hebrew school
programs is less time than is spent in kindergarten learning the
alphabet!
It's remarkable, though, how you so precisely stated the problem
with and the importance of learning Hebrew—particularly that of the

siddur, Tanach, and classical texts, considering how recently you had
become involved with the Jewish community.

SZ: The truth is that the passage embarrasses me, even now, because I
have never managed to attain the proficiency in Hebrew that I knew—
know—to be so invaluable. There was still more to the entry:

> At the same time, though, I would not want to see services entirely in
> Hebrew. Not now, anyway, because not all of us know Hebrew well
> enough to express ourselves in it, or would even understand if it were
> the language of our instruction. It is important to pray with an under-
> standing of what is spoken, in the language in which we can best com-
> municate with God. And we must learn with understanding or it is no
> learning at all. To sum up: The vernacular is important for communica-
> tion between man and God and God and man as the individual—but
> between God and the Jewish community, I believe, Hebrew plays a vital
> role.

DK: Even in the times of the Talmud, the rabbis had to deal with
people's limited linguistic education. There's a discussion about
which prayers, if any, can be said in the vernacular and which must
be said in Hebrew. Your last observation I find intriguing, though I'd
probably argue that between God and the Jewish community, Hebrew
is the essential, perhaps the only, means of communication.

SZ: I understood that if all Jews knew Hebrew, then any Jew would be
"at home" in the synagogue with other Jews, even when he is halfway across the world from where he lives. I didn't understand the
deeper connections of Hebrew at that point.

DK: Well, then, your observation about being "at home" is quite true.
In Jewish mysticism, by the way, Hebrew is the language of creation.
Just as human speech is the outward expression of an inner essence,
so God's "speech" (the ten times we find "God said" in the story of
Creation) expresses the Godliness that sustains creation. The Hebrew
letters, through their combinations into words, form the channel for
Godliness to create and sustain a physical reality.

SZ: The journal continues:

One thing I have "missed" in Jewish worship is the sense of deep emotional experience. Maybe that is because I still feel self-conscious, and hold myself back from "letting go" because I still feel so unfamiliar with that aspect of Jewish services. Nevertheless, I feel that it is an important part of the religious experience even though it is not the main one. And, seeing the responses of my own peers in religious matters, I am convinced that the nurturing of heartfelt involvement in faith will become increasingly crucial in not losing Jewish youth to the lures of secular thought or the highly emotional enticements of other religions. Of course, I still am certain that emotion cannot be the central issue, and one should not, I believe, regard it as such.

DK: Often, I think, we confuse the problem of religion as an emotional experience with religion as fun. What lures Jewish youth to "secular thought or the highly emotional enticements of other religions"? Some think that they provide more thrills, more instant gratification, so Judaism must compete on that level. I don't think that Judaism can or should. Rather, the media and secular thought seem to "win the war" precisely because Judaism is superficially presented as an accretion of hollow ceremonies and a collection of the trite and the trivial.

Of course, Jewish youth—teenagers and young adolescents—want to enjoy themselves. But I think they also want to find meaning and be meaningful. If the Judaism of their childhood is irrelevant and indifferent to that search, then they'll look elsewhere.

The first requirement, though, is that the Judaism be authentic.

SZ: But that is my point. Authentic Judaism—*Shabbos* dinners, sitting in the sukkah, celebrating Simchas Torah—are all examples of "heartfelt involvement" that rightfully and naturally engage the person's emotional involvement.

DK: By the way, I noticed the change in approach from your earlier entries. Here you recognize that "I still am certain that emotion cannot be the central issue, and one should not, I believe, regard it as such." You could not have made that statement earlier. You'd realized, unconsciously perhaps, a basic Jewish value, that the mind rules the heart. Hence the need for law, and commitment actualized (*mitzvos*). This is true even when the mind has to rule itself, so to speak, go beyond the rational.

SZ: Yes, and that is not always an easy task. It explains why learning is so important. For the mind to rule the heart, it must have the strength—the authority, so to speak—to overrule the heart. Only learning, Torah knowledge, can provide this. Maybe I understood that, too, as I tried to come to terms with what Torah was:

> Yet another area I want to relate to in this statement is that of Bible, the Holy Scriptures. It is probably here that I am least able to discuss intelligently. What has taken scholars centuries to even begin, I do not aim to summarize here. As yet I am still trying to reconcile myself to some solid viewpoint of the Bible. Once I believed that every word was miraculously preserved as from the very mouth of God, infallible and absolutely correct. Now, though, my experiences with Judaism are causing me to amend that view, and it is becoming more difficult to ascertain my exact beliefs. I can say this, though, I believe that the Bible is at the very least man's account of God, and more than that, the account of the divine by great people who merit great respect. I believe that God does communicate with man, whether to his ear or to his heart—here I cannot say which. The Bible, it seems to me, is an account of a living dialogue between God and man. In the Bible I believe is an absolutely incomparable moral ethic which evokes a confession of Divine origin. If the moral laws of the Bible were not spoken by God to man, they were minimally established by man out of fear of God. Without faith in God, without fear of God, there is no absolute basis for true morality, and it will tend to be replaced by a false morality of expedience. In this false "morality," I am afraid, will be man's greatest downfall.

DK: Again, very cogent observations. You'd obviously spent a lot of time thinking about these issues. Such thoughts and discussions are not as rare among the college and post-college age as some tend to think. That alone should be a hopeful sign. It means that, if they can be shown the truth of Torah—through logic and experience—they'll be likely to try living Jewishly, or at least, to add a *mitzvah*.

The Divine origin of the Torah has been debated for millennia. Yehuda HaLevi's *Kuzari*, among other classical texts, lays out some basic philosophical positions. It seems to me that the disenfranchisement of Jewish youth you mentioned earlier has two root causes in "modernity," though of course, neither is particularly modern. One is the so-called "scientific" slant on the Torah. The other is the historical and literary denigration—the one you mention in your journal entry here.

This argument has been bought and promoted throughout much of Jewish life, in both synagogues and universities. Ironically, its first assumption, that modern historical and literary research prove the composite, inaccurate, late nature of Torah, is absolutely false. Literary studies long ago rejected the assumptions still current in much of so-called biblical criticism. In fact, the current trend looks for inner and dynamic narrative unity, tacitly admitting that such approaches as source criticism cannot speak to historical origins.

We can't prove or disprove the Divine origin of Torah any more than we can prove or disprove the existence of God, simply because both are theological assumptions. But if we accept the theological reality of revelation, then the "philosophic" evidence (history and narrative analysis) support the theological assertion of the Divine origin of Torah.

SZ: Now I'm beginning to understand why it is so hard to have a frame of reference in a vacuum, without teachers to give guidance.

We've almost finished this entry. It concludes:

The Bible is not all law, of course, and at times it becomes for me a prayer book, a song book, a book of history, adventure or philosophy; but most of all it is a book of answers to the questions of human life, and a book of challenges to human answers.

Having said that which I perceive about Judaism in general, I will conclude with some comments of a more personal nature.

It is a difficult time for me right now, because, although not in actuality Jewish, I have come to ever more identify with Jewish life. It is difficult for me to find a solid identity in this situation. This is surely one of the facets of my desire to convert, and within that, I think is a real desire to be under religious guidance and instruction. I want to study, to learn, to seek out an understanding of God, and of life. I want to seek, assisted by the wisdom of others who understand better than I, what the search entails.

Perhaps in time I will see things differently than now, but I pray, that as my perception changes, it will enable me ever more clearly to perceive God, and His will and His demands on my life, to the end that I might serve Him in honor and love every day of the life that He shall grant me to live.

4
Conservative, Part 2

DK: We've talked about the different approaches to questioning (and doubt). How did you respond to this during your conversion process?

SZ: As far as questioning goes, there was still a lot of baggage left over from my earlier experience, where I had learned not to question too much. I felt that one should not ask questions of a religious authority. One had to give the impression that there were no questions. "Just believe what you are told." Of course, now I know that this is not at all a Jewish approach.

DK: There's a famous explanation of the Jewish people's response at Sinai: *Na'aseh v'nishmah* (we will do and we will learn). The Talmud explains that the Jewish people declared they would first observe the commandments, and then, as much as possible, learn the reasons behind them. Even if they didn't understand, however, they would still do. So I guess that Judaism's tenet is "Just *do* as you are told." The reason for that is clear: Action is essential.

As we've discussed, "Believe what you are told" means that you're not competent enough to think on your own; "Do as you're told" means that the task takes precedence. "Believe what you're told" isolates the individual, cutting off communication even—perhaps especially—from others who also believe what they're told. "Do as you're told" unites individuals into a community; sharing the experience of doing binds them together, enabling them to share, explore, and question. (We need only think of team sports or, better yet, an army.)

Doing is learning; experiencing is understanding. A lot of questions disappear and a lot of doubts get answered as we act. Discipline does that. We can say that *halacha* actually frees the mind to ask honest questions, to pose real problems.

The impulse to question *rather than* to do comes from the *yetzer hara* (evil inclination); "Why" tricks us into neglecting or missing a *mitzvah*. On the other hand, when we respond to the command, the *mitzvah*, with "how," we "gain the name of action," joining ourselves to the One who commands. This attachment (*devekus*, in Hebrew) leads to a "why" that deepens our unity with the Creator.

There are two kinds of "why." One is constructive; the other is destructive. But a "religious authority" should recognize which is which and be able to answer each accordingly.

SZ: When that doesn't happen, though, it can be difficult. There were a couple of times when I asked the rabbi a question in group settings and received replies that made me wish I hadn't asked. I decided that it was easier to hide my ignorance than to risk exposing it. An important lesson was there: The teacher really holds the key to the student's ability to question. It was very different from the experience I had many years later with another teacher who painstakingly helped me to re-learn how to ask. It's an issue of trust.

DK: True. As the Talmud says, a short-tempered person can't teach. Often a student learns more from how a teacher handles an "I don't know" or "I forgot" [the student's or the teacher's] than from the deepest lecture. It's important to recognize where the question—or lapse—comes from.

On a related note, I've had a lot of students start with, "This is probably a stupid question . . ." That's a clear signal that it's an important question to them, but sharing it makes them feel uncomfortable or embarrassed. They divert the discomfort or shyness to the question, ready to disown it if it fails to communicate their need. "It's not me, it's the question." But there *is* a real need behind the so-called "stupid" question.

SZ: You asked about the conversion process. I think I viewed the conversion process kind of like getting citizenship. There was a period of study, a ceremony, and then you were proclaimed a "citizen"—Jewish. The spiritual element seemed rather hidden, though.

DK: The citizenship analogy is a good one. Done right, of course, the spiritual element is there in the study, there in the ceremony; there in the *doing* of the conversion itself. After all, the convert becomes not just a physical citizen of the Jewish people, but a spiritual citizen of the descendants of Abraham.

SZ: Perhaps the key phrase here is "done right." But you are correct; the spiritual element is necessarily a major element in the conversion process.

DK: By the way, were there other converts studying at the same time as you? What were they like? What were their attitudes?

SZ: Apparently there were, but they were not part of the confirmation class. When it came to the actual conversion there were three, maybe four of us. At least one conversion was connected to a marriage; the other I don't know. Evidently the rabbi didn't send everyone to this class. I don't know why; I didn't ask.

DK: You mean that there wasn't a conversion class in addition to the confirmation class?

SZ: No. The only formal classes I had were the confirmation class and the introductory Hebrew class, which I took because I wanted to. I know that in some communities there are now classes, often dubbed "Introduction to Judaism," that serve as conversion classes in addition to giving Jews with limited backgrounds a taste for Jewish history, traditions, and lifecycle celebrations. Through reading, and through the confirmation class, I got most of that, but in retrospect I feel "cheated"—like the whole process was just "hoops" that I was given to jump through to make sure I was more or less serious. I sensed an underlying attitude that, unfortunately, made me feel that conversion must be "no big deal."

DK: Conversion *is* a big deal. But how to convert and who to convert—and who is qualified to convert—has become, over the last thirty years, a major issue and point of division within the Jewish community. Sanctioned assimilation (both formally and informally) and the consequent rise in intermarriage have made "Who is a Jew?" a controversial and internally threatening question. An acquaintance of mine once phrased the point rather nicely. The conversion controversy centers around not "Who is a Jew?" but "Who is a rabbi?"

But did the community also think that conversion was "no big deal"?

SZ: I'm not sure. One thing I did notice, though, was that most people in the congregation seemed to assume that a conversion was for the sake of marriage. They seemed to find it quite strange that someone would convert for "no reason." To be honest, that is a very common attitude among Jews of every persuasion. There is a reaction of surprise: "Oh, you converted *before* you met your husband?" It's very disconcerting.

DK: I'm sure it is. Unfortunately, it also reveals why intermarriage, improper conversions, and the abandonment of any Jewish identity have reached epidemic proportions. Ironically, a person ought to convert solely for "no reason," that is, only because he or she has *mesiras nefesh*—self-sacrifice—to be close to and obey God.

Maybe I should ask what the journal entries were like at this point.

SZ: There is a lot of confusion in the journal between me seeing myself as Jewish and seeing myself as not Jewish. My concern with not being Jewish was one of "rights and privileges, and membership." I felt that it was a little presumptuous to refer to myself as Jewish, like I was invading "their" territory. On the other hand, by this time, I could see myself as nothing outside of Jewish. I saw myself as Jewish, and just needed them to see me that way too. I wanted and needed acceptance, for (as I saw it) acceptance alone stood between me and Jewishness. Acceptance was the rubber stamp of official approval on what I already had chosen for myself.

DK: Probably most converts go through a period of being and not-being, of feeling they are or should be Jewish, yet knowing they aren't yet. It must be very frustrating. It's that in-between stage, isn't it—that period of transition, not unlike adolescence or being engaged. The process of transformation may indeed be the movement to a higher level of acceptance (by oneself as well as others).

The Torah tells us that there are three situations when a person starts anew, when all transgressions are forgiven: converts when they convert, a bride and groom when they marry, and an individual when he is elevated to community leadership. Interestingly, these all require public confirmation of a change of status.

But how did you feel at that point?

SZ: At that point, it was more awkward or uncomfortable than frustrating. It was like waiting for citizenship papers, the expectation more of a transition than of a transformation.

You had asked earlier whether I had thought the process would take as long as it did. No, I don't think so. First, I didn't understand that Jews don't really care whether or not someone becomes Jewish. Second, I really thought there would be a lot more personal interest, talking to me individually, and the like. It soon became quite evident that the course of conversion was going to follow the curriculum of the confirmation class. "Okay," I figured. "That's how conversions are done, if that is what the rabbi says. Why question?"

DK: Are you saying that the course of study was an "easy A," as students say?

SZ: It was not challenging or difficult, but I still tried to take the studies very seriously. I guess you could call it an "easy A," but then, what you get out of learning is proportionate to the effort you invest. Outside of the courses, I was still pondering life.

I wrote an entry about the time in which I began to confront the enormity of what I was about to undertake. It concluded:

Pursuing truth and casting out falsehood are often two different matters. . . . I felt I knew the truth. Now it seems to me that it is not so simple, that truth is not learned in one easy step.

In truth, I am a little afraid. Afraid that alone I will not have the nerve to really stick up for the principles required of me. How much can I endure? That remains to be seen. Now I can only take one step at a time. The next step, and the next. If I meet a cliff will I jump? If I meet a river will I swim? Is that the next step? If not I will not answer now.

DK: You were right: Whether a convert or a *baal teshuvah*, we can walk only one step at a time.

SZ: I guess that the time had come for me to confront the fact that this road would not always be an easy one. I recognized how weak and vulnerable I was alone. What I did not realize was that a Jew does not travel alone.

DK: Ruth, the paradigmatic convert, said, "Where you go, I shall go." But God has said that to the Jewish people as well. Or, as the Talmud puts it, the Divine Presence went into exile with the Jewish people.

SZ: This was a difficult time for me. Maybe I was beginning to feel the first pain of what it meant to leave behind the traditions of my family. It was lonely. It was transition. Where did I belong? Whose celebrations could I share? I was uncomfortable where I was wanted—with family, and (seemingly) unwanted where I was comfortable—with Jews.

In the end, as the journal says, I realized that I could take only one step at a time. Anything else would overwhelm me.

5
Thoughts and Feelings

DK: We ended the last chapter with some journal observations about the difficulties of your transition. Are there any other thoughts or feelings from that period? I imagine that your conversion became a reality for friends and relatives then.

SZ: It did. I didn't talk much with my parents about it. They seemed resigned to my decision, and, for the sake of peace, I decided that the less said, the better. In fact, my life changed very little, other than becoming involved in synagogue activities and going to services. I think this was as I wanted it, because I hoped that if I showed my parents that there was nothing "strange" about being Jewish, then they would accept it more easily.

DK: An instinctively smart move.

Our transitions require us to be sensitive to the discomfort and insecurity of those who have supported us. Of course, we should stay on the "long-shorter" path to truth; but, in the midst of our enthusiasm, we have to respect those who showed us where it started; that means letting them travel at their own pace.

So it's important to make things as "unstrange" and inclusive as possible. Sometimes we forget not only how long and hard the path is for both converts and *baalei teshuvah*, but also how threatening and confusing it is for family and friends, for those who have not yet chosen the long-shorter path.

SZ: I'm sure that is true. Of course, my family and friends were not Jewish, and for them the long shorter path did not necessarily mean conversion to Judaism. That was something I also had to learn to accept. Was my chosen path threatening or confusing to them? Maybe a little, and it must have become more so a number of years later . . . but all in good time. This was a path that I needed to follow. I may have been aware of the difficulties I was causing others, but, in a sense, I was somewhat helpless to do anything about it. The best I could do was to minimize their trauma.

DK: You're right that if the difficulty belongs to someone else, you can't do anything about it. There's a difference between being a catalyst and being a cause.

Okay, let's move on. Where are we?

SZ: It was January 1975. I had been studying for conversion for a little over three months. The issues and difficulties of the holiday season were behind me. I had dealt with them, making a lot of mistakes, "falling down" on the path. Still, I learned from my failures and was ready to move on. It was in this spirit that I wrote the following piece in the journal:

I do not know how much I will succeed in writing, for of late my pen has found itself strangely silent when I most wanted to speak.

Does love sometimes find itself growing cold for apparently no good reason and then again grow warm, even warmer than before for no better reason? Can God be at once stranger and lover?

DK: The cycle of love, of emotional involvement, has been observed by poets and philosophers, physicians and politicians, for centuries. In *Pirkei Avos* the rabbis tell us that for any love that depends on something, once that "thing"—that attraction—vanishes, the love ceases; any love that does not depend on a particular condition will never cease.

SZ: But will even this unconditional love grow and diminish? I felt such undulations, the surge and vacuum of attachment to God. I sensed them then and I sense them now, twenty years later. They are not a "vanishing," but rather a closeness and a distancing. There are times and days that I simply feel "nearer" to God. Still, this is emotional, isn't it? And emotion is not an arbiter of truth or falsehood, of right or wrong, or of what is holy or profane.

DK: Answering the first point first, given that we are finite, the capacity of our love is also finite. So, yes, although the love itself—the bond emotional and spiritual—endures, its expression—the feeling of it—will wax and wane. That's the nature of the physical. (Obviously, God's "feeling of it" is as infinite and eternal as He is.) The rabbis long ago recognized this reality. That's why Judaism mandates and regulates cycles—national, yearly, personal, and familial. The *halacha* of cycles places our waxing and waning, our back and forth in a context of meaning and a structure of significance. It cycles us into a deeper appreciation and acceptance of, and participation in, the spirituality of our relationships.

Obligations create the foundation of a relationship; carrying them out with love intensifies and reinforces the relationship. Thus, a relationship founded on love founders, while one founded on duties—*mitzvos*—remains consistent and inviolate. However, in order for a relationship to grow, to live, it must, as the Baal Shem Tov emphasized, be permeated with love; otherwise, it's like a room full of souls without wings.

This brings us to the second point. While the emotional is not an arbiter of truth, truth cannot be expressed without emotion.

SZ: So it is our obligations, the *mitzvos*, that steady the relationship through the cycles of love—and of life.

DK: Judaism sanctifies the cycles of life, be they the cycles of nature, the cycles of history, the cycles of our selves—biologically and intellectually. *Taharas mishpacha*, the laws of family purity, not only recognize the feminine rhythms, but sanctify them.

Where were we?

SZ: We were talking about cycles. At that time in my life, I was learning about many of the Jewish lifecycles, but not their deeper—sanctified—meaning. As for boundaries, we crossed them with equanimity, seeing them as confining, not emancipating.

DK: Boundaries are essential to sanctification. Without them, there can't be sanctity—differentiation. In Judaism, *halacha* defines the boundaries.

I'd like to see more of that journal entry.

SZ: Of course. It moved from gentle musing to a love song to God, then back again:

It has not been easy for me the last couple of weeks, my love for God, that fire which sometimes burns so intensely, was dimmed. There is no real reason, it just was. Maybe it was all emotional. The fire again is burning. Faith carried me through a dark period, now the light is reappearing.

> God, I love You.
> But sometimes when I try to express it,
> The words just don't come out.
> Sometimes I pick up my guitar
> And begin to compose songs to tell You of my love for You,
> But the songs fail the task.
> Yet there surely is one song You hear
> Whose melody is total silence:
> The love-laden cry of the heart
> Carried on wings of faith unto You.
>
> God, I love You.
> And if I can be no more eloquent than that,
> It will have to do.
> I love You my King, my Father, my Lord,
> And I want more than anything
> To live a life which pleases You.
> To follow You in love,
> To go with Your people,
> To worship You,
> Wholly, only and forever.

Sometimes I think about this conversion to Judaism and I wonder if I am doing the right thing. But, I am sure I am. Despite any ghost of the past,

I am certain, beyond doubt, that I do and must and shall believe in One Holy God; His Holy Torah, and in His promise to Israel. I don't know why I believe these things, but I do. And maybe the best answer to "why?" is just because they are true. And truth, after all, is really the end of all my search.

DK: I don't know. While the poem is clearly from the heart—and you can't argue feelings—the last paragraph seems a bit like rationalizing. You're asserting—or believing—what you need to prove, as the logicians would say. Truth must be believed *and* believable.

SZ: Maybe it was rationalizing. Certainty takes study, learning, and knowledge—far more than was available to me then. What I had learned was only enough to send me down the path, confident that I would find truth on the way.

At its core this was a love song, words expressing the failure of words to contain the feeling of love. It was about loving God, a love that flowered seemingly without explanation, about a faith that blossomed without my fully understanding why.

David, we've talked about the need to know that God exists, a rational, lucid recognition of God's reality, but at this point, I don't think I had that. This was an emotional cry, an expression of feeling, not of logic. Was it wrong? Was this shallow?

DK: What and how we feel shapes our perception of reality. As the Alter Rebbe explains in *Tanya*, love and fear are the wings of the soul, enabling it to move—to soar. We need to make sure that we see correctly, not through a distorting lens. Perhaps we can say that the emotional cry itself is never wrong, but its expression, the speaking of it, may sometimes be "worded" wrong.

The cry itself, as you said, is from the heart. Prayer is called the service of the heart, because it should make feelings into servants of action.

So, to answer your question, whether it was shallow: From those emotions—or the expression of those emotions—did you grow emotionally, intellectually, and spiritually? Did it somehow become the source for more *mitzvos* or more careful observance of what you were already doing? Note that that didn't have to happen immediately or in a predictable manner.

SZ: Yes, the emotions and feelings were at the heart of a commitment that, when put to the test years later, survived. Such concerns continue to resonate in my life, though. What if I can't live up to my aspirations?

DK: I don't know that the answer is very reassuring, because it requires some distancing, some introspection and retrospection. As with the Jewish people, such self-evaluation or sanctification is framed by history and a teacher.

I will say this: The truth-test of Judaism is the *mesiras nefesh*—the self-sacrifice—that is the commitment of the Jewish people, the heritage of Abraham. If, as you say, the emotions in that piece express your acceptance of the commitment—an unconditional acceptance that manifested itself years later, then they *did* reflect a change in character—a transformation, a *teshuvah*, that already existed, at least in potential.

SZ: Most of this entry I could write again today, except that because I have had the opportunity to learn, I would have a much better idea of why I believe the things I do. So, knowing what to do gives me the capacity to express that *feeling* (of "loving God") in the *doing* of concrete *mitzvos*. In a sense, turning love from an emotion into actions, liberates its power—makes it real. I only wish I had understood that back then.

There is so much in this entry, so many themes, and it evokes so many questions, even now. Oh well . . . I guess we'd better get back to 1975.

DK: You've taken us about halfway through the learning-for-conversion process. How was your social life during this time? Your work life? Relations with parents, other friends?

SZ: Things were actually going quite well. I was still in the apartment, so I had a fair amount of independence. I visited my parents quite frequently, since they were so close by. Paula and I had become very close. We spent a lot of time together. She often came to the synagogue for Friday night services, and then we'd get together over coffee and talk. We talked about a lot of things, but even with her, I never really tried to explain my "deeper" religious emotions. She never saw my journal, for instance. I still kept a lot of my thoughts to myself.

DK: I think that most people keep their thoughts to themselves. Everyone feels that they feel deeply. While the "deeper" emotions of all kinds run parallel in us all, we also know there's a difference that makes *our* "deeper" emotions unique, and therefore ours.

SZ: Paula and I talked about work a lot. She worked at the courthouse, and I was still a teller at the bank. I wasn't particularly thrilled with my job, but it paid the rent. I was still on a part-time status, which meant that I didn't get a lot of benefits. I didn't really trust the management there, either. Many of us felt that women were not treated fairly. At one point I was considering working with NOW (National Organization for Women) to file a class action suit against the bank. In the end, I didn't have the pluck to do it.

I guess the independence made me a bit of a feminist, and I was rather cheered whenever I saw situations where women succeeded in "leveling the playing field" with men. That was certainly true at work, and it was also true at the synagogue. On *Shabbos* morning, I felt quite happy being given the opportunity to lead *Adon Olam* [a hymn that ends the service] with another young woman.

DK: I'm a little surprised, actually, that the issues of feminism and religion and women's role in Judaism haven't surfaced earlier. But then, they play a critical role later on, don't they?

SZ: Very critical. I still struggle at times with these issues. However, it was at a different level back then.

Once, I think it was at about this time, there was a period of rough winter weather. One Friday night there were not even ten men [a *minyan*], but a dozen or so women, who showed up for services. Someone had a *yahrzeit* [anniversary of a relative's passing] and had come to say Kaddish [a prayer recited on a *yahrzeit*, among other times]. The rabbi unilaterally decided that, from that point on, women would be counted in the *minyan*. He said: "The men who are not here have made this decision. Had they been here, it would not have been made."

At the time, I thought that the rabbi had done quite a marvelous thing and that womankind had taken another step forward for religious equality.

DK: "At the time. . . ." That's an open line if I ever saw one! Do you want to discuss these issues now or leave them for "that other time"?

SZ: I think it's important to talk about them now. At least, let's begin.

DK: Well, I'll say this much. The rabbi's decision, aside from being halachically wrong, doesn't make much sense logically. Where does he get the authority for it? A rabbi "in the field" is not supposed to make his own rules; he is supposed to provide guidance according to the laws and rules of Judaism, the *Shulchan Aruch*.

Furthermore, what's the basis for it? Since someone didn't fulfill their obligation, I'll change the obligation? According to that reasoning, I could also make pig kosher!

Also, contrary to being a wonderful thing, I think it was quite insulting to the women there. Had the men been there, the women wouldn't have counted. In other words, on their own, they weren't good enough. The men had to fail first. Either women should be counted in a *minyan* or they shouldn't, regardless of the men's actions. The issue should be decided solely according to the principles and methodology of *halacha*, as practiced and codified and maintained over the centuries. Otherwise, it's not a Jewish decision. And that insults both Judaism and women.

The whole incident strikes me as a paradigm of what's wrong with certain forms of "feminism" and the "feminist critique" of Judaism.

SZ: Really? From our perspective, we gave the men a chance and they blew it; they dropped the ball and we picked it up. But also from our perspective ("at the time," of course), this was tradition, not *halacha*; after all, you don't read in the Torah, "Thou shalt not count women in a *minyan*." Besides, we reasoned that even if there was an interpretation to that effect, that it was made by a bunch of insecure men with vested interests in keeping women down. As we saw it, the rabbi wasn't changing anybody's obligation, he was just making sure that the "job" got done. We didn't believe we were second-string. We felt that we were "just as good" but had never even been given the opportunity to audition. What's fair is fair, after all. Wasn't it time for women to stop being compared to children and slaves? How would you have answered us?

DK: This may be one of those deceptively long beginnings. That paragraph contains three assumptions. The assumptions are false, but behind them are three "fair" questions—issues that bother a lot of people.

First, when you say "This was tradition, not *halacha*," it assumes that a practice falls into the "Fiddler on the Roof"-type of tradition, that is, the quaint but archaic customs good for a nostalgic sigh or smile, but that we're too "enlightened" to need. But how much *halacha* did any of you know? Were you really educated enough to make that judgment, if it could be made at all? Also, we've talked a lot about *mesiras nefesh*, self-sacrifice, being *the* characteristic of the Jew, an inheritance from Abraham to every Jew and convert. Part of *mesiras nefesh* means putting aside "our perspective"—however apparently reasonable or emotionally satisfying—and accepting the Torah's perspective, defined by the Talmud and the *Shulchan Aruch*. (All this leaves aside the question of any inherent value to tradition.)

As a teacher, I know that students may ask questions, expecting answers to be reasonable before accepting them. Students may also ask questions because they've already decided from their perspective that they "know better" and want to show up the teacher. Starting from "our perspective" (whatever it is) seems to lack the humility necessary to learn or to do.

A second assumption is that the Torah is subject to interpretation and that, therefore, almost any "reading" is valid. This is the "That's what it means to me" freshman English syndrome. In a way, this is just another disguise for reasoning by emotion, which we've discussed. (I suspect that reasoning by emotion is also a form of arrogance, the opposite of *mesiras nefesh*.) The truth is, there are rules for interpretation. There are also clear literary and legal conditions for and definitions of interpretation.

The *application* of Torah principles to changing social conditions (as opposed to *altering* of Torah to changing social conditions) follows a well-defined procedure, structured by logic and a spiritual jurisprudence. I may not like something in Torah, but *halacha* or *minhag* (tradition, custom) doesn't give me the right to change it. Also, denigrating the source ("a bunch of insecure men" was the phrase) doesn't affect the Jewish validity—the spiritual truth—of the idea or practice. That's just an obviously fallacious *ad hominem* argument. Too often we confuse taste with tradition, fashion with faith. An opinion is not a reason.

Finally, there's the reading of history that assumes women were considered "second-string." For every talmudic quote that seems to be a put-down of women, there are at least two that extol women. Most statements that seem pejorative either are taken out of context or are simply observations of human nature. Certainly the Talmud has many such observations, positive and negative, about the dynamic nature of people in general and many different groups in particular. (Of course, we haven't even mentioned the issue of the sanctity of the Talmud, the different assumptions about its inherent *kedushah*. But that's a critical difference in approach.)

Failing to recognize the rhetorical structure contributes to such misunderstanding. Judging Torah and Talmud with a kindergarten-level Jewish education (what most Jews who go through Hebrew school and bar mitzvah get) doesn't help, either. This leads to reading, often unwittingly, from a Christian or secular perspective—which most critics, even Jewish ones, do. The worst problem, though, is coming at Judaism, Talmud, and tradition with a preconceived bias: agenda first, facts later—if at all.

SZ: Yet underlying even that may be a question of whether or not the Talmud is authoritative. That issue became critical for me later on, and I plan to discuss it when we get to that point. For now, though, what about that comparison of women to children and slaves?

DK: You're referring to a statement in the Talmud concerning groups who are exempt from the obligation to recite the *Shema* and put on *tefillin*. It's not a comparison. It's a statement of categories. Mourners are also exempt from certain *mitzvos*. Nor are these three always exempt from the same *mitzvos*; women are obligated in *mitzvos* from which the others are exempt. The whole issue of exemptions and obligations is discussed at length in the Talmud, codes, and commentaries. Further, there are *mitzvos* that only a kohen can do, as well as ones from which he is exempt. Such statements must be understood in context. I'd recommend, among other books, *Jewish Women in*

Jewish Law (Meiselman) and *The Modern Jewish Woman*. Anyway, each group is exempt for a different reason, but the reasons are rarely discussed by those who attack Judaism. Feminists simply point and say on this subject, "That's bad." One may just as well walk into an operating room, point to the surgeon, and say, "That's bad."

I'll say it again. Such an approach not only misreads Torah, but is insulting to women.

I think that's enough of a beginning for now, though.

SZ: Yes, for now. Regarding the rabbi's decision, he may have given us a sense of equality, but he did not teach Jewish values or *halacha*. He "solved" the problem, but did not succeed, in this instance, to lead as a Jewish leader, or to teach as a Jewish teacher.

Ethics and moral challenges, including feminist issues, place us on a very slippery slope. We can grab onto the rope of Torah with both hands and climb up, but as soon as we let go and reach out for a handhold outside of *halacha*, we find ourselves in an extremely precarious position: We have a handhold, but nothing more. Sometimes it leaves us nowhere else to go but downhill.

By the way, the synagogue wasn't a complete bastion of feminism. I still saw that there were limits on what women could do; I don't recall that they were ever called for an *aliyah*. It didn't bother me. I figured that, in good time, those who decided such things would "come around to a proper way of thinking."

DK: Do I hear an echo of "our perspective"?

SZ: Of course. That's where I was at that time. I think it is where many Jews still are.

I saw feminism—"equal opportunity for women and men"—as a positive value, something that would improve Judaism.

DK: Actually, I'd agree with the value of the statement "Equal opportunity for women and men," but the statement's incomplete. Equal opportunity to do what? "Equal opportunity" doesn't—or shouldn't—mean the opportunity to be exactly like someone else. It means the opportunity to fulfill one's purpose in life, one's God-given role in creating a dwelling place for Godliness in the physical realm. It means that everyone has an equal opportunity to be valuable in God's eyes (and, therefore, in their own eyes, as opposed to the eyes of the world), regardless of the external circumstances, provided they do what God wants, not what the self wants.

SZ: I don't think that I really distinguished between a woman's role and goals in Judaism, and how they were viewed in secular life. Considering that I'd never bothered to learn much about women in Judaism, it was a pretty pompous thing to do.

DK: Well, we all have our pomposities, I guess. And, unlike so many, you did bother to learn. But that's years in the future.

SZ: So it is. That part of my story is best left until then. Let me just add that if there was any vindication in this for me, it was that the other women at the synagogue seemed to take the same "liberated" attitude: They were Jewish, so I assumed that this was a solid Jewish stance. There was no one teaching me otherwise.

6

The Ceremony

DK: Before we get to the actual conversion, are there any "last thoughts"? Any events or feelings we need to cover?

SZ: I think I've given you a pretty clear picture of the situation. I thought, at the time, that I had learned quite a bit about Judaism. The problem was (and it is a common one) that I didn't *know* what I didn't know. In hindsight, of course, there were some serious deficiencies.

First of all was the approach to *mitzvos*. It was more in the category of, "Of course the speed limit is 55 mph; sure, I realize that I can get a ticket for going faster, but 'everybody does.'" Likewise: "Sure there are *mitzvos*, and a Jew is supposed to do them, but. . . ."

DK: But everyone ignores them?

SZ: Right. That was the attitude.

There were also omissions of fact and history, the kind of learning that fills in the holes and strengthens our knowledge, that fortifies our commitment to our people, our land, and our God; the kind of knowledge that validates what we are taught. For example, there was a journal entry from about this time where I gave lip service to "the wisdom of sages and teachers devoted to God." The truth is that I had never studied what these sages had to say. If anyone had asked me who Yehuda HaNasi was, for instance, I would have returned a rather blank stare.

DK: That was a fault in your education, then. Certain names should be fluent on the tongue. A sense of history—not just knowing dates, though that's important—would have given you an understanding of what Jewish continuity really means. I've mentioned this before, but history is Judaism's "prooftext."

By the way, another Yehuda—Yehuda HaLevi, author of the *Kuzari*—deals with authenticating sources.

SZ: That's very important, because our actions reflect how seriously we take our sources. It may well be that we didn't take Torah—and *mitzvos*—as seriously as we should have because, at some level, we hadn't accepted them as God's direct instructions to us. I'd almost suggest that we didn't take God seriously enough. But the recognition of God's authority and involvement in our lives is a consequence of accepting Torah and *mitzvos* rather than the other way around, isn't it?

DK: Perhaps. I think it actually works both ways. To truly recognize God's authority and involvement in our lives means to learn Torah and observe *mitzvos*, and vice versa. A lot of times I hear people complain—or jest—"Why doesn't God speak to me?" The immediate response is, well, do you speak to Him? Do you learn Torah? Do you perform *mitzvos*—observe *Shabbos*, put on *tefillin*, light candles, pray three times a day? It reminds me of the attitude of some students I've had. They want the credit for mastering the subject—an "A"—without doing whatever it takes to actually master the subject. The guidelines are clear; just because I don't like them or don't understand them doesn't mean that they don't work.

So you're right: If we want "God in our lives," we have to accept Torah and *mitzvos*. Again, it's the action that creates and communicates the meaning. Put another way, the reason for *mitzvos* is that they establish and maintain the relationship between God and the Jewish people.

Thinking about it, I'm a little surprised that this—and at least some of the halachic details—weren't taught. I just don't expect a "laissez-faire" approach toward *mitzvos*, not even if "Everybody ignores them."

We can be pretty sure that the inner, mystical reason—that *mitzvos* are the clothes of the soul—weren't taught either, were they?

SZ: No, not even mentioned. In fact, I'd say the opposite: I had the impression that such mysticism was almost foreign to "real" Judaism, and that any notions I might have to the contrary were just relics of past beliefs.

DK: That's part of what I'd call the secularization of religion. We've become uncomfortable with the demands a "sense of wonder" makes on us. The mysticism—the inner teachings of the Torah—gives vitality to the details of *halacha*. And it's those activities, the *mitzvos*, that raise us above the mundane and the animalistic.

SZ: It's something that I'm only now beginning to appreciate. If love and fear of God are the wings of the soul, then it is the *mitzvos* that empower and give direction and purpose to its flight.

DK: So how do you feel about what you learned?

SZ: I look back with some sadness and loss. There was so much more to Judaism; so much more to learn, to feel, to live. I didn't know.

DK: No, you didn't know. But it sounds like few, if any, in that community knew, either. The "curse" of our times is not that we're ignorant (and unobservant). It's that so many are *unaware* of their ignorance, how far they live from the relationships, faith, *mitzvos*—and ethics—of their ancestors and of Judaism itself.

SZ: Yes; and, unfortunately, because there are so many Jews who are in this state of unawareness, that level of knowledge (and observance) is often accepted as "normal Judaism." I know that we'll be talking about this problem later, so let's get back to 1975.

Pesach came very early that year, the end of March. The synagogue had planned a community seder for the second night of Pesach, and I made plans to go.

I want to point out something that may not have been obvious in our discussion of the conversion process. I originally approached the rabbi about conversion sometime before Rosh Hashanah. So that means that, after indicating my desire to convert, I had passed through Rosh Hashanah, Yom Kippur, Sukkos, Chanukah, Purim, and now Pesach, plus a great number of Sabbaths. And yet, never once was I invited to see how the holiday (or *Shabbos*) was observed in a home atmosphere. Why? Maybe because there was no significant recognition of these days outside of the synagogue. Maybe because no one bothered to ask. Maybe I was still too much of an "outsider." To be honest, I don't know.

DK: Well, I don't know either. We've talked about the need to experience, to have *daas*, in order to know and understand. I'm sure that some member of the synagogue had some aspect of *Shabbos* observance. Twenty-plus years later, it's hard to determine the reason you weren't invited to anything, whether justified or not. All we can do is point to the differential between the ideal and the event, recognizing that the ideal, in this case, the *mitzvah* of *hachnassas orchim* (inviting guests), has proved to be a practical, obtainable goal.

I suspect that if you asked those people today, they'd probably say something like "We didn't know," or "We thought you wanted to keep to yourself." Or else they'd explain about some personal problems. Being a "lamplighter" isn't easy, but it's being cognizant of—and doing—these little acts of kindness and goodness that will bring *Moshiach*.

It sounds like you're a little bitter.

SZ: I was. There are several things about that whole conversion process that I reacted to with feelings of resentment and sadness. It's important to recall the "mirror" concept, especially in light of your comment about keeping to myself. I did do that somewhat—shyness, mostly—so it is not surprising that that which was a deficiency in myself I was most aware of in others. And, of course, the best thing to do now is to take a lesson from the experience, not to dwell on it or be bitter about it.

DK: True. The purpose behind a bitter experience is not to make us bitter, but to teach us a lesson in our *avodah*, our service of God, to increase our humility and devotion, as it were. A painful encounter can be a stimulus to growth if we use it to break our ego, so to speak, to appreciate and learn from our mistakes, to recognize our limitations. On the other hand, if we use it to defend ourselves, to excuse our faults—even to blame our errors and failures on others—then it becomes a barrier, preventing development of our relationship with God.

By the way, since your conversion took place after Pesach, the holiday of redemption, it's appropriate to point out the conjunction of themes, as it were: Passover, redemption, family, and inviting guests ("All who are hungry, let them come and eat" is the spiritual and physical theme of Pesach), Torah, conversion, and *Moshiach*. They intertwined for you then; they intertwine now—as they always have—for all Jews.

SZ: Yes. Still, the path sometimes has had some rough starts and difficult turns, like the first night of that Pesach. I had found what privacy I could in the apartment that I still shared with a housemate: My seat was a pillow on the floor at the foot of my bed, and my table was a trunk covered with a white pillowcase. There I sat, trying to make a seder. I had a Haggadah and some matzoh and wine, some horseradish, and a bit of each of the rest of the symbolic foods for the seder plate. I read the whole Haggadah. I did whatever I could as best as I could figure out. It was a very lonely experience. I wondered what it must be like to have a seder with a family, at a real table. I wondered what the songs sounded like. Most of all, I wondered how I would ever learn these things. After all, I knew that the conversion was coming up, probably within a month.

DK: I don't know how to react to that. I can't imagine anyone reading this, or hearing you tell about it, without getting angry or wondering why no one—especially the rabbi—invited you to a seder. After all, Passover is *the* family holiday. As I mentioned, "All who are hungry, let them come and eat." That means Torah, the "bread" of the soul, as well as actual matzoh and chicken soup.

SZ: It is very difficult for me to "revisit," too. Such pain runs deep; tears sometimes span decades. Sometimes there's little that can be done, except to try to understand and accept that what's done is done.

DK: I have to ask, just to clarify: Didn't you have any friends in the synagogue? In six months, surely someone had taken an interest in you.

SZ: No. I had acquaintances, people knew me, spoke to me at the synagogue, but no one reached out to help me learn what being Jewish was all about.

DK: You had a lot of courage, deciding to continue after such a lonely Pesach. You must have been discouraged.

SZ: In a sense, yes. It's the frame-of-reference again. I didn't realize then that I ought to have been invited to a seder. That wasn't the issue. I cried because I was alone and because I felt so inadequate even to the simple task of a seder. I cried because I was afraid that there was a whole side of Judaism, of family life and celebration, that I might never know. In the end, there was nothing to do but wipe away the tears and go on with the Haggadah.

As far as courage goes, it wasn't that. I wanted so much to be Jewish, really Jewish, that there was only one direction I could go. If the road seemed longer, more difficult, or lonelier than I'd expected, well, I just had to dry my tears and get on with it. Determination, or maybe need, might better describe what drove me. And, besides, it was only one night.

DK: Did you go to the community seder the second night?

SZ: Yes, I did, and it was a very nice event. There was a large turnout. There was a lot of singing, a very smooth telling of the Haggadah, and enjoyable banter during dinner. I really enjoyed the whole evening. It was the last big event before the conversion would take place.

DK: Then I think we should talk about the conversion itself. When and how did it happen? Any journal entries about the event, just prior to it or after?

SZ: Surprisingly there was only one, and that was a few weeks before the actual conversion. The piece in the journal went like this:

In about a month I will be a Jewess. It is still difficult to comprehend how it all came about, for much like my physical birth it all seems natural that I am coming to this birth. I am neither afraid nor impatient. My anticipation is real, but calm. Perhaps it is best that way for I am not anticipating the event of conversion so much as the life that will be demanded after it. I have learned many new things, but now I want to learn more. I have seen and learned of many great accomplishments of Jews and I expect more accomplishments in the future, from them, from me. I have only scratched the surface of understanding Jewish life. I want to learn to probe the depths and to know, to understand, to comprehend in fullness, each and every facet of this jewel of the Jewish faith. An impossible task to complete? Admittedly true, but not too great a task to begin. But how, and by what road? That is my question. I await an answer.

DK: It sounds like, psychologically, you were already past the conversion. The test was over, and you were just waiting for the official results. So there's nothing left but to contemplate life with "certification." You don't sound very excited or nervous. It's almost as if the conversion will give you license to breathe easy for a few months, to start a slower path of learning and doing.

SZ: No, I don't think it was that. I wanted the conversion so that I could finally "go in the door." It was very much like being in a womb, waiting to be born, to be recognized as a person—or, in this case, as a Jew.

DK: The need to be validated.

It is worth repeating that the rabbis tell us that there are three times in a person's life when all past transgressions are forgiven, when they become spiritually pure, transformed into a new state of being. These are when a person marries, when a convert converts, and when a person is elevated to high office.

So what do you think of that entry now?

SZ: With that marvelous gift of 20/20 hindsight, I find it a little painful to look back on what I wrote there. This is because of the almost childlike trust that was there, especially in the opening statement. I stood ready to receive a precious jewel, a diamond whose facets reflected the hopes and trials, the faith and dedication, the sacrifices and victories of *am Yisroel*. When one knows that that jewel will, in a moment of truth, be cast to the ground, shattered into a million fragments, exposed to be nothing but glass. . . . It hurts.

It isn't the right time to say more. Let's push on.

DK: So at last we come to the conversion itself. An important milestone in your life, obviously. Why don't you describe your feelings, what happened, and how it went?

SZ: I had so much of the "formula" right. I understood that this would be like a rebirth. I understood that things would be expected of me as a Jew that were not expected of me as a gentile. I was willing to commit myself. I wanted to be part of the family. I knew that there was a lot I still didn't know.

DK: What did you think would be expected of you as a Jew? What did you think you would have to do?

SZ: What did I think would be expected of me as a Jew? I had rather "global" aspirations, like *tikun olam* [repairing the world]. I saw a responsibility to help bring justice and truth to humanity, to behave in a way that was beyond reproach, because whatever I would do, I would do as a Jew. Maybe that, more than anything, was what I was committing myself to: to be Jewish in the world's eyes, even in the face of anti-Semitism and misunderstanding; to be Jewish even if it caused difficulty between my family and me.

DK: That's how God describes the Jewish people: a treasured nation, one the other nations will point to and say, if we observe the commandments, "This people exemplifies Divine wisdom and holiness. Let us go and learn."

SZ: But those aren't the specifics you were looking for, are they?

DK: In part. I also wanted to know what would be different about your life. What were you committing to?

SZ: It's back to the details, the *mitzvos*. I can't tell you that I was expecting to keep the *mitzvos*, because I had not learned what, or how important, the *mitzvos* were. I wish I could tell you that I made a commitment to keep kosher and not to do any of the thirty-nine *melachos* [categories of work prohibited by the Torah] on *Shabbos*, to say a *brocha* [blessing] before and after eating. I wish I could, but I can't—and I am truly embarrassed by that fact. Sure, I wouldn't eat pork or seafood, and I wouldn't actually go to work on Saturday, but that is about as far as it went. It was about the same level that I perceived others were keeping.

DK: Understandable, if regrettable. Only a *tzaddik*, or someone attached to a *tzaddik*, can rise above their environment on their own.
Was there a timetable for the conversion?

SZ: I knew that the rabbi wanted to complete the conversion before the confirmation class graduated.

DK: It sounds like there was some urgency.

SZ: The rabbi wanted me to be able to participate with the confirmation class graduation, and probably felt that it was important for me to be Jewish when I did so, since each confirmand took an active part in the service. Perhaps he also wanted to get the conversions out of the way before summer vacations started and schedules got hectic.

DK: Let's assume the best of motives. So, after Pesach. . . .

SZ: So, just after Pesach, the rabbi told me that he was planning to go ahead with the conversion at the end of April. I was quite happy, of course. He spoke to me for a few minutes, and explained that I would need to go before a *Bais Din* to answer some questions, and then he would arrange for a *mikvah*. He reviewed the material that I should expect questions on: The *Shema*, the calendar, the dates and significance of the various holidays, major biblical figures, and my own commitment to Judaism to the exclusion of any other religion. I felt like I was studying for a final exam. Still, it was exciting to think that I was finally going to be Jewish.

DK: Aside from feeling like you were taking a final exam, did you know all the questions you were going to be asked? Did the course of study challenge you? Did it prepare you to *live* as a Jew?

SZ: The questions were mostly taken from what we'd studied in the confirmation class, so I was pretty comfortable with them. I had to review the dates for some of the holidays, and get the order of the months straight in my head.

The course of study did not particularly challenge me, and it most certainly did not prepare me to live as a Jew in the most important and fundamental ways.

DK: We'll talk about that as we get to it. Okay, then what happened?

SZ: I told Paula, who was quite happy to share my elation. I told her that the rabbi said that there would be a sort of kiddush after the conversion and that I should bring some wine. He suggested that I get some "Rose of Sharon" wine, since the Hebrew word for "rose" is *shoshana*, the Hebrew name that I would be given.

DK: Any significance to the name?

SZ: My English name, Susan, is derived from Shoshana.

We were supposed to bring some cake or cookies along, too.

DK: We? Who's we?

SZ: Me and the other people that were to be converted at the same time.

The rabbi had also told me that I'd need to cover my head for the service, so I needed to get a hat.

DK: What service?

SZ: After going to the *mikvah*. As near as I could figure out, it was when we officially got our "names."

Of course, I invited Paula to join me for this event, and she happily agreed. I hadn't made any other close friends at the synagogue, so she was the only person who would be "there" for me.

DK: The conversion wasn't a public event, was it?

SZ: It wasn't in the synagogue bulletin or anything like that. We were welcome to bring friends along to wait with us and attend the kiddush afterwards—moral support, I guess, and someone with whom to celebrate.

So the appointed day finally arrived. We would-be converts gathered at the synagogue to face the *Bais Din*. We were called individually into the rabbi's study, where we sat in front of the *Bais Din*, which was composed of the rabbi, the cantor, and one of the officers of the synagogue. After I was seated, the questions began. They were exactly what I'd been told to expect. "Can you read the *Shema*? What does it mean? When is Pesach? What is its significance?" I was there for about ten minutes. The *Bais Din* was satisfied, and I was excused and asked to wait in the social hall until everyone was finished. Then we were ready to go to the *mikvah*. We got into our cars and went to an apartment complex that had an enclosed pool. We changed into our swimsuits and stepped into the water. The rabbi instructed us on the procedure, making sure that we submerged completely and got our hair wet. A few of us went in at the same time. We dunked, then repeated a solemn statement of commitment and dedication to God and Torah, Judaism, and the Jewish people; then we made a blessing and dunked again a time or two.

DK: I don't know what to say. A swimming pool is not a proper *mikvah*. And only one person at a time should have been converted. (Also, a *Bais Din* has to be *shomer Shabbos*—meaning, observing the laws and restrictions.)

SZ: The rabbi was willing to use a swimming pool for a *mikvah*. I had no reason not to trust him. I guess that converting us together was more efficient.

DK: I hate even to ask this, but were all of you female?

SZ: There were about three women and one man. I don't believe that he went into the pool at the same time we did, though.

I didn't understand the significance of the *mikvah*, just that the rabbi said that it was something we needed to do. I felt like I was becoming a part of the Jewish people, though. "It's like crossing the Red Sea," I thought.

DK: That's a good way to think of it, but it's rather disturbing to hear that you hadn't been taught the significance of the *mikvah*.

SZ: True, but as the saying goes, "Ignorance is bliss." We stepped out and were declared to be Jewish. We changed into our clothes and returned to the synagogue for the kiddush.

DK: How did you feel? What were your feelings from the time you went into the *"mikvah"* until you returned to the synagogue?

SZ: I felt that I had finally "arrived," that at last I could be part of this family—that I would be accepted. Now I could say "yes" when asked if I was Jewish, instead of struggling with how to answer.

DK: When you got back to the synagogue, what happened?

SZ: Well, first we went into the small chapel for a short service.

DK: Consisting of what?

SZ: The service was very short. As I recall, it consisted of a few blessings, the *Shema, Shehechiyanu* [the prayer thanking God for bringing us to this particular auspicious time], and a few words from the rabbi. We also got our Hebrew names and the conversion certificates, which stated that we had had conversions in accordance with the laws of Moses and Israel, and that we had gone before a *Bais Din* and immersed in a *mikvah.*

DK: Well, we know that a swimming pool isn't a kosher *mikvah.* Beyond that, the laws of Moses and Israel require a Jew to keep *Shabbos,* kosher, and the like. (Therefore, a convert has to observe all these laws from the moment of conversion.) But let's not spoil the moment. What happened after the service?

SZ: After the service, we went into the social hall and had some wine and cake. I guess that this kiddush was to celebrate the *"mitzvah."*

It felt good to have finally "made it." At last, I could stop *wanting* to be Jewish and just *be* Jewish. I felt like I had finally caught up with who I was supposed to be.

There is no journal entry about this event. That really isn't so surprising, since I most often turned to my journal when I was having an emotional struggle. At this point, everything seemed wonderful.

7

Afterthoughts

DK: What are the positives from your conversion experience?

SZ: The most important thing was a solid commitment to being Jewish. As part of the conversion—actually, at the *mikvah*—we took an oath that we would be faithful to God, Torah, and the Jewish people. I meant it as an irrevocable promise; whether I fully understood all that it entailed is a different matter.

    Of course, I learned some things along the way: the basics of Hebrew, the melodies and words of many songs in the services.

    The dedication of some of the congregation to Soviet Jewry helped me understand that *am Yisroel* is a global family. And I learned that, at least sometimes, *mitzvos* are important.

    What I learned from my Conservative conversion was that being Jewish was important. It was a gift of birth or a privilege of "becoming." From that point on, Jews were not just God's chosen people, they were *my* people, too.

DK: Powerful and important lessons—and issues that will resurface later. Before we go on, are there any issues or questions we've raised that we need to finish discussing?

SZ: There is one continuing theme that we have touched on before: How can a person know whom to trust? How do we—if, in fact, we can—stand above our own ignorance and emotional investment to choose a teacher? How do we uncloak our guide and see whether *emes* [truth] or *sheker* [falsehood] is leading us down that path?

I guess that the "simple" answer is that the teacher is committed to Torah and *mitzvos*, but when that teacher is *defining* what Torah and *mitzvos* are, that answer is not enough. My Christian teachers would have defined Torah as the predecessor of their religious texts. The Conservative rabbi might have defined Torah as a divinely inspired guide to a righteous and moral life. Still other rabbis would have insisted that it was a holy dictation from God at Sinai.

How can I, as a seeker of truth, know whom to believe? What are the questions that will allow me to authenticate my source? Are there questions that can transcend that ever-present "frame of reference"?

DK: Whom can we trust; how do we choose a teacher; whom do we believe?

There's no simple answer to this. If there were, many of the controversies and conflicts that form and constitute history wouldn't exist. Yet, paradoxically, history itself answers the questions. Of course, waiting a hundred years to know whom to believe doesn't help those of us living *in media res*. At least, however, it gives us a starting point: Which teachers and texts have been authenticated by history? Knowing this, the seeker of truth can then ask: Does my text simply and humbly support and develop the ideas of the historical text? Does my teacher follow and teach the rules and methodology of the authenticated teachers?

So you've already answered your question, in a sense. The teacher must be committed to Torah and *mitzvos*; that's a *sine qua non*—an absolute minimum requirement. Your comment, ". . . but when that teacher is *defining* what Torah and *mitzvos* are, that answer is not enough," indicates a method for testing both the commitment and the trustworthiness of the teacher.

For by what right does the teacher make such a definition? The Torah defines itself; indeed, anyone who comes to add or subtract from it is a false prophet. If one claims that it's a matter of interpretation (i.e., that Torah is no more than "a divinely inspired guide to a righteous and moral life"—a claim not the province of one denomination or philosophy, by the way), then again we refer to the verdict of history. Even if it's only "a matter of interpretation," Jewish history—Judaism itself—has already limited, defined, and established what are *legitimate* interpretations, and how to arrive at and apply them.

Torah and *mitzvos* do not exist in the abstract. The Jewish people have survived and continue to exist because of their observance of *mitzvos*—*Shabbos*, *kashrus*, family purity, and the like. Whether we want to explain this spiritually or sociologically, philosophically or historically, it's a fact. There have been movements in the past—for example, the Sadducees, the Karaites—that have tried to eliminate or modify the basics and methods of the Oral Law. All such efforts result in either the destruction of the group or its mutation into something non-Jewish.

If the "teacher" is going to legitimize activities that have been proscribed by the Talmud, Maimonides, and the *Shulchan Aruch*, we should ask why. Torah is not academics; it is the rules and substance of our relationship with God.

You asked how we can stand above our own ignorance and emotional investment to choose a teacher. In a sense, we can't ignore our emotional investment; nor should we. The question, in fact, reminds me of some "debates" I've had with college students. "I've been there" doesn't always answer "How do you know?"

But again, by recognizing what our emotional investment—the boundaries of our emotional comfort zone—is, and what the teacher's is, we can assess the agenda, so to speak. It's not easy, though. And when are we mature enough to begin?

Torah emphasizes the importance of humility, the value of putting aside one's ego. The trick is to do so without repressing one's intellect. In other words, we have to put aside the ego while simultaneously examining the logic and results of the teachings. We have to ask, but we also must know when to ask in order to learn and when to ask in order to challenge. *Naaseh* ("we will do") comes before *nishma* ("we will understand"), but both are necessary.

It's not easy to be so rigorous or so honest. Convenience confines commitment.

Let's see. Next you asked: "How can I, as a seeker of truth, know whom to believe? What are the questions that will allow me to authenticate my source?"

The first question we've already answered, to some extent. First you have to make sure that you *are* a seeker of truth, and that means putting aside your ego, understanding the axioms of a system and examining the logic of application and methodology. If belief is to be more than an undifferentiated opinion, then both experience and history must support it.

Questions that authenticate a source? I'd start with two, I guess. One: How are its claims verified? Two: If we take its position to the extreme—insist on consistency and observance by all—what results? Anything else?

SZ: We've used the term "soul" a number of times, almost naively assuming that it means the same thing to everyone. There's something special about a Jewish soul, isn't there?

DK: Well, we're all individuals, but every Jewish soul is truly a part of God above. That is, there's a *pintele Yid*, a spark of Godliness that every Jewish person shares, so to speak.

SZ: I had an ulterior motive in asking the question.

Given what you say, for a gentile to become a Jew, it is necessary to have a definable process by which the soul undergoes a transformation, because their essence, their soul, is changed and becomes "a part of God above." Certainly, this is something that only God can accomplish.

What I am trying to say is that a person cannot simply choose to be Jewish; that person must also be "chosen," spiritually invested with a soul (or spark) from outside the self.

DK: Exactly, although the soul isn't changed so much as invested with "a part of God above." The Godly soul of the Jew, the inheritance from Abraham, is the soul as "the breath of God." That's the spiritual dimension. The physical–social dimension (the conversion process) concretizes this infusion, gives it reality in space–time. (That, of course, is what every *mitzvah* does: gives the spiritual space–time reality.)

Simply put, without commitment to that covenant, the commitment that bears the name of action (i.e., submitting to the yoke of the *mitzvos*), one cannot become a part of the Jewish people. And only a person who is a part of the Jewish people can have a soul that is "a part of God above."

SZ: When I was waiting for the conversion, I wanted—needed—acceptance, for—as I saw it—it was only acceptance that stood between me and Jewishness. Acceptance was the "rubber stamp" on what I already had chosen for myself.

But with even the cursory understanding of the soul that you presented a moment ago, it becomes quite clear that acceptance—by me, the congregation, or any other person, for that matter—is not sufficient to effect a conversion. The acceptance has to come from the Source of the transformation, the Source of the soul: God.

So, again: "How can we know the mind of God, if not through Torah?"

The conditions for Divine acceptance are spelled out only in Torah—*halacha*. Contrary to my perceptions at the time, conversion is not a "rubber stamp," but a transformation achieved only in accordance with *halacha*.

That is why a person can't just declare himself to be Jewish, why a rabbi and a *Bais Din* must oversee the conversion, and why an impeccable attention to halachic details plays such a vital role.

DK: It goes without saying that the rabbi and the *Bais Din* must be observant, committed to all the halachic "details," *because they come from God to the Jewish people through the Torah that was given to Moses at Sinai.*

SZ: A person can't become Jewish simply by running up to a *Bais Din* and shouting, "I believe!"

8
The Next Stage

DK: What happened next? On a practical level, how did your life change?

SZ: Almost nothing changed on a practical level. Emotionally, I felt more at ease, of course. I understood that I was now a full member of the congregation. I could join in to whatever level any other woman was permitted, without the restrictions that applied to non-Jews.

DK: I guess that, in one sense, practically nothing should change. When a child becomes bar or bat mitzvah, after all, what does he or she do differently? They simply perform publicly what they've practiced privately.

That's the point, though, isn't it? We become what we practice. Exercise becomes experience through the transformations, the rites of passage—be they conversion, bar or bat mitzvah, or marriage—that confer responsibility.

If, as Judaism claims, rituals (*mitzvos*) are repetitions that build the relationship and demonstrate the covenant between God and the Jewish people, obviously they are innately important. Therefore, we must learn how to do them—through study and practice—in order to create a spiritual reality.

This also means that the *details* of the rituals are also in and of themselves significant, for the very details of observance determine, as it were, what the spiritual reality will be.

SZ: You're right. "Who we are" does not determine our actions so much as our actions determine who we are. While the common attitude is "I'll do it when I feel like it," the reality is that I won't "feel like it" unless I do it.

DK: True. An animal—and the animal soul of man—has the attitude of "I'll do it when I feel like it."

Desire by itself, the "I feel like it," can move us to *kedushah*, to holiness, as well as toward the "other side." But the *yetzer hara*—the evil inclination—adds the twist "I'll do it when," turning *mitzvah* as imperative, a submission of will, into *mitzvah* as prerogative, a degradation of will, and thus into a violation of the *mitzvah*.

The words of Hillel, "Don't say 'When I have free time I will study,' for perhaps you will never have free time," apply to doing *mitzvos* as well.

SZ: Of course, it helps if someone has taught us what it is we are *supposed* to do. At that point, Judaism was a religious philosophy and a social outlook. I'm not sure how one practices that, especially since uniquely Jewish routines and rituals—the details—didn't play much of a role in my everyday life. Even though I was intellectually aware of the existence of a few details, I really hadn't come to appreciate their importance. I certainly didn't view them as linchpins of Jewish life.

I want to emphasize that my view of Judaism was very "synagogue-based." My personal life followed the lifestyle of Jews I knew in the community. As a result, I didn't keep kosher or dress or act in any particularly Jewish manner. Every Friday night and *Shabbos* morning I faithfully attended services, but essentially for six days a week my Jewishness was defined by the star of David that I wore around my neck. My conversion had tied me to the Jewish family and community, but not to *mitzvos*.

DK: That paragraph of yours says a lot about the condition of Jewish belief and practice, for, as you say, your personal life understandably followed the pattern set by the community.

Anyway, it sounds as though things got pretty quiet after the conversion.

SZ: There was no religious awakening or intense searching. I had my conversion certificate. I was content.

Shortly after the conversion, a group of Orthodox Jews from Seattle came to our synagogue. Besides a rabbi, there was a group of young men, probably college-age. They were dressed in black suits and hats; the rabbi had a beard. They looked seriously Jewish to my uninitiated eyes. I don't know why they were there. I don't know what group they were affiliated with. I just know that they were there at that kiddush after *Shabbos*-morning services.

It was a different sort of kiddush. Everyone started singing songs in Hebrew that I hadn't heard before. I tried to "fake it" and sing along, too. That seemed to distress one of the young men; I had no idea why. After joining in one song whose melody I found especially captivating, this fellow turned to me and said, "Well, are you satisfied? Do you know what you were singing?" I felt intimidated by the tone of his questions, and meekly answered, "No."

"It was 'A Woman of Valor,'" he replied, making it clear that he felt it wasn't entirely appropriate that I should have been singing it. I felt so embarrassed. I shrank into the background and had no interaction with them the rest of the time they were there.

DK: *He* should have felt embarrassed.

I'm reminded of the story of the Baal Shem Tov concerning the shepherd boy and Rosh Hashanah services. One Rosh Hashanah, an ignorant shepherd boy, seeing all the townsfolk hurrying to *shul*, followed them. Now, his religious education was sorely lacking, to say the least. But when he saw everyone praying, he wanted to pray, too. So he poured out his heart the only way he knew how. He whistled. Before the congregants could throw him out for disturbing the decorum of the service, the Baal Shem Tov, who was in that synagogue, came up and hugged the boy. "His sincere, heartfelt prayer broke through the gates of heaven," the Baal Shem Tov explained.

How much better had the visitor asked you the same questions not with annoyance, but understanding. Imagine the same words with a different tone! (As we said before, words from the heart go to the heart.)

SZ: I wish that the Baal Shem Tov had been there then. Unfortunately, this was my first impression of what religious Jews were like. My response was fear, embarrassment, and perplexity.

DK: What a shame. Of course, religious Jews also are only human. As you said, the fellow was young and perhaps inexperienced. Still. . . .

SZ: Soon after that, our rabbi pulled me aside. He said that when he told us to wear bathing suits for the *mikvah*, he had expected suits that were much briefer than the one-piece swimsuit I had worn. "It covered so much. It would be a good idea for you to talk to this rabbi from Seattle the next time you go there and go to the *mikvah* again."

DK: Strange. Clearly the rabbi felt uncomfortable and was making an excuse for not doing it right. Obviously, that visit disturbed him. But the *mikvah* itself hadn't been kosher to begin with. (That's the problem with symbolic Judaism: a *mikvah* or a swimming pool, this style of bathing suit or that; it doesn't matter, since the act doesn't mean anything in and of itself. It's only symbolic.)

I'm surprised by your rabbi's reaction. I wonder what prompted him to make that suggestion, to plant the seed of doubt in your mind. His response raises some questions, perhaps only rhetorical: Why wasn't he bothered before their visit? If he was, why didn't he act otherwise? What was it about the visit that motivated him?

SZ: They will have to remain rhetorical questions, I'm afraid. The rabbi never gave me a hint of why he was bringing the issue up.

In fact, his concerns made no sense to me, and after that little incident with the visiting group, I had mixed feelings. On the one hand, I wanted to call the rabbi in Seattle, if only out of respect for our rabbi; but on the other hand, I was afraid to do so. Rabbis were still frighteningly authoritative, unapproachable figures in my mind. I never did contact the rabbi in Seattle. Emotionally, I was not prepared to deal with any barriers to what I had waited so long to attain. I reasoned that my rabbi had merely suggested this *mikvah* thing, and that he wouldn't have signed the certificate if there were any real problems.

DK: Well, just going to the *mikvah* wouldn't have changed anything, without practical changes in your life—that is, *mitzvos.*

I suspect you realized that something was wrong, otherwise your rabbi wouldn't have suggested this *"mikvah* thing." But it put you in an almost impossible dilemma: The very person who certified your Jewishness now suggested that there was a problem with his certification—or with yours.

Who wants to have their life's dream, their life's work, their soul itself, suddenly snatched from them? Your very understandable reluctance came from the deepest sense of self. If, after all you'd been through, there was a problem, you weren't yet Jewish, you'd been deceived—how could you continue? You couldn't go back, of course, but to go forward meant admitting that falsehood still loomed over your shoulder—or over the shoulder of someone you trusted.

Your situation reminds me of the Akedah—Abraham's near-sacrifice of Isaac. At the moment when his life's work was complete, so to speak, when he had proved the truth of his efforts and existence, came the demand for one more sacrifice, a sacrifice beyond reason or understanding. (Of course, as our commentators explain, that readiness to sacrifice was necessary to make all else true.)

SZ: You've perceived my emotions very well! I was facing a question of not only whom to trust, but *when* to trust. Did I believe the rabbi on the certificate or in a briefly spoken message? More like Jonah than Abraham, I couldn't handle the challenge, so I ran away; I rationalized my way out of the emotional conflict—almost. Deep inside me, maybe it never went away.

There are only a couple of journal entries at this point. They both express my frustration about the gap between what I expected Judaism to be and what it seemed to be in my life and in those around me. In fact, they mirrored internal frustrations, my failure to achieve that connection with God that still seemed just out of reach.

DK: I'm not sure why, if you'd reached a lull, a sense of ease, you'd feel frustrated. How did it seem out of reach?

SZ: The lull was a sense that I didn't have to pursue Judaism anymore because I had found it. The frustration came because what I had *found* didn't match the depth and fervor that I had *expected*.

DK: Okay, let's look at the journal entry.

SZ: Here it is:

> Lest We Forget . . .
>
> If the world is forgetting God,
> Then I fear for the world.
> And if man has forgotten how to love God,
> Then I pity man's loneliness.
>
> Where is the fire, my God?
> Where is the pillar of light
> Which guarded Israel by night?
> And where is the fire inside,
> The fervor, the passion for You?
>
> In a world of words and words
> In deafening cacophony
> Have we forgotten how to pray?
> In the noise of modernity
> Have we forgotten to listen to You?
> Let us not forget, Lord;
> For the forgetting of You is death.
> Let us live O God,
> That we may survive this wilderness
> That we once again know that fire
> Which will guide us and guard us,
> That we may enter the promised land
> Once again,
> And in a new way.
> And the promised land?
> A whole world . . .
> That remembers You.

Though I'm not sure that I recognized it then, this poem was a reflection of my own turmoil, the lack of fire and fervor in my own faith.

Despite the conversion, I was still wandering in the wilderness, looking for a clear path to God.

DK: It certainly reflects a sense of bewilderment and confusion. It seems that you're looking at your ennui and wondering where it came from. (Of course, it's hard to remain enthusiastic about things that are only symbolic.)

SZ: My "ennui"? What's that?

DK: Fatigue. I find it in phrases like, "Where is the fire, where is the pillar of light," the repetition of "forgetting."
    What happened next?

SZ: Summer came and I had accumulated a bit of money and some vacation time. I wanted to take a trip around the Pacific Northwest, and asked Paula to come along. One of our stops was in Vancouver, British Columbia. We arrived there on Friday and checked into a motel near the beach. Just before sunset, we drove off to dinner at a spot recommended in our tour book. On the way we passed through a Jewish neighborhood. There were a lot of Jews in *kippahs* walking along the sidewalk, some with family in tow. I had mixed feelings. I felt a little guilty; after all, this was *Shabbos*, and going out to dinner probably wasn't the most Jewish thing to be doing at the moment. I felt a little envy, perhaps, for these folks who had succeeded in making Judaism so important in their lives. And I remember thinking how religious they must be that they would choose to walk, rather than drive, to their synagogue. A part of me wanted to get out and join their peculiar parade and see where it led.

DK: Your *yetzer tov* (good inclination). Rashi comments that when Rebecca was pregnant with Jacob and Esau, whenever she would pass a house of study, Jacob would pull her in that direction; whenever she passed a house of idol worship, Esau would pull her in that direction.
    One reason you didn't follow them is that only a part of you wanted to get out and join. *It* wanted to *get out*. When that "part" was able to pull *all* of you along, you did join the "peculiar" parade.

SZ: Yes, years later I did, and we'll get to that. However, that evening I kept my thoughts to myself and said nothing to Paula.

When we got home, it was the beginning of July. I wrote this entry in my journal:

> God must once again become
>> the imperative for human existence.
>
> Man must no longer ignore his Creator
>> He must remember.
>
> A revolution must take place among the few
>> for the sake of truth.
>
> And the many must follow
>> and establish justice for all time.
>
> Despair must not overtake faith.
>> God is forever.
>
> We can and must establish justice and truth
>> and make this earth holy.
>
> But we must begin now
>> the task cannot wait.
>
> Today we must walk toward light
>> lest darkness overtake us.
>
> We must believe in God.
>
> We must live like we believe in God.

What strikes me most about this entry is how universal, as opposed
to "Jewish," it is. Nothing in it speaks of a unique mission, of *mitzvos*
or specific acts, just a demand for justice and truth for the sake of
God. Not that that is bad; it just isn't Jewish. You'll see that all the
things I wrote in my journal in this period of life reflected this idealistic universal theme. The infusion of Judaism, *mitzvos*, into everyday life was totally absent.

DK: Judaism has always had a universal component, looking toward
the complete and final redemption, the messianic era. What so many
(Jew and non-Jew) forget, overlook, or distort is that the way to that
idealistic reality has always been, and can only be, through *mitzvos*.

SZ: Perhaps some forget, overlook, or distort; others just don't know. They haven't been taught. That was my situation back then. Even so, as someone who had supposedly studied and learned to become Jewish, I should have been aware of that. It should have been part of me. The journal entry suggests that it wasn't.

That September, I moved back home. My housemate had decided to make other arrangements, and I couldn't afford the apartment by myself.

DK: Did your move back home create any conflicts? How did it affect your observance, your Jewishness?

SZ: There weren't any real conflicts. My folks were very accommodating about my decision. Since my observance, as I explained earlier, was so minimal, not much was affected by my coming back home.

DK: Now that your parents and old friends saw you as a Jew, how did it affect your relationships? Were there any tests or trials, any emotional upheavals?

SZ: No. It seems strange, doesn't it? Here I had seemingly achieved the identity for which I was searching, the beliefs that I had been willing to risk my soul to attain and for which I had hoped and waited, and now . . . nothing.

You asked about relationships. No one seemed to care much one way or the other about my conversion. It was more of a "So what?" attitude. I think that is probably because they saw conversion to Judaism in the same light as conversion to any other religion: a mental decision, not an event. I didn't do anything to dispel the notion. I didn't discuss the conversion with my parents or other family. At some very deep level I think I felt embarrassed over my decision to become Jewish, and to reject the traditions of the family I was born into.

DK: Maybe what you felt was a discomfort similar to the rabbi's. If the conversion was, in fact, only a mental decision without any practical difference, why did you do it? Back home, faced with your non-Jewish family that lived pretty much as you—now considering yourself Jewish—lived, maybe you had to ask yourself, "What was the point?"

SZ: No. I never asked what the point was. To me, becoming Jewish, gaining that link to *am Yisroel,* having a way to affirm a faith in One God, was of such paramount significance and importance to preclude the question.

The embarrassment stemmed more from my inability to explain to my family the inner motivations that led me to conversion.

DK: So in September 1975 you were settling into living back home. How were the High Holidays that year? I'm sure that they were different than the year before.

SZ: The High Holidays were more meaningful that year. I had a better idea of what they meant, and I understood that this was a time of judgment. This was my first Yom Kippur as a Jew.

I took it very seriously. Something about the day itself causes us to take a sober look at life. Maybe that is why so many people come to synagogue on that day, if on no other. We need each other for support and strength as we become painfully aware of our own inadequacies. It helps to know that we are not alone.

DK: I'd like to think that at some point on Yom Kippur, even for a little while, most people experience the sense of *cheshbon nefesh*—spiritual accounting—you mention.

Let's get back to what was going on in your life. After the High Holidays, where did you find yourself, so to speak?

SZ: Back at work. I was getting pretty frustrated with my inability to get anywhere. Here I was with a college degree in Russian and a minor in political science, working as a bank teller. I began to explore some other possibilities.

I wanted to apply for a job that would use my Russian, which was starting to get rusty from lack of use. I decided to take a refresher course at a local state university while waiting (I hoped) to hear of some job offers. I also applied to the University of Washington for the Russian Area Studies graduate program beginning in the spring quarter of 1976.

Eventually, one of the government agencies to which I had applied asked me to come in for an interview and all the attendant paperwork and background reviews that went along with it.

I knew it would be a while before I would hear about a definite job offer, so I went on to the graduate program in Seattle. I chose to live at the Russian House because of its proximity to campus and because I needed to keep up my language skills. Soon after I got there, I began to look for Jewish connections.

There was a Chabad House a few blocks away from the Russian House. They had a *Shabbos* dinner every Friday night, and anyone was welcome. At the suggestion of a casual acquaintance, I began going there.

DK: Being Lubavitch, I'm very interested in your experiences there. Considering your previous experience with "black hat and beard," I'm surprised (pleasantly, of course) that you went so willingly.

SZ: All I knew at the time was that some Jewish organization called Chabad was being nice enough to invite students to services and to *Shabbos* dinner. I didn't know anything about Chabad before I went; I didn't even know that they were religious. So there really wasn't any reason that I would form an association between it and the other "black-hat" group. To me, Jews were Jews; some more religious, some less. Getting all the "labels" sorted out takes time and experience. (Truthfully, I *still* can't keep most of them straight.)

DK: Truthfully, I don't bother. We can separate philosophies and label movements, but the differences between Jews are secondary— even irrelevant—to the common Godly soul we all share.

Legitimate Jewish *minhagim* (customs) need to be respected and preserved. These differences, like those between Ashkenazim and Sephardim, actually enhance Judaism by revealing the "seventy faces" of the Torah. In the same way, there may be philosophies or approaches that emphasize certain aspects of Torah (while, of course, stressing the importance of observing all the *mitzvos*); these, too, contribute to the totality of Judaism.

When it comes to individuals, however, and movements that try to define them for political or institutional reasons, we're better off following the example of the Rebbe Rashab (third Lubavitcher Rebbe), who, in a discussion with one of his distinguished followers, a wealthy diamond merchant, began praising a simple but honest God-fearing fellow. "Why do you make so much of him?" the merchant asked.

"He possesses fine qualities," the Rebbe replied. "I don't see it," the merchant said. Later, the Rebbe asked to see the merchant's diamonds. Obligingly, the merchant spread them out and began to point out their fine qualities. "And this," he said, pointing to a particular stone, "is a superlative gem." The Rebbe said, "I see nothing in it." The merchant said, "Ah, Rebbe, with diamonds, one has to be a *mayvin* [expert]." The Rebbe replied, "And with *neshamos* (souls), one also has to be a *mayvin*."

Every Jew is a superlative gem.

We should all spend less time on labels and more on *mitzvos*, *ahavas Yisroel*—and on being lamplighters.

Anyway, what did you think of the service? Was it the first Orthodox service you attended?

SZ: Yes, and there were some surprises. I had heard of men and women sitting separately, but this was the first time I had encountered a *mechitza*, a six-foot-high curtain dividing the men's and women's sections. It was a side-by-side *mechitza*, so I didn't perceive it as a "put-down" of women. It didn't bother me at all.

DK: That's interesting, because the *mechitza* is a common excuse or point of attack. You were still a bit of a feminist then, weren't you? Why didn't it bother you? After all, it prevented you from participating as you had in the synagogue at home.

SZ: There were a few reasons, I think. First, this was not a synagogue, but a house, so the *mechitza* was portable and didn't seem all that severe. Also, everything seemed different, unlike any other *Shabbos* experience I'd had. I was too busy trying to get oriented to worry about participating! Besides, I didn't go there looking for problems. I went to be with Jews on *Shabbos*.

I enjoyed spending *Shabbos* at the Chabad House. The singing and general atmosphere was liberating. Of course, the food was good, but that was secondary. Food I could get anywhere. To find this spirit was more rare.

DK: If we're doing our job, less rare. But can you be more specific?

SZ: Besides singing, there was Torah. The rabbi always talked at the meal. Sometimes he was funny, sometimes serious, but always we felt uplifted when we left. What struck me most was how different this expression of Judaism was from that I had experienced before. It seemed more "real" somehow.

DK: Sounds like a typical Chabad House. Did you get a chance to talk with the Chabad rabbi?

SZ: The rabbi at the Chabad House was very nice, but I never got to know him well. He often walked out to the edge of the campus and spoke with students passing by. I wish I had stopped to talk to him. We occasionally exchanged greetings, but little more. I still couldn't begin the conversation, but I remember that I really wanted to talk. I kept hoping that he would make the first move and get me to open up. I wasn't even sure what I wanted to talk about, which is probably why I was so hesitant to approach him.

DK: A shame. As a *shaliach* (emissary), I'm sure he would have liked talking with you and answering questions. It's hard, though, to know who to approach and when.

SZ: I was afraid of two things: imposing on the rabbi's time, and not knowing whether it was considered "proper" for a woman to talk to a rabbi. I just wanted permission. That spring, I often timed my comings and goings to when and where I knew the rabbi would be around campus. But I mostly stayed on the periphery, never quite coming close.

DK: Well, you know now that it's no imposition and that it is "proper." *Hashgocha pratis* (Divine Providence), I guess.
What about Pesach that year?

SZ: I was in Seattle during Pesach. I went to the seders at the Chabad House. What a difference from the lonely Pesach a year earlier! It was joyful and serious at the same time, and there was a sense of togetherness in the experience that was almost palpable.

DK: As it should be. Were there any journal entries? Did you have any sense of what made the difference, or have any motivation to explore it further?

SZ: There was nothing in the journal about it. I never had the time to explore the different spirit that I found there. There were so many things I saw that I didn't understand—the different sort of praying, saying a blessing after meals, washing—and that no one ever stopped to explain (no, I didn't ask) that I spent most of my time trying to get oriented to the practicalities.

DK: It can be overwhelming, but it is to be hoped, in a positive way.

SZ: My memories of it are good ones. I was still a *"Shabbos* Jew." Friday nights and Pesach were the only times I really had a connection with the Chabad House or the other students there.

DK: That's true of a lot of students. Sometimes it takes a while for the seed planted on a Friday night to grow into other aspects of one's life.

SZ: After Pesach, I received a job offer with the government. I made arrangements to begin work in July. After the semester ended, I went back home and, with a lot of help from my parents, started making arrangements to move. It was exciting and frightening all at the same time. The hardest part was knowing how far away I would be from my family.

Near the end of June 1976, the movers came and took the small collection of furnishings we had put together, and, a few days later, I kissed my parents goodbye and boarded a plane to Friendship International Airport in Baltimore, Maryland.

9
In Laurel

DK: So in June 1976 you left home and headed East.

SZ: Yes, and with the arrival of my flight on a hot and humid Baltimore night came a new phase of my life, far away from home and college and the relative security they offered. I was on my own.

DK: How did you adjust to life on your own in Maryland?

SZ: I had no choice but to adjust quickly. The first week I bought a car, tracked down an apartment in Laurel, purchased basic household needs, and moved in. Of course, I still felt overwhelmed in unguarded moments, but on the whole the excitement and novelty made the process easier. I started work about a week after my arrival.

DK: I think that the excitement of starting a "new phase" when you're young and single compensates somewhat for being inexperienced and overwhelmed. Of course, that's part of being or becoming an adult.
Still, those starting out—whatever the new phase entails and whenever it occurs—deserve a lot of credit, recognition, and encourage-

ment. As the Talmud says, all beginnings are difficult. Making that beginning, though, leads to another talmudic saying: "If someone says to you, 'I put in the effort and failed,' don't believe him; 'I didn't put in the effort and succeeded,' don't believe him; 'I tried and succeeded,' believe him."

Anyway, what kind of work did you do?

SZ: Generic government translation stuff. Nothing very exciting, but I liked the work well enough, and the salary was attractive. It gave me a chance to use my language skills, and there were a lot of young men and women about my age working in the same area.

DK: Maybe sitting and translating wasn't very exciting, although it can be quite an intellectual challenge. But the working conditions certainly sound as if they were, to use your word, "attractive."

How did you find and fit into the Jewish community in Laurel?

SZ: It turned out that there was a small synagogue just up the street from the apartment, maybe just four blocks or so. The community was quite new, and wasn't affiliated with any branch (Reform, Orthodox, Conservative, Reconstructionist) and, mostly for financial reasons, had no rabbi. The cantor led the services on Friday night, and there was a small independent Hebrew school that they had also organized.

The members wanted a focal point of Judaism on Friday nights, and Hebrew school for their children on Sunday mornings. On the one hand, being Jewish and passing Judaism along to their children was important; on the other hand, they wanted Judaism on their terms.

DK: Maybe we should keep the concept of a "focal point" as, well, a focal point. Notice the focal point(s)—or priorities—of this community in the making. They might have protested being characterized as wanting Judaism on "their terms." They couldn't afford a rabbi, so they started with communal worship and basic education for the children. What's wrong with that?

Nothing, of course. Those are basic elements—focal points—in creating a community; without the sociospiritual interaction and training of the young, there is neither community nor continuity.

And yet, the *Shulchan Aruch* tells us that, before building a synagogue, a community should build a *mikvah* (so that women can keep the laws of family purity). In other words, Judaism must proceed from the family to the synagogue, not the other way around.

How did this congregation compare with the one in your hometown? They were both small congregations. Besides that, though, what were some of the similarities and differences?

SZ: The congregation in Laurel was much smaller, younger, and less diverse. It didn't have any structured learning for adults. As a result, the emphasis on Judaism "for the sake of the children" seemed even more pronounced in the Laurel congregation. Also, there wasn't a focal figure—a rabbi—to provide religious leadership for the Laurel congregation. While that was problematic in that everyone had their own idea of what the "rules" were, it also meant that there was less of a tendency to "pass the buck" and leave everything in the rabbi's lap.

In fact, many—probably most—of the congregants in Laurel seemed to take the synagogue "personally." There was a broader level of involvement by a greater percentage of the members. Many seemed to look at the synagogue as their "baby." I guess that when you give your time and energy to a cause or an institution, it matters more to you than just paying dues.

DK: Definitely.

SZ: What seemed to be a common denominator among many in both congregations was that being Jewish was something you did at synagogue. In the synagogue, you socialized with Jews; outside it, you gave no hint that you were Jewish. At the synagogue you prayed, thought about God; outside it, you scarcely gave religion a thought. Judaism was like a mental *tallis* that we carefully unfolded when we walked into the synagogue door, and just as carefully folded away when we left.

DK: I like that image—a mental *tallis*. Of course, some of us wear a *tallis katan* [a small *tallis*] all the time, which would make your metaphor even more striking.

Again, you've noted a significant point: the compartmentalization of synagogue Judaism. Here, I "do" Judaism; there, I "do" work; in this place, I "do" family. It's not a Jewish approach, though. Rather, whatever one does needs to be done Jewishly.

SZ: The exception to this was the political side of things—concern with Israel, Soviet Jews, anti-Semitism. Yet I'm not sure whether these things carried us and our Jewishness outside the synagogue and into the world, or whether the world carried them to us and put them at our doorstep so that we simply could not ignore them.

DK: Probably both. Note that politics itself is external, public. We might say that politics, the synagogue, the yeshiva, and Hebrew school are the masculine side of Judaism. Kashrus, *Shabbos*, *taharas mishpacha*—the three "proof *mitzvos*"—are found in the home and are the feminine side of Judaism. Guess which side actually preserves Judaism? Guess which side will bring *Moshiach*?

Anyway, did you have any Jewish contacts aside from the congregation?

SZ: I found a second contact with the Jewish community through work. I worked in a building near a military base. Every Tuesday, the chaplain, a Conservative rabbi from Baltimore, came down to the base's Jewish chapel, and folks from the base and from the agency where I worked came for "Lunch with the Rabbi." Those who attended ranged from Orthodox to Reform. Most were "regulars," but every week two or three new faces would show up.

Before lunch, there was a short service—just the *Amidah* and *Aleinu*. After the prayers, we'd have a simple kosher lunch that was prepared by one of the volunteers at the chapel. Then the rabbi would talk about a topic of Jewish concern, we'd do the *birkas hamazon*, and then would head back to work. From start to finish it was about an hour.

I really looked forward to the Tuesday lunches. It was both a social and a religious outlet. It was nice to be with a group of Jews outside of *Shabbos*.

DK: Were there journal entries during these two years?

SZ: There was only one entry from this whole time. It was a piece I wrote about Rosh Hashanah. It went like this:

ROSH HASHANAH

On this Rosh Hashanah, the birthday of the whole world,
I would like to think all tears would vanish and
   in their places be joys and joys.

I would like to think that the great missiles could carry only flowers
   to the lonely and food to the hungry.

I would like to think that for at least this day (and just maybe, all of
   its tomorrows) all the violent storms would be calmed and gentle
   rains would give drink to a thirsty land.

I would like to think, on this Rosh Hashanah that all hatred, bigotry,
   injustice, inhumanity and indifference would be replaced by love,
   overcome by it forever.

On this day when the world was made in eons past I would like to
   think that man has not forgotten his task to help God complete the
   world.

On this Rosh Hashanah, I would like to think that the fruit of every
   vine and tree would beget itself a hundred times and no child ever
   cry from hunger again.

I would like to think that there would no longer be slaves—
of men or of nations, that freedom would be the precious stone
   worn in the crown of each man, the pendant on the neck of each
   woman.

On this day of Rosh Hashanah, the day when the world was made,
I would like to think that we would celebrate a thousand, thousand
   more.

On this Rosh Hashanah, I would like to think all things perfect; and
   all that is imperfect, turning, changing and being perfected.

On this day of Rosh Hashanah I would like to think the world at
   perfect peace among men and God, among men and men, among
   men and nations.

On this day of Rosh Hashanah, I would like to think the world too
   holy for evil.

On this day of Rosh Hashanah,
I would like to think that all of this is possible,
Because God answers man,
And because man answers God.

SZ: It was simplistic, perhaps, but at the same time very hopeful; at once a recognition of the problems we face, but optimistic that somehow, someday, the problems would end.

DK: Actually, it's full of an important Rosh Hashanah theme: *Moshiach.* We blow the shofar on Rosh Hashanah both to crown God as King and to express our heartfelt yearning to be reunited with our Father. But the prophets also tell us that the sound of the "Great Shofar" will proclaim the era of redemption. (In fact, one of Saadiah Gaon's ten reasons for blowing the shofar on Rosh Hashanah is that the shofar reminds us of and is a prelude to redemption.)

So you captured a basic theme of Rosh Hashanah.

I imagine that the lack of journal entries indicates that life had begun to settle down. What other changes—Jewish ones, particularly—occurred during this time?

SZ: Well, I made the decision to try to keep a kosher home once I moved.

DK: Why?

SZ: My decision to keep a kosher kitchen was simple: I wanted any Jew to be able to eat in my home. I never wanted anyone to turn away because my home was not kosher. Not that my apartment saw many guests—it was just the principle of the matter.

DK: That's an admirable motive. The willingness to accommodate others, to respect a different level of observance, is part of *Ahavas Yisroel* and *hachnosas orchim* [welcoming guests], two very important *mitzvos.* (In a way, *hachnosas orchim* is a branch of *Ahavas Yisroel.*)

Once we get past the institutional politics, most Jews naturally extend themselves for another Jew. I know several people who don't keep kosher but will go out of their way to provide kosher meals for guests who do. They're willing to do this even for people they don't know very well.

Of course, it would be better if they kept kosher themselves, but that's not the point. First has to be consideration and respect, even and especially for those with whom we disagree, even and especially if they're doing something wrong.

And you took the extra step. You had *mesiras nefesh* and made your kitchen kosher on the chance that someone might need such a facility.

This reminds me of a true story. A very learned rabbi named Yosef lived in the times of the Alter Rebbe. At one point Rabbi Yosef was offered a comfortable rabbinic post. Being a Chassid, he asked the Alter Rebbe whether he should take it. The Alter Rebbe responded, "For your *neshama* [soul], it's better that you should be a wagon driver." Rabbi Yosef accepted the Alter Rebbe's advice and turned down the position, but he couldn't bring himself to become a wagon driver.

His wife, seeing his distress, asked Rabbi Yosef what the problem was. When he told her, she said, "I don't see the problem. Since the Alter Rebbe says you need to be a wagon driver, that's what you should do." She immediately pawned her jewelry to provide the funds for him to buy a wagon and horse.

At first, none of the other wagon drivers took seriously his request to be taught the trade. Eventually, though, he learned how to manage the horse and all the other necessary skills. Between trips, he'd study. In fact, he kept up his routine of long davening and morning study.

Many years later, Rabbi Yosef dropped off a customer at an inn some distance from home. In the same city, an impatient merchant needed a wagon to take him on some important business in another town. The innkeeper told the merchant that the only wagon driver was Rabbi Yosef, who never left before noon. The merchant, needing an early-morning start, tried to bribe and threaten Rabbi Yosef, but to no avail. He resigned himself to arriving later than he'd wanted.

What made it harder for the merchant was that he, too, was Jewish, although for many years he had observed no *mitzvos* and lived exactly like his non-Jewish neighbors. Although he had come from an observant background, he was now too "modern" for *mitzvos* and laughed at the simplicity of the religious.

That night, the rooms of driver and merchant happened to be next to each other. Rabbi Yosef had the custom of saying *tikkun chatzos* [midnight prayers mourning the destruction of the Temple]. The sincerity of what the merchant heard through the wall touched something deep within him. The next morning, he approached Rabbi Yosef and asked to put on *tefillin* and be taught how to do *teshuvah*.

Afterward, Rabbi Yosef visited the Mitteler Rebbe (the Alter Rebbe's son), who had in the meantime succeeded his father. The Mitteler Rebbe wrote a book on *teshuvah* specifically for this merchant. He also told Rabbi Yosef, "My father turned a rabbi into a wagon driver to save the *neshama* of another Jew. Now I will turn a wagon driver back into a rabbi." (Rabbi Yosef soon thereafter got a prestigious rabbinic post.)

The principle of helping some other, unknown Jew with *mesiras nefesh* is the basis of *Ahavas Yisroel*. I see your decision to keep kosher—before you had any awareness of *kashrus* as a *mitzvah* from God—as coming from the same source.

So what did it take for you to keep kosher?

SZ: That meant driving about forty-five minutes to get to a kosher butcher. Back then, most of the meat didn't come soaked and salted, like now. I had to take it back to the apartment and do it myself. I had never taken a class on how to keep kosher. I'd just read in a couple of books how to do the basics, so I did the best I could.

DK: You probably didn't realize the *mesiras nefesh* required. I'm sure your friends and co-workers thought that you carried your dedication to an extreme.

SZ: It wasn't like that. Actually, most never knew about my keeping kosher. I don't recall ever being chided for it, certainly not by other Jews. They didn't hold to it themselves, but they never suggested that I shouldn't. Besides, there was a certain satisfaction in it for me. It was something that I was doing just because I was Jewish, at a time when there wasn't all that much Jewish about my life.

DK: So you tried to keep your home kosher—on your own. What about outside your home?

SZ: I still ate non-kosher outside. Even though I ate out, I never ordered pork or seafood, or pepperoni pizzas. *I* decided what *kashrus* was in my life, often defining the limits as I went along. I felt only a little guilty when I ate the prime rib along with the baked potato and sour cream; the boundaries were flexible.

DK: Let's not forget that you were trying. You were making a conscious effort to grow in your observance of *mitzvos*. Since you still approached the commandments as folk customs rather than commandments from God, and since you didn't have a rabbi or mentor, of course the boundaries would be flexible.

SZ: It seemed to me that I was doing at least as much—probably more—than most of the Jews in the community, so I didn't really have an incentive to go any further *kashrus*-wise.

DK: Of course. If I may quote Pirkei Avos: "Rabbi Nehora'ey said: 'Exile yourself to a place of Torah—and do not assume it will come after you—for it is your colleagues who will cause it to be clearly established with you; and do not rely on your understanding.'" He was talking to the scholars and sages. How much more so does this apply to the rest of us!

Aside from participating in the synagogue's services and trying to keep kosher at home, did you do any other Jewish things during these two years?

SZ: I tried to work on my Hebrew skills at home. With practice they improved, but not much. I knew that I needed to find some formal instruction. Near the end of 1977 I registered for the evening Ulpan class at Baltimore Hebrew College. Our teacher, Shulamit, was an excellent instructor. The class was entirely in Hebrew from the beginning. I thoroughly enjoyed it. We learned through pantomime, singing, conversational practice, skits, and the like. We learned modern Hebrew, but it was a tremendous help as I began trying to decipher other texts. It is amazing how such an ancient language can be adapted to fit our far more technological world.

DK: The basics of any language are relatively easy. You're talking more about adaptations or additions of vocabulary rather than grammar or the fundamental word list.

After the initial excitement and adjustment wore off, how did work go?

SZ: At work, I had an opportunity to go to a semester program at a university in Washington, D.C. I got paid a full salary while attending school full-time. It was supposed to be a top-notch program, one of the management's favorites, but I thought that it had some serious deficiencies. I wrote a highly uncomplimentary critique of the course, suggesting that there were better ways for the government to be spending the money. I don't know whether it was that bluntness, but soon after, I was drafted for shift work.

DK: Indeed, it may have been the whistleblower's dilemma. There's something to be said for anonymous review. Did this have an effect on the Jewish part of your life?

SZ: Shift work meant a rotating schedule of six days of work followed by two or three days off, then a switch in shift and another six days' work. That was a real strain on the mind and body, because sleep patterns had to be readjusted almost weekly. There were a lot of problems with the schedule, but fortunately I was able to finish the rest of the Ulpan classes by attending a combination of daytime and nighttime classes to fit my schedule.

I didn't always make it to services during that period. My attendance at Tuesday luncheons was sporadic. I ended up in pretty much a do-it-yourself mode of Judaism. I kept up with current events on the radio, and listened to shortwave broadcasts from Israel quite often.

DK: You accomplished a lot in your first two years on the job and away from home.

Did anything else of interest happen?

SZ: That summer, I happened upon a demonstration of an Apple computer at a local convention. I was absolutely fascinated by this wonderful little gadget, and made up my mind to get one. I went to the credit union and arranged for a consumer loan, trekked into a tiny shop in Georgetown, plunked down my money, and left with my prize: a 16K Apple computer that loaded its programs from cassette tape. Since it used a television for display, I went out and bought one of those, too.

DK: You were a few years ahead of me. My first was a 64K Apple II.

SZ: I was also a little involved in amateur radio at that point (it was one of my father's passions), and was working on a program for Morse code practice. One day, while I was working away on it, someone knocked at my door. My visitor lived in the apartment below mine, but we hadn't met before. He explained that he had been tuned into channel 10 on his television and had seen my name pop up on the screen. After checking the mailboxes in the lobby, he came up to learn what I was up to. It turned out that my computer was radiating into his TV, and he just happened to be tuned in when my name was displayed by the program. I was embarrassed, but my guest was nice about everything. Joe introduced himself, and we talked for a while. I liked him immediately. We had a chance to talk a few more times over the next couple of weeks. Joe never said right off that he was Jewish, but mentioned that his parents wanted to go to Israel. "A good sign," I thought. I assumed that he had figured out my allegiance from the large batik wall hanging—a star of David—on my living-room wall.

It may sound strange, but already I knew that I wanted to marry him.

DK: You haven't said anything yet about hoping to get married. In fact, we haven't discussed that at all.

Regardless, how you met is a clear example of *hashgocha pratis* [Divine Providence], isn't it? Here you and Joe had been neighbors—for how long?—but had never met. Now, if you hadn't bought the computer and hadn't been typing your name, and he hadn't been watching a channel that picked up the computer's radiation. . . . It's easy enough to see that the "coincidences" are more than that—at least if we have faith in God.

Hashgocha pratis, while a fundamental concept in Judaism, is also rather complicated. We'll have to talk about it some more later.

What happened next?

SZ: Happily, when I got back from a visit home to my parents, Joe and I started seeing each other. I finally figured out that his family was Jewish when he told me that his father had been president of his synagogue for a number of years. We spent much more time together after that.

DK: What was Joe's interest in Judaism, his level of observance? I imagine that that would have been important to you, as well.

SZ: Joe wasn't very religious. Like me, Joe kept kosher at home, but outside we ate in non-kosher restaurants. He didn't go to services at the synagogue, and I didn't press the issue. In fact, I stopped making any effort to attend services myself. We'd often go out on Friday or Saturday nights to dinner or a movie instead. As time went on, I had very little contact with things Jewish, except for the Tuesday luncheons. I guess that, on some level, I was trying to keep in his favor by adopting what I perceived as his level of observance.

DK: That's not unusual. I've seen it happen lots of times. We naturally try to make ourselves compatible. The level of observance can go up or down, depending not just on who is "most eager," but also on who is "most committed."

SZ: In the end, I completely dropped out of the synagogue, not only because of my changing priorities, but also because the synagogue itself was changing.

The congregation had decided to get a rabbi. That meant that they would have to affiliate with a branch—Reform, Conservative, Orthodox, or Reconstructionist. Representatives from each of the branches came in to present their case.

The rabbi representing the Reconstructionist movement came. I especially remember that night, and how he described his—and I assumed the Reconstructionist—view of God. My understanding was that his notion of God was a name we gave to our internal yearning for meaning and purpose. It was not the notion of God Who created the world, or God Who brought us out of Egypt, or God Who is involved in our daily lives. I was shaken by what I heard. When the synagogue affiliated with the Reconstructionist movement, I resigned immediately. I did not want another cent of mine to support such a philosophy. I didn't go to the synagogue anymore after that.

DK: The issue of a personal God has vexed theologians for centuries. How can God be both immanent and transcendent, both the Lord of the universe and the God of the Jewish people?

Yet that unity is the basic declaration of Judaism. The unity of God's transcendence and immanence (or God as He surrounds all worlds and as He fills all worlds) distinguishes and identifies Judaism. It's the "battle cry" of the Jewish people: *Shema Yisroel, Hashem Elokeinu, Hashem Echad* (Hear, O Israel, the Lord Who is our God, the Lord is One).

Interestingly, all the great issues of theology—evil; the suffering of the righteous; defining ethics; prayer; life after death—require and depend upon a personal God, that is, a deity that must be described as "God Who. . . .

What was Joe's feeling about all this?

SZ: Joe and I didn't talk much about religion, either. Somehow I'd gotten the notion that he wasn't interested in the subject, and I didn't want to endanger our budding relationship by pushing it.

10
Married

DK: Obviously, things went the way they were "supposed to." Was Judaism an issue?

SZ: To some extent, yes.

DK: Let's explore that. When did you feel it was appropriate to tell Joe about your conversion, and how did he react?

SZ: I felt very comfortable discussing my conversion with Joe. He readily accepted me as a Jew. The details of the conversion, if we discussed them at all, were never an issue. Joe, it seems, accepted me—and my Jewishness—based on what he saw: I kept kosher, I had been active in the synagogue, was learning Hebrew, and so on. If it looks like a rose and smells like a rose. . . .

DK: I assume that Joe's parents also learned about the conversion at some point. How early in the relationship did that occur?

SZ: Joe told his folks early on. Because his parents felt quite strongly against intermarriage, I'm pretty sure that they were relieved that I was Jewish, convert or not. I still cared a lot about Jewish and religious issues, so even though it wasn't the main focus of conversation when I saw his parents, we did talk about those things.

DK: Were there any discussions about intermarriage, conversion, and the like? Did these affect your relationship with your future in-laws? Obviously, there are many details parents are interested in when their children get married. Was this just one of those details, or was it something more crucial?

SZ: We didn't talk about intermarriage much. I knew that they were against it, but then, isn't anyone who cares about the future of the Jewish people? The conversion was, I think, a "significant detail," but not in a negative sense. That a person would choose to be Jewish shows a certain commitment to living a Jewish life, raising Jewish children. I think they understood that. If "proof is in the pudding," then I'd say I passed the test, because after Joe assured his parents that I kept kosher, they were comfortable eating in my apartment when I had them over for dinner.

DK: In other words, it was just one of those details prospective children-in-law get scrutinized about.

SZ: Well, Joe's father showed some concern about my conversion. He asked to borrow the conversion certificate to show to his Orthodox rabbi. I gave it to him. He showed it to his rabbi, who told me when I asked, many years later, that he had tried to trace the rabbi who did the conversion, but was not able to find anything on him. At the time, Joe's father returned the certificate without indicating that he had any serious concerns.

DK: Did Joe's father's "interest" raise any doubts or concerns for you, especially considering the "warning" the rabbi who converted you had given you?

SZ: Deep inside, yes, but it was nothing I could bring to the surface, nothing to which I could give voice. I simply didn't know enough to recognize potentially serious problems. The certificate was dated, signed, and official. It never occurred to me that it would be questioned. I proffered it eagerly to Joe's father, believing that it would satisfy his rabbi. For many years I believed that it had.

DK: You said that you spoke with Joe's father's rabbi years later. Since your hometown had only one synagogue and it wasn't Orthodox—even if its rabbi was no longer there and couldn't be located—on what basis did this rabbi not raise any questions?

SZ: I'm not sure. I do know that this rabbi was—and is—very well respected in the Jewish community. I wrote to him once and asked about it, and he chose not to discuss it further. I trust that his reasons for not doing so were good ones.

It's important to keep in mind that we aren't talking about nineteen-year-old kids living at home. We were independent adults who had already made some serious decisions about our lives. What if the rabbi had said that the conversion was a problem? Would it have mattered? Or would it have caused friction within the family?

DK: Good questions. The answers depend, I guess, on how *you* would have reacted.

That said, there's something to be gained from looking at a particular situation as an example. We can derive some principles from examining a variety of "what ifs."

Maybe we should rephrase your questions. You asked what if the rabbi had said that the conversion was a problem, and whether it would have mattered or would have caused friction within the family. Maybe, instead, we should ask: When a rabbi raises a question, should we listen, and to what extent? When there is a conflict between principles and feelings, what kind of resolution should we seek?

Since most of us are neither prophets nor *tzaddikim*, how much authority should we grant a rabbi? And, to return to one of the questions you've asked throughout, how do we know we can, in fact, trust this particular rabbi?

SZ: I'll tackle your last question first. We trust a rabbi who is demonstratively committed to Torah and *mitzvos*, both publicly and personally.

DK: I wasn't necessarily looking for answers; the questions were meant to be rhetorical or at least just food for thought. But as long as you've started. . . .

Your answer (which I agree with, of course) is quite different from your responses earlier. Do you remember asking how we know whom to trust? You've given us a set of criteria, but I'd like to turn the question around: Why do we trust such a rabbi? Or perhaps I should phrase it this way: Aren't you putting things in reverse order? For if I don't accept *halacha* to begin with, how does the rabbi's commitment—or anyone else's observance, for that matter—prove him trustworthy? In other words, how do you know that observance of Torah and *mitzvos* are the baseline criteria?

SZ: It may be as simple as opening one's eyes to fact and history. While so much of society is falling apart at the seams, Jews have historically maintained strong communities with positive values in terms of education, low crime rates, family life, and so on. There has to be a key to this phenomenon; given the tremendous diversity of the Jewish people and the places they have lived, the one obvious link is a commitment to Torah observance. I guess it is the same way we judge anything: If something produces the desired results predictably and consistently, then we accept it—and the people who promote and encourage it.

DK: Well, that's pretty close to what the answer is. To phrase it differently, Torah and *mitzvos* are the basic criteria by which to judge a claim for trust (trustworthiness) within Judaism, because they are the only historically proven guarantee of Jewish survival and because they are an objective, nondenominational standard of measurement.
The next question was. . . .

SZ: How much authority should we grant a rabbi? I'd say that it depends on the particular situation. In matters of *halacha*, the rabbi is supposed to be an expert; his title is given precisely to allow him to decide points of Jewish law. A good rabbi will not pretend to an expertise that he does not have. We should take his words with at least the same degree of seriousness as we would take those of a doctor. There is a similarity: The physician is concerned with maintaining personal and communal physical health; the rabbi, with personal and communal spiritual health.

DK: This means, as well, that we have to know what questions to ask. In other words, we must acknowledge our ignorance, on the one hand, and be able to make sense of the answers, on the other. If we allow a "feel-good" answer—an emotional prescription—to satisfy an intellectual need (or vice versa), we're back to where your journey began. But we have to recognize our limits as well. By the way, do you see how we've come to establish the "goodness" of what I'll call contextual dependence?

SZ: I think so. We are complex beings, and it is important to sort out which of our "needs" is driving us. Religious needs must be dealt with within the framework of *halacha*, so the answer to your earlier question is clear: When a trusted rabbi raises a halachic question, or provides a halachic answer, we should listen.

You also asked, "When there is a conflict between principles and feelings, what kind of resolution should we seek?" The easiest thing for me to say is that Jews must always stand on principle, or, rather, on *halacha*. Yet, unless a person has already accepted the authoritativeness of the principle (Torah and *halacha*), he or she will most likely let emotions overrule it.

If that's the case, then the resolution between principles and feelings *must* take place at a very deep and fundamental level, to wit, "What is our view of Torah?"

DK: Absolutely. Put another way: Can there be revelation? If so, what demands does it make on me?

These are not new questions, of course. They're dealt with by Rabbeinu Saadiah Gaon, Maimonides, and Rabbeinu Bachya ibn Pakuda (*Duties of the Heart*). One of the ironies of our age is that however well-educated we may be in matters scientific and political (although, often as not, secularism leads us to confuse arrogance with knowledge), we remain ignorant of our tradition's responses to the central questions of our existence.

How can we have a view of Torah if we haven't studied it, haven't experienced it the way Jews have been doing for thousands of years? We have the right to demand that the answers make sense, but we also have the obligation to accept Judaism's principles and practice.

How did we get to this point, anyway? Oh, we began with a "what if": What if your in-law's rabbi had raised questions, had made Torah-based demands?

It's the kind of question you've faced before. At every juncture, it seems, there's a "what if" that might have led. . . . Well, Divine Providence leads us to where we need to be.

SZ: Perhaps it's no different than when I didn't take up the *mikvah* issue with the rabbi in Seattle. If things seem to be going well, why look for trouble? On the contrary: Close one eye to truth if you must. Maybe we were all doing a little of that. Still, like I said, it's all speculation.

DK: True. It also points out that affiliation and labels aren't real Jewish issues.

But was Judaism itself an issue while you and Joe were dating?

SZ: Judaism really wasn't an issue for us while we were dating. In a lot of ways, we were stereotypically assimilated. We managed to find a connection with our Jewishness on Rosh Hashanah and Yom Kippur, at Chanukah, and during Pesach. The rest of the time. . . . Well, like I said, Judaism wasn't an issue.

DK: While those are the typical "connecting points" during the year, far too many Jews don't find a connection even at those times.

But do you think that your own observance—or growth, or interest, call it what you will—increased at this time?

SZ: Unfortunately, exactly the opposite occurred. I think that, as I always had, I was trying to take cues on what "Jewish" was from the Jews around me. Since Joe became my closest and most constant Jewish influence, I took what I saw of his Jewishness externally and adopted the same "level." I was a bit puzzled that he didn't go to synagogue services, but beyond that, I saw no real conflicts.

DK: Fair enough. All of us either adopt an environment or create one (or get "caught" in a tension between the two). I think that we have to try to recognize which "mode" we're in, and make sure that it's the appropriate one.

So how long did it take to work all this out? How long between your meeting and your engagement?

SZ: In December 1979, about a year and a half after we had met, Joe proposed to me. We were in his apartment watching television when he shut off the TV and popped the question. I was thrilled, and of course said yes. We called our parents, and everyone seemed pretty happy about it. Originally we planned to get married at the end of August, but we found a house that we liked at the end of February. We decided to move up the wedding to March so that we could move in right away. I'm afraid that this took Joe's mother by surprise: She had just gotten the engagement notices, and already we were talking about a wedding—in three weeks! She was more than gracious about it, though. She even helped arrange for me to borrow the wedding gown of the daughter of one of her friends, which was a tremendous help in terms of both time and money. My folks did some fast changing of plans and made reservations to fly back East.

We had already decided that it would be best to have a very small wedding in Maryland. It would be easier for my folks to deal with a Jewish wedding if they weren't overwhelmed by huge numbers of Joe's relatives; besides, neither of us wanted a big affair.

DK: I was just going to ask about your parents. How did they react? Did they have any questions, doubts, reservations?

SZ: Except for the short notice, which turned out to be pretty inconvenient for their schedule, they never raised any questions. The conversion was already a few years behind me at this point, so the fact that I was marrying a Jew came as no surprise to them. I had told them a lot about Joe (all favorable, of course), and they seemed very happy with my decision.

DK: Tell me about the wedding itself.

SZ: We asked the rabbi who served as the base chaplain to officiate at the marriage. He asked us to come and talk to him before the date, which we did. His comments were mostly on understanding the importance of the act, comments that he hoped would help make our marriage successful, and instructions on the technical details of the ceremony itself. He asked us a few questions—I don't remember any about my conversion—and then we left. I don't know how much we got out of the session, but it was painless, at any rate.

DK: Since his comments centered on the importance of marriage, did the rabbi discuss any *mitzvos* that might help make it successful? You were already keeping kosher; did he recognize that?

SZ: *Mitzvos*? I don't think so. We did talk about raising any future children as Jews, and about joining a synagogue. He talked about give-and-take in marriage relationships. He didn't talk about observing *Shabbos*, about *kashrus*, or about *taharas mishpocha*, or make a connection between those things and a successful marriage. I certainly didn't either, at the time.

DK: You had no reason to, since you hadn't been taught. But a rabbi has an obligation to at least inform people about *mitzvos* such as *taharas mishpocha*. How can a young couple choose to keep *mikvah* if they don't know what it is?

Anyway, back to the wedding.

SZ: In the end, we got married at the rabbi's synagogue. Those who attended were my folks, Joe's folks, a half-dozen of his relatives, and a few friends. Altogether, there were maybe twenty of us. We had to hurry the ceremony a little because there was a bar mitzvah rehearsal scheduled right after us. After we finished the ceremony, we went to a nice restaurant and had dinner in a private banquet room. There were no musicians, nothing really fancy. I had ordered the wedding cake from a local supermarket. My folks generously paid for the reception.

So that was it. We were married, and two days later moved into a new house from our two separate apartments. We didn't get very far into unpacking, since we were only one week away from the beginning of Pesach. We hurried to get the kitchen ready for Pesach and then headed for New York, to Joe's family, for the seders.

DK: Was your new home kosher? How did Joe feel about it?

SZ: It was as kosher as my apartment ever was—maybe a little more, since we *kashered* the stove and cleaned the kitchen thoroughly for

Pesach. We used the dishwasher as it was, deciding that we'd wash dairy dishes in it. Joe had always kept kosher in his apartment, too. The level of *kashrus* for both of us was about the same (i.e., very lenient on dairy products, candy, and the like). There was never any doubt that we would continue to keep a kosher kitchen. Between the two of us we had lots of dishes, even a minimal set for Pesach.

DK: As a newlywed, you went to New York for a family seder. That must have been pretty exciting.

SZ: Absolutely! It was my first *real* family seder. The first night was at Aunt Helene and Uncle Norman's house out on Long Island. We stopped on the way to pick up Aunt Rose, and Aunt Esther and Uncle Max. It was at least an hour's drive, my first experience with what Jewish holiday traffic could do to New York expressways. By the time we got there, the festivities had already commenced. Joe's grandmother, who exemplified the word "spry," was doling out her marvelous latkes. Conversations of the latest family news surfaced like bubbles in a glass of seltzer, each lasting only until a new one took its place. I was overwhelmed by the number of folks who arrived: Wendy, Robby, Eric, Michael, Joyce, Uncle Sonny, Aunt Bobby, Aunt Bev, and Uncle Eddie. There were names and names, and a hug and kiss from just about everyone. And there were the last-minute preparations for the seder, the *haroses* and *maror*, setting up the plate, getting the matzohs ready. It was a little overwhelming!

Finally we sat down and began to tell the story of how we were brought out of Egypt with a strong hand and an outstretched arm. . . .

Despite the occasional—Okay, maybe not so occasional—disruptions to the seder, it was a special experience for me to be together with the Jewish side of my family at a uniquely Jewish celebration.

DK: It's certainly far different from the first seder you experienced. By the way, did any of the family know about your conversion?

SZ: As far as I knew, no. No one mentioned it. I felt very much welcomed as a full member of the family.

We were at Joe's folks' home for the second seder. It was easier because we didn't have to shlep anywhere in a car. And it was much quieter without the full complement of relatives. Joe's father led the seder, as he has continued to do every year since. Of course, Joe's mother had prepared a major feast for the seder, as she has every year since.

Then, before we headed back to Maryland, Joe's mother fixed us a cooler full of Pesach food: chicken cutlets, latkes, fruit, soda, chips, matzohs, and a ton of packaged goods. I remember thinking that the Jews leaving Egypt never had it so good!

DK: A good way to start a marriage.

SZ: It sure was. As Pesach 1980 came to a close, we began our married life with full stomachs and hope for the future. In May, we headed off to a delayed honeymoon in San Francisco.

DK: Did marriage change your views any? How did it affect your life (aside from the obvious)?

SZ: Joe and I had known each other for over a year and a half, and had spent a lot of time together. We were both already twenty-seven years old and had been working in professional jobs. For those reasons, I think we approached marriage with an understanding of the responsibilities and commitments involved. Before we got married, we had both expressed our mutual view that marriage was a serious lifetime commitment. I wouldn't say that it changed my views all that much, but now whatever we each undertook, at some level we undertook together.

Marriage probably affected our lives the most in that each of us needed to consult the other before making significant plans and decisions, as it should be in any marriage. And we recognized that marriage wasn't always going to be "easy." It was something that we each had to work at.

As I look back, I know that we both wanted to include our Jewishness in our married life, at least as a foundation. That's why the Jewish wedding was important. It was a commitment before God. I wonder if that isn't part of what makes a Jewish marriage special.

DK: Certainly that commitment is part of what makes a Jewish marriage special. I'm sure you've heard the famous *midrash* about the relationship between a man, woman, and God. Briefly, the Hebrew word for man is spelled *aleph, yud, shin* (pronounced *ish*); the word for woman is *aleph, shin, hey* (*ishah*). In Hebrew, man and woman share the letters *aleph* and *shin*, which spell *aish*—fire. *Yud* and *hey*, however, spell one of the names of God. Thus, if God—the *yud–hey*—is not part of the relationship between a man and a woman, what is left is *aleph–shin*: *aish*, a fire that consumes and destroys itself.

SZ: An apt description. If you were to counsel a couple on their upcoming marriage, what would you tell them about building a strong marriage? We wanted God, Jewishness, to be a part of the marriage, but it didn't happen, at least not at first. How do we make sure that God is part of the relationship? For that matter, what *is* a "Jewish marriage"?

DK: We can answer both questions at once, of course, because they're really different ways of phrasing the same idea. As such, the answer has two parts—an external framework and an internal dimension.

The external framework, as with all things Jewish, consists of the *mitzvos* governing marital relations. The *halacha* of marriage sanctifies the cycles of self and involvement, creating borders of responsibility and respect. First, of course, are the laws of family purity. The *Shulchan Aruch* tells us that before we build a synagogue, we should build a *mikvah*! Yet, for many years, unfortunately, family purity was a "silent *mitzvah*." That is, while many Jews knew the basic rules and principles of *Shabbos* and *kashrus*, even if they didn't observe them, few Jews outside the Orthodox "enclaves" knew anything about the *mitzvah* of family purity, or even that there were laws governing marital relations.

That's changed in the last twenty years or so. It was one of the *mitzvos* the Rebbe emphasized in his campaigns. Now, of course, there are some wonderful books and videos on the subject. I know of people who don't keep *Shabbos* or *kashrus*, but do observe *taharas mishpocha*.

Beyond *taharas mishpocha*, however, are the obligations of husband to wife and wife to husband.

SZ: Are the obligations changed if one partner isn't Jewish?

DK: A good, and highly charged, question. In the sense that all of us deserve respect, no. But a Jewish marriage connects the generations, forms a link in an unbroken chain that stretches back to Sinai and to Abraham and Sarah. Intermarriage destroys the continuity—not just physically, but spiritually.

Earlier, we talked about dependence. A Jewish marriage assumes spiritual dependence, one on the other (though the man is the more dependent). Judaism emphasizes that husband and wife are two parts of one soul, each enabling the other to be whole, complete. (We could spend a long time talking about the various aspects and implications of the term *shalom bayis*—literally, a "peaceful house.")

Spiritually, however, Jew and non-Jew are different. So while there can be a physical partnership, there can't be a spiritual one. Intermarriage, by definition, can't be the joining of two parts of one soul, because the two individuals have categorically different souls. (Of course, if the non-Jewish spouse converts . . . but that's another discussion.)

Of course, finding the right mate is hard. The Talmud says that, since the splitting of the Red Sea, God has spent his time on a bigger miracle: matchmaking.

Still, a Jewish marriage requires the whole man and the whole woman—the *aleph-yud-shin* and the *aleph-shin-hey*. The laws of marriage and marital relations, both the physical and economic as well as the ethical, often seem dry and unromantic. But Judaism long ago recognized the truth that Tevye and Golda made into a cliche. Golda's answer to Tevye's question "Do you love me?" simply catalogs all the mundane details—we might even say drudgery—that they've shared. And after twenty-five years, if that's not love, what is? True love, as defined within a Jewish marriage, comes from living within the framework, from depending on your spouse.

SZ: I also remember one rabbi teaching that our love for a person grows by what we are able to give to them, not what we are able to take from them.

If I understand, then, you are saying that there are three components in a successful Jewish marriage: the initial compatibility (God's matchmaking); a solid commitment and dependence on each other (the hard work); and a mutual acceptance of *halacha* as the basis of that commitment (what makes the marriage "Jewish").

DK: I think that sums it up well. The Jewishness of a marriage, like the Jewishness of anything else, develops from the Torah and *mitzvos* within it.

So, once you were married, how Jewishly involved were you two?

SZ: Jewishly, we didn't get much more involved than we had been. One thing we both felt strongly about was that we needed to join a synagogue. It wasn't that we wanted a place to go to services or to find a social circle; we both felt that as Jews we had a responsibility to support the general Jewish community, and felt that the synagogue provided an appropriate focus for that support. We decided to join the Conservative synagogue.

11
Children

DK: After the honeymoon, you and Joe settled into what might be called a normal married life. There was the routine of work; you had children. The next few years were quiet, weren't they, especially after the turmoil you'd been through?

SZ: Yes, these were quiet years, especially in a religious sense. Joe and I were both working full-time. In addition, Joe had entered an evening program to earn a master's degree in computer science. That didn't leave us a lot of time for much else.

DK: Why don't you tell me a little about how you lived, some of the challenges you encountered, how having children changed your lives, Judaism's "role"—those kinds of things.

SZ: We lived in a very nice two-bedroom home in a housing development located in a rural area of Maryland. We enjoyed eating out and going to movies on the weekends. Joe played on a softball team. We were close friends with some of the other players and their wives; one of the men was best man at our wedding. This couple pretty much initiated the "baby boom" among our friends, something that couldn't help but make us think. Before marriage, we had discussed the issue of children, and had decided that we would prefer to wait at least a year before trying to have any. At first, I didn't think I wanted to have children at all. I remember wondering at how much our neighbors gave up to accommodate their children, and thought life would be a lot easier if we stayed "just the two of us."

I guess I was being selfish in looking at just my own needs and contentment when considering whether to have children.

DK: Yes, but in that you were a product of the times. But at all times, in Judaism, children are a blessing.

SZ: I certainly see the truth in that now that I am a mother.

DK: Anyway, while I'm not surprised at your diffidence, I wonder whether your Jewish learning—or just your sense of Jewishness—had any effect at this point, any pull toward having a family.

SZ: It did. I wanted my existence as a Jew to mean something beyond myself. I saw children as the most obvious and important way to accomplish that goal. These thoughts were a seed that grew into some real emotional challenges later on.

DK: We'll get to them "in their season." Let's get back to your "settling down" stage. The Reconstructionist synagogue wasn't for you, so you joined the Conservative one. What then?

SZ: We still went to New York for Pesach, and for the first couple of years split our attendance on Rosh Hashanah and Yom Kippur between Maryland and New York. After joining the Conservative synagogue, we attended the Friday-night services occasionally. It was at those services that Joe first sat in a mixed-seating service. He didn't object, but later told me that it seemed a bit strange. I thought the atmosphere quite normal, and in fact thought that sitting separately would have been more uncomfortable.

DK: Misconceptions about the *mechitza* create one of the biggest barriers, if you'll pardon the pun, to an open-minded consideration of an observant lifestyle.

SZ: I agree. If you remember, the *mechitza* at the Chabad House hadn't been so much of an emotional barrier to me, maybe because everything was so new. Now that I was attending my father-in-law's *shul* for some holidays, I began to think of the *mechitza* in rather negative ways.

DK: A lot of those negative ways—unfortunately shared by many Jews—come from assimilated thinking patterns. Separations can be used to discriminate or to bond. Sisterhoods, fraternities—we organize along natural support lines.

Of course, the reason for the *mechitza* goes well beyond sociology. But let's get to this in order. You said that the Chabad House *mechitza* wasn't an emotional barrier, but the one at your father-in-law's *shul* was. Why?

SZ: I guess my outlook had changed. My father-in-law's *shul* had a balcony above the main sanctuary and a *mechitza* in the lower level, where the *minyan* normally held their *Shabbos* services. Undoubtedly influenced by some of the sex-equality issues pervading secular society and by the egalitarian nature of the Conservative synagogue, I concluded that the *mechitza* was demeaning to women: "They" either kept us in the "attic, like bats in a belfry," or put us behind a wall to keep us from intruding into their religious "old boys" club. Of course, I never really *asked* why it was there.

DK: So it wasn't so much the *mechitza* (although obviously some *mechitza*s are more "accommodating" than others) as the non-Jewish sensibilities you had absorbed. Since you weren't at a Chabad House any more, or at your father-in-law's *shul* very often, your standard naturally was the "sex-equality issues" and the "egalitarian" stance of the Conservative synagogue.

I've talked to a lot of college students about this. You'd be surprised how sophisticated they are, and yet they have responses similar to yours. In response, I'm reminded of the old commercial: "Try it, you'll like it."

SZ: Yet I did "try it," and I left angry, feeling demeaned and degraded. Why? Because I didn't understand it and I made up my own theories as to why the *mechitza* was there, based on the standards and experience of the non-Jewish world. So, "trying it" isn't enough. One also needs to learn, to comprehend, the real reasons the *mechitza* is there.

DK: Well, what did you expect to feel? You entered with a preconceived definition of what should happen in a synagogue. That definition was imposed by the "social and political forces that surround us," as you put it. I'd be surprised if you felt anything else. I guess I should have qualified that flippant comment.

When I said "Try it," I meant that one has to understand as well as do. Although when the Jewish people received the Torah they did say "We will do" first, they also said, "We will understand." While one has to know the rules of the game, so to speak, what the purpose is, before being able to play well—or to enjoy playing at all—one also has to be open to the rules, to changing one's perceptions—and preconceptions.

SZ: So what are the rules of this "*mechitza* game"?

DK: It goes back to the unique role and responsibility resulting from inborn—Divinely created—differences. We must first acknowledge that prayer is primarily spiritual, not social. Prayer is not "family time," or a time "to see and be seen," except by God. That said, we need to discuss a few precepts before getting to the *mechitza*.

Prayer is essentially a private act, a communication between the individual and the Almighty. In fact, the model for prayer is Hannah; the most profound moment of the prayer service is the *Amidah* (also known as the *Shemonah Esrei*), when we stand in silent devotion.

Of course, there are also some communal prayer obligations. The reciting of Kaddish, *Borchu*, the reading of the Torah—all require a *minyan*. Without going into the details of why, women are exempt from positive time-bound *mitzvos*. They don't have to put on *tefillin*, for instance. Participating in a *minyan*—a communal prayer service—is a positive, time-bound *mitzvah*. Of course, women are also obligated to pray daily, but they are freer to choose when. (Nothing prevents women from praying in the synagogue with the community, and they are encouraged to do so. They merely aren't obligated to.)

Obviously, books can be, and have been, written about this subject, but I'll just deal briefly with the "*mechitza* issue." Even in a communal setting, most prayer is private. When talking to God, we try to eliminate distractions and recognize our own limitations. The word *mechitza* comes from the Hebrew word for "half." During prayer, we have to recognize our incompleteness. But the Torah tells us that husband and wife are one soul, two halves completing one soul. With a spouse next to us, we can't recognize our incompleteness and have the sense of submission we should.

Furthermore, sexuality is a powerful force. Our awareness is naturally, even unconsciously, drawn to members of the opposite sex. During prayer, that's not appropriate. Our focus should be on the words and on the Divine Presence. Mixed seating, potentially and actually, makes that difficult.

Boundaries are important. Isn't this what we mean when we say, "I need my space"? The *mechitza* gives men and women their spiritual space.

It's important to remember, though, that the *mechitza* and the synagogue service itself—can't be taken in isolation from the rest of Judaism. As we've said before, Judaism is first and foremost family-based and family-oriented. Without a thorough understanding and appreciation of that, the whole synagogue business gets viewed through the wrong lens.

That's probably as good a way as any to get back to your family life. You said earlier that, at first, you didn't think you wanted children. When and how did that change?

SZ: After the first year of marriage, we started talking about children a little more. We talked about the responsibilities, the costs, the loss of our "freedom" to pick up and go whenever we wanted. In the end, we decided that there was no "logical" reason to have children, but at the same time realized that there is more to life than logic. We didn't decide to have children because it was logical, or because it was a *mitzvah*, but because somewhere, deep down, we knew that it was the "right" thing to do.

DK: Of course, it's a *mitzvah* to do the right thing.

I'll bet your discussions weren't as logical or as straightforward as you've described. There must have been a lot of emotional, non-rational conversations. In the end, such decisions often are made simply because one wants something. Such an act of will (or desire, if you prefer) expresses itself first in feelings and emotions, rather than logic.

Did you really say to yourself, "We ought to have children," or did you say, "I want children"? Then, when forced to explain that want (internally or in dialogue with Joe), the natural reason seemed to be, "We ought to."

SZ: Actually, our discussions *were* pretty straightforward. You're right, though; in the end, it was very much a case of "want." I wanted children in spite of what seemed like "logical" reasons (from a selfish standpoint) not to have children. I don't know where the "want" came from, but it is a powerful force. Happily, this time the want was for good.

DK: It's no coincidence that "want" means both will and lack, or that the self is sacrificed for the want.

Anyway, having made that decision to have children. . . .

SZ: Having made that decision, we found a preparation-for-parenting class that was offered through the local YWCA. It was a small class, five or six couples. We were the only couple that was not already expecting a child. It took the instructor a little by surprise. By the time the class ended, I was pregnant. The next class Joe and I took was a natural-childbirth class. I continued working up until the first of May that year, about a week before I was due.

I'll spare you the mother-to-be stories. Suffice it to say that David Michael was born on the afternoon of Friday, May 7, two days before Mother's Day. Our lives now forever changed, it was clear from the start that that illogical, deep-down feeling had been correct.

DK: Were there any journal entries from this period?

SZ: In fact, a number of years passed during which I didn't write anything in the journal. I wasn't struggling with any major spiritual or emotional challenges, which always seemed to have been the catalyst for writing in the journal. Even David's *bris milah* didn't inspire an entry.

DK: Was David's *bris* your first experience with the ceremony?

SZ: Yes. I was, to borrow a phrase, clueless. Harry, from the Tuesday lunch group, gave us the name of a *mohel*. Joe arranged for him to come to the house for the *bris*. I had never been at a *bris*; I didn't know what was expected or, beyond the physical surgical act, what would occur. Joe's folks had come down from New York. Harry was also there. We spoke together in our living room for a few minutes; then the *bris* was done on our dining-room table. For some reason, I ended up having to be right at my son's side. There were so many emotions I felt at that point. I felt bad for the pain that my son was feeling, almost guilty for making him go through it. At the same time, I knew that this was something that had to be done. There was no option. I held the wine-soaked gauze to his lips and fixed my eyes on his. I felt bad, in a way; I didn't think that a mother should have to watch such things.

DK: I know a lot of men who don't watch.

At a *bris*, there's a sense of urgency, an awareness of continuity, a celebration of community and common self-sacrifice.

SZ: My feelings weren't all negative. I felt proud, fulfilled, that I had finally achieved a crucial goal in my life, to continue my Jewishness through children.

DK: This was, in part, what I was getting at when I asked you earlier if Judaism had any pull toward having children.

SZ: Yes. I always had felt that, as a convert, I was somewhat meaningless—a soul dangling in history with no link to the Jewish past, no link to the Jewish future. Now there was a connection; now there was meaning. Now I felt that I had a role, in a very real and physical sense, to the future of Judaism.

DK: I'd argue strongly against the meaninglessness of a convert. Conversion automatically creates a link to the Jewish past. Of course, only children create a link to the Jewish future, but that's true for all Jews.

Your last sentence summarizes much of the "theme" of our discussion here: that every Jew (and, indeed, all existence) has a Divinely ordained role; that creation leads to redemption through our *mitzvos*; that we all must be not just a link to the future of Judaism, but the creators of it (through our Torah and *mitzvos*); and that women already, in a very real and physical sense, are creators of the Jewish future.

So, how did having David change your life—Jewishly, I mean? (The diapers and the sleepless nights are obvious.)

SZ: We didn't go to synagogue at all after that, except for Rosh Hashanah and Yom Kippur. It didn't make sense to drag a baby to services, and neither of us was likely to go alone. I returned to work after about five months, leaving David in daycare with a family living on the base near work.

Life went on. We socialized with the small group of non-Jewish friends that Joe had known from before our marriage. These friends quickly got used to the fact that we didn't eat seafood or pork, and they were careful to serve only beef or chicken when they invited us to dinner. As a rule, I tried to keep Friday nights as family time, and we generally didn't go out then. For a couple of years, that was the extent of our public expression of Jewishness.

DK: What about the holidays—Rosh Hashanah, Yom Kippur, Passover, Chanukah?

SZ: We celebrated those holidays (although not Sukkos, Shimini Atzeres, or Shavuos) as a family. Rosh Hashanah and Yom Kippur, if we didn't go to New York, we would get a babysitter for David and attend services at the Conservative synagogue. Passover was almost always with Joe's family in New York, though one year we did it alone, just the three of us. Chanukah tended to focus on family. We lit candles, of course, and bought presents and *dreidels* and chocolate *gelt* for David. I even learned how to make *sufganiot*—jelly doughnuts. Messy, but definitely a hit.

Anyway, we did celebrate a number of the holidays; *Shabbos* wasn't one of them. I guess that we took Judaism on our terms, when we wanted, how we wanted.

DK: Would you say that you became typical assimilated American Jews?

SZ: I'd say that we had a lot of company. . . . Still, we were members of a synagogue and tried to keep a kosher kitchen. There were still connections.

DK: During this time, did you ever reflect on your journey? Did you think: Yes, this is where I wanted to be, spiritually?

SZ: Sometimes. I didn't really know what the possibilities were. Judaism was what I saw other Jews doing, coupled with my halting attempts to find traditions with which my children could "connect." Occasionally I wondered how it was that I had lost that same "feeling" for God that I had had before the conversion. It seemed like the "real world" just got in the way of spirituality.

DK: It tends to do that if we let it. That's why we have to make our Judaism, our "feeling for God," as physically real as the "real world." Our feeling for God has to be as mundane and material as the "iron curtain" of selfish "real-world" activities. In business, reality is in the details. In *mitzvos*, the feeling for God is also in the details.

We'll come back to this later. But let's move on in your family life.

SZ: Julie was born in July 1985. We named her after Joe's grandmother, Julia. She was given the Hebrew name Yehudit Rachel at a naming ceremony at my father-in-law's *shul*.

With Julie's birth, we had outgrown our two-bedroom house. Though David, who was now three-and-a-half years old, acquiesced to sharing his room with his baby sister, we recognized that the arrangement was at best a stop-gap. We began to look for another house. I had three concerns in the location of the house: First, it had to be close to our pediatrician, whom I had come to like very much; second, it shouldn't be too long a commute to work; and, third, it had to be within a reasonable drive to the synagogue.

My interest in proximity to the synagogue was driven primarily by concerns for the children. David was almost old enough to enter the nursery program at the synagogue. I was eager for him to have that opportunity. I also wanted both children to eventually have the opportunity to go to a Hebrew-school program. In many ways, I was at a loss to know just what it meant to educate a Jewish child. I had not grown up in a Jewish home. Everything was guesswork. Maybe I just hoped that he would learn in Hebrew school what I did not know how to teach at home.

DK: Again, you project a sense of urgency and confusion, of knowing what needs to be done (here, to give your children a Jewish education), but not knowing how to do it. It seems to have been a pattern in your life.

I'd think this time would be a bit different, though. True, you hadn't grown up in a Jewish home, but your husband had. True, you never went to Hebrew school, but the other members of your congregation had. This time you had resources.

SZ: Resources, but not the courage to ask for help. I felt embarrassed that I didn't know very much. There was a facade that I was trying to protect.

DK: I also suspect that part of your eagerness for David to learn was an eagerness to learn with him. You could safely get the Hebrew-school education you never had, which you felt caused a gap in your Jewishness.

SZ: You suspect correctly.

DZ: So what happened with the house-hunting?

SZ: We found a place in Bowie. Actually, it was a cornfield at the time, but we saw a model of the house and the planned development and decided to go with it. This was in a part of the city that was in the beginning stages of development. There were townhouses and single-family homes, a small convenience center, and, about a half-mile down the road, a Reform synagogue. That wasn't much of a concern to us at the time, since we were comfortable enough with the Conservative synagogue, which was about four miles away.

The next year David began attending a preschool daycare program, and we enrolled him in the Sunday nursery-school program at the Conservative synagogue. His classes provided more than just a learning experience for him, though. In many ways, I found that I focused on the little fragments of Jewish tradition that he brought home from school. Somehow, I had become reluctant to discuss religious issues. I don't know if it was out of doubt, or embarrassment, or a simple lack of familiarity. At times, it was almost as though I needed the permission of a child to affirm the importance of being Jewish.

DK: That's not unusual. The sages talk a lot about the purity of children. When God came to give the Torah to the Jewish people, he demanded a guarantor. The Jewish people suggested first the Patriarchs, then Moses and Aaron. God rejected each one. Only when the Jewish people pledged their children as guarantors did God give them the Torah. When *Moshiach* comes, we will interrupt almost all *mitzvos* to rebuild the Temple—except for the teaching of children.

The Rebbe emphasizes that parents should spend half an hour a day thinking about and planning for their children's Jewish education. It's obviously the key to our survival. In fact, the latest statistics show that the two most important factors in fighting assimilation and intermarriage are, for children, lots of Jewish friends and a day-school education. I think that the two are related.

But I'd like to go back to your vicarious education. Why do you think you'd become reluctant to discuss religious issues? After all, it had been a major facet of your life; your search even led you to find your husband.

On some level, of course, we can say that your search now led you inward, or that the spirituality became hidden in the practical difficulties of living and of raising children. And yet, as soon as David went to Hebrew school, you immediately refocused on questions of tradition and religion.

By the way, was the doubt or embarrassment similar to your earlier encounters with those barriers to your spiritual search? What were some of the things that you weren't familiar with at this point?

SZ: Why had I become reluctant to discuss religious issues? To be honest, I think that I was questioning whether God was real. My very belief in God was beginning to fade. I began to think that talking about religious questions was just not done in "normal" life, in normal conversation, that maybe nobody believed anymore, despite what they said in synagogue. Maybe I projected my own doubts onto others, but on the other hand, no one talked about God anywhere but synagogue, anywhere but in services.

At least at Hebrew school the children still learned about God. I didn't want to lose my faith. I was grasping for a connection with no risks.

The doubt and embarrassment were different, I guess, because they hit at very basic issues. Not just what I didn't know, but that which I wasn't sure if anyone, myself included, took seriously.

I wanted to talk to the rabbi about my feelings, but I was afraid. Afraid of facing myself, afraid of exposing my lack of faith, and, most of all, afraid of sounding "stupid."

Hebrew school was "safe." It was okay to talk about God with children.

DK: You also said that you focused on the little fragments of Jewish tradition that David brought home from school. Can you elaborate?

SZ: When David brought home a homemade "Torah," we could talk about the Torah. When he colored pictures of Moses carrying the tablets, we could talk about the commandments. The rest of the time, we didn't discuss these things. I looked at it almost like I viewed the "tooth fairy": something I was willing to play along with for the children, but was not truly convinced of myself.

DK: Given your experiences, that's a pretty strong statement. The innocence of children reveals truth to adults, doesn't it? It seems that as long as we can maintain our veneer of sophistication, we can "indulge" in certainties.

I find it telling how you phrased this, that when your son brought something Jewish home, you could talk about Judaism. You said earlier that you almost needed the permission of a child to affirm the importance of being Jewish. There's no "almost" here, is there?

SZ: No. There was no "almost."

DK: Let's ask why. The answer will also tell us a lot about the reaction parents have to children who become *baalei teshuvah*, return to an observant lifestyle. In a way, we're talking about a difference in degree, not in kind. Your son brings home a homemade "Torah" and you can talk about Torah itself. But imagine that he had said, "Since the Torah says to keep *Shabbos*, I want *Shabbos*." What then?

Maybe it's part of the *chutzpah* of the generation before *Moshiach* that the children will teach the parents. Whatever the reason, we as parents live for our children's approval, don't we? So we have to "know better." Being a cynic, having "been there," gives us some assurance and authority. "When I was your age" or "wait till you grow up" sets up a hierarchy in our favor.

Torah itself, however, creates a different hierarchy. Before "Honor your mother and father" comes "I am the Lord your God," "You shall have no other gods," "Do not use God's Name in vain," and "Keep the *Shabbos*." If we accept the Torah, we can't be autonomous. So we bargain with Torah. "Okay, God," we say, "we'll let You in for the children, but only enough to keep a sense of continuity." Continuity. That's a big word in official Jewish circles these days. But without action, there's no commitment.

Being physical, we connect with what we do, and with others who do the same. Have you ever talked with a friend you haven't seen or spoken to in ten years? We immediately go back to things we did together and start looking for things that we can do together now. If, say, we played bridge then but don't now, it's harder to maintain the connection, to keep the continuity.

We could almost make a chart of what we've just talked about. On the one hand, the "isms" of modern life—selfishness, upward mobility, assimilation, sophistication, and cynicism; on the other hand, Judaism, self-sacrifice, children, continuity, innocence, and wonder.

SZ: Innocence. . . . There were times when I wondered how I would answer if one of my children asked me straight out whether there was a God. Like so many others, I had lost almost all contact with Judaism in everyday life. I had, in a sense, turned my back on the throne; it was no wonder that I failed to see the King. Yet my child would hold up a mirror in front of me, and I could see the reflection of majesty in it. So, despite the struggles, had they ever asked, I would have told them, "Yes, there is a God."

DK: Yes, and your child would also hold up the mirror of your younger, searching self—the one that knew where home was. Our souls, like our children, always know how to come home.

We can expect our intensity to level off, but it's a little sad when our *emunah*, our trust and faithfulness, dries up. I guess that's part of what the Baal Shem Tov meant when he said that he wished he could pray with the simple pure faith of a child.

Anyway, now that David reawakened your "inner child," so to speak, did you allow it to explore again?

SZ: In indirect ways. I became a little more involved in the synagogue. I was pretty active in the Sisterhood. My big task was being in charge of the annual Chanukah party for a couple of years. We prepared the food in the kitchen. Everything was kosher. The rabbi popped in regularly to make sure we were doing things right. The parties were always a big success, drawing about 140 people.

DK: That's great. What else?

SZ: I remember attending only one adult education class while we were members there. That was a beginners' class for the *Shabbos* service. The rabbi taught us for an hour about the meaning and importance of the various prayers and parts of the service, and then we would join the regular *Shabbos* service in the sanctuary. At the end of the class, which met for a number of weeks, we were each given an *aliyah*, men and women alike.

Women were generally counted in *minyan*s at this synagogue. The only exception was that if the man saying Kaddish objected to including the women, then they would not be counted.

The rabbi was a very warm and helpful person who, on many occasions, did his best to encourage the congregants to put more emphasis on Jewish observance in their lives. I can't speak for the rest of the congregation, but it didn't have much of an impact on us. We were still far more likely to be shopping on Saturday than to be at a service.

DK: Here's the difference between a sermon and a story. Simply being told what's right (no matter how much emphasis the rabbi, or anyone else, puts on it) won't change us much because we usually know what we ought to do. When, however, something affects us personally— moves us, touches us even vicariously, then there's the possible impetus for change.

SZ: I wonder how much I understood even the "ought." There was a lot I didn't know, even more that I misunderstood. But let's continue.

David attended Hebrew school at the Conservative synagogue through second grade, but the number of students in the program was quickly dropping off. David was the only child left who was entering third grade, and I was concerned with the obvious lack of Jewish peers at this synagogue. Looking to the future, I wondered how I could ever demand that my children date only Jews if I had never given them the chance to get to know any.

DK: Were there any reasons for the small number of children? Was membership dropping as well?

SZ: There was rather a split between the older members, whose families were already grown, and the younger members. Nothing hostile; just a lack of common interests and needs. As the children began to "disappear," I learned that many younger families had left the Conservative synagogue and had joined the Reform temple near us. It had a very large number of students and a well-organized program.

    I began to think that it was time for a change.

12
Reform

DK: The time had come to make a change, you said. Were there any other factors besides the Hebrew school situation?

SZ: Hebrew school—more specifically, the lack of other Jewish students at the Hebrew school—was my overriding concern. I spoke with Joe about the possibility of joining the Reform congregation. He was quite unenthusiastic. I tried to rationalize my position: Socially it would be better for the children, I reasoned, and, besides, we were behaving like Reform Jews anyway (we didn't observe *Shabbos*, didn't eat kosher outside) so why not just live up to the fact and join a Reform synagogue?

DK: What does a "Reform" Jew behave like? You kept kosher; in that, how did you differ from an "Orthodox" Jew? I'm not trying to be facetious. Although there are obvious (and some not-so-obvious) differences between the Orthodox, Conservative, and Reform philosophies (and the sanctioned practices that result therefrom), the individual is not the movement. I always find these types of labels disconcerting because they're meaningless. There are Jews and there are *mitzvos*. All Jews do *mitzvos*. Labels make categorical differences, whereas in truth the differences are of degree, not kind.

I'm not sure if that's really relevant to your decision-making process here, but I've confronted that type of "reasoning" too often to be comfortable with it.

SZ: Well, the fact is that I looked at the folks who were members of the Reform congregation and decided that *that* was Reform. "That" was a minimal observance of *Shabbos*, lack of concern about *kashrus* (remember that we didn't keep kosher outside the home), and generally allowing religion into one's life only when it was convenient or socially inviting—the attitude that while one should be proud to be Jewish, Judaism shouldn't interfere with "real life." I'm not saying that this is what Reform *is*, only that that is how I perceived it. It is also how I saw us behaving at the time.

DK: You've just illustrated what we might call the "great dichotomy": the difference between a philosophical platform, the leadership's promotion of it, and the laity's practice of it. Is X how people practice it, how the leadership presents it, or how it's printed? Maybe it's some combination thereof. Clearly, though, the more distant the three are from each other, the more problematic is the philosophy, the leadership, or both.

Something else I'd like to pursue at another point is your observation about the congregants, which really applies to many Jews from all denominations: They were proud to be Jewish, but felt that Judaism shouldn't interfere with "real life." I've encountered it before, of course, but I always wonder what it means. If you're not doing anything, what is there to be proud of?

That may be an unanswerable question, or one that we should think about and discuss later.

Anyway, given Joe's background, how did he respond to your arguments?

SZ: Joe questioned me about the choice. Up until that point, the Conservative synagogue had seemed to be the best compromise between the Orthodox Judaism he had grown up with and saw as authentic Judaism, and what I perceived real Judaism to be (mixed seating, optional *mitzvos*).

DK: How different, in fact, were these perceptions and realities? That's actually a bit of a rhetorical question. Your phrase "real Judaism" emphasized, for me, the poignancy and truth of the "great dichotomy." To some extent, we all separate our "real life" from "real Judaism." It's a problem that's at least as old as Elijah. You'll recall that, after defeating the prophets of Baal, Elijah demanded that the Jewish people stop sitting on the fence. If Baal is god, follow him, Elijah declared, but if the Lord is God, follow Him. A strange demand, considering that, having won, he could have simply demanded loyalty. But Elijah recognized that the greatest danger was not following a false god. In that case, once one was taught or realized that it was false, the same faith could be redirected to the one true God; but if a person sat on the fence, separating "real life" from "real Judaism," then his or her *emunah* could never be true or complete. So if we separate our "real life" from "real Judaism," how real is either?

Anyway, you were saying that Joe gave you a bit of a hard time.

SZ: Given the situation, we saw no better alternative to joining the Reform synagogue. There was no Orthodox presence in Bowie, so I never considered moving in that direction. We certainly didn't want the children to grow up rejecting Judaism because they perceived themselves to be the only Jews around, that they had to literally leave town to find Jewish peers. Joe went along with my scheme, if only for the children's sake, and we joined the Reform temple a half-mile down the road. The rabbi of the Conservative congregation called the Reform rabbi to make sure that we weren't "recruited." I tried to assure everyone that we were doing this by our own choice. To be honest, I wasn't thrilled with myself for making the transition. I sensed that, spiritually, I was headed in the wrong direction. I knew that I was trying to score points by moving the goalpost to the ball. On the surface, though, it seemed the pragmatic thing to do.

DK: Your lack of excitement probably should have told you something, although circumstances certainly made the move seem reasonable. Yet we all talk ourselves into things, citing "pragmatic" reasons that our instinct tells us is just self-indulgence. That tendency to "move the goalpost," as you put it, arises from the internal battle we've talked about before. It's a type of laziness that gives in to the *yetzer hara*.

SZ: Yet what was the internal battle here? Although in hindsight it seems misguided, I thought I was doing the right thing for my children. I wanted them to be in a group where being Jewish was "normal." I wanted my children to grow up Jewish, feeling proud to be Jews and valuing and understanding their history and heritage. A vague sense of discomfort, an instinct, couldn't compete with what I saw as the best available way to achieve that aim. In fact, I probably would have dismissed that instinct as selfishness.

DK: But that's exactly the internal battle. We don't always recognize it while it's taking place; at least, we don't always see it in front of our faces. But if there had been no such internal battle, if you had been completely convinced your choice was right on all levels, you would have been content. You wouldn't have sensed that, spiritually, you were headed in the wrong direction.

   How did the transition go?

SZ: David and Julie took the transition in stride. They were happy to be so close to their Hebrew school, and to have so many other children around. Their goals were more social than religious.

DK: Often the social goal *is* a religious one, and vice versa—and not just for children.

SZ: That's not to say that they didn't identify as Jews, but the distinctions between the two synagogues were lost on them. Probably what took them most by surprise was the rabbi wearing a robe.

   We started going to services at the temple pretty regularly on Friday nights; there were no services on Saturday mornings.

DK: Why did you start going regularly now, when you didn't at the Conservative synagogue?

SZ: The children were older. Julie was in kindergarten and David was in third grade. They were able to handle the services a little better. I was also getting more serious about giving them a Jewish education. I wanted them to understand that prayer is as much a part of Judaism as Chanukah. Maybe I was trying to justify the move by jumping in with both feet, hoping that a greater involvement would lead to greater acceptance.

DK: Greater acceptance of whom, by whom, and, to complete the triad, for whom?

SZ: I meant that I hoped the involvement would lead to *my* becoming more convinced, more accepting, of the choice I'd made to affiliate with a Reform synagogue.

  The services were different from what I had been used to. Most of the time we were either engaged in responsive readings or listening to the cantor, a woman, as if we were at a concert. There were a few prayers (or parts of them) done in Hebrew, but mostly the service was in English.

DK: In Judaism, a religious service shouldn't be a performance. *Chazzanus* [the art of cantorial singing] is not opera.

SZ: It seemed strange to me. It was so close to a church service, so orchestrated. Still, I had made the decision; I had to deal with the consequences—good or bad. I told myself that this service was just as valid and was done with just as much sincerity as any other; that it wasn't worse, just different, and that it would take some time to adjust to it.

DK: Of course, sincerity doesn't equal validity. Truth is made of sterner stuff.

SZ: The Torah portion was photocopied so that we could follow along as the rabbi read a section of the weekly reading.

  At the end of the service, the rabbi said Kiddush and asked a family to say the *hamotzi* over the challah. The children were invited to join in, each of them getting a piece of challah or a sip of grape juice. I thought it was very nice to include the children like that.

  The people were friendly. At the Oneg Shabbats—a time of socializing that followed the services—we became acquainted with a number of people in the congregation. David and Julie made acquaintances with the cookies and punch, along with the other children.

Altogether, the services had a kind of "churchy" feel to them. Joe later told me that he didn't even consider it a service—"not a Jewish one, anyway." When we attended High Holy Day services a year later, the atmosphere was even more striking: In order to accommodate all the people who came for Rosh Hashanah and Yom Kippur, the service was held in an auditorium at the community college. It was truly like attending a concert, a soprano and a tenor offering almost operatic renditions of the most holy prayers accompanied by the rich tones of the organ. I didn't like it at all; it all seemed overly melodramatic, and I found the environment disruptive to personal prayer and introspection. The atmosphere was more one of performance than of personal encounter.

DK: One's synagogue comfort zone depends on what one sees as the purpose of prayer, and on how often one prays. The Hebrew word for prayer, *tefillah*, has many meanings, though they're all related to the concepts of introspection and devotion. Public prayer in Judaism has historically been structured to support the individual's self-judgment and effort to be attached to the Divine, not to distract him or her from the imperative, "Know before Whom you stand."

I take it that the regular Friday night services weren't quite as disruptive.

SZ: No. Actually, I quickly adapted to the regular Friday-night services. In fact, except for a few things (a different prayerbook, the organ or guitar accompanying the female cantor, and *Shabbos* candlelighting after sunset), the services weren't all that much different from the services at the Conservative synagogues I'd attended in the past.

DK: The differences between the services result from the differences in philosophy of the various movements. Thus, ironically, religious services tend to separate the Jewish people, rather than bring them together. The movements make their ideological stance in the synagogue, their "seat of power." In order to identify itself, a religious group first makes a new prayerbook, a text around which the lay people can be gathered. The philosophies are usually not of interest to the "common man."

What we see happening is that people choose a style of worship (or a Sunday school), not a philosophy. True, there may be some social considerations when joining a synagogue, although the active members tend to be welcoming regardless of affiliation. Generally, though, Jews identify with, and identify their Judaism as, a type of synagogue service.

Someone once said that if all the synagogues were closed for a hundred years, but the home-centered *mitzvos* were observed, Judaism would survive just fine; it might even be better off. (I wonder what would happen if, instead of asking what type of synagogue another Jew belonged to, we asked which *mitzvah* he or she emphasized.)

SZ: Or if we asked how important *mitzvos* are in his or her daily life.

DK: Let's get back to the reason you changed synagogues in the first place. Did the Hebrew-school program meet your needs?

SZ: Let's see, what were our needs? I wanted my children to learn Hebrew, to understand why and how we celebrate the various holidays, and, most important, to reinforce a faith in God and foster a sense of unity with the Jewish people. (That my expectations closely mirrored the curricula of my conversion studies is probably more than a coincidence.)

Hebrew school began that fall. We enrolled both David and Julie in the program. Each grade had ten to fifteen students. The temple had just hired a new principal, a dynamic young woman with a Conservative background. Several of the teachers were parents of students; others were hired from outside. The children went to school one or two days a week: three hours on Sunday morning for everyone, and ninety minutes on Wednesday evenings for the students in fourth grade and beyond. They split the session time between Hebrew and Judaica (history, customs, holidays).

DK: In other words, a typical Hebrew-school program.

SZ: By the end of his year in third-grade Hebrew school, David had learned to read and print about half of the Hebrew *aleph-bet*. He couldn't yet read prayers or blessings. I was rather disappointed; I had expected more.

DK: You had high expectations. It's hard for children to learn much in the typical Hebrew school. Even those who want to be there on Sunday mornings (or after school) and whose parents are supportive don't have the time or continuity to absorb much. The wonder is not that they learn well, but that they learn at all.

SZ: I was more concerned than David seemed to be. Then, the parent of another student—a very gifted girl—confided in me that she was also upset by the lack of progress. We approached the principal with our concerns.

I should have realized that speaking up to complain in a synagogue was like stepping forward to volunteer to do something about it. I'm not sure exactly how it transpired, but somehow I ended up agreeing to teach the fourth-grade Hebrew class the next year.

This was truly a case of one who knows *aleph* teaching *aleph*. I had to brush up on my Hebrew. It had been a long time since the Ulpan classes. I did the best I could. I was committed to one thing: that the students who left my class would know what the Hebrew words meant, as well as how to read them. Our goal was that each student would know several blessings by the end of the year, and would be able to read a paragraph or two of Hebrew for the class service. Some students were more successful than others.

DK: This brings back memories of when I taught Hebrew school. I've known a lot of dedicated teachers and administrators. However good the programs are, though, they're just not enough. Sunday-school Judaism can't survive; I'm convinced of that. Judaism has got to live in the home and be part of the curriculum every day.

SZ: You're right. Judaism has to be an all-day, every-day commitment. We can't merely send our children to school four or five hours a week and assume that we have discharged our responsibility as Jewish parents. Our personal example is the most powerful teacher. If we have abandoned Judaism in everyday life, how can we ask our children to do any differently?

As a teacher, it was obvious to me that most of the better students—the ones who really tried—were from families who put a priority on things Jewish. The ones from families that made little effort were often the same children who didn't come to class because of a Scout meeting or a conflict with a soccer game, or whatever. It wasn't just the absences—we didn't move so fast that it would be difficult to catch up—it was more the attitude that Hebrew school—maybe Judaism in general—wasn't all that important, so why bother? I guess that the parents must have agreed, or the children would have been there.

DK: Where do you think the children got the attitude? The critical question is, where did the parents get such an attitude? But what you're describing is the result of Sunday-school Judaism, and it doesn't matter with which movement the synagogue's affiliated.

SZ: I see your point. In fact, some of these parents were graduates of Hebrew programs run by Orthodox synagogues a couple of decades earlier. It was the same thing: a few hours a week in class, attend *Shabbos* services, become bar or bat mitzvah, and you've reached your goal, passed the test, know it all. Now you can leave learning behind and get on with your life. Hebrew school leading to bar and bat mitzvah becomes a rite of passage. And that mentality carries on to the next generation, if the next generation even stays Jewish.

DK: No, not a rite of passage. A rite of passage means that after completion or survival one has a new status. One is expected to be responsible, reliable, involved. Bar or bat mitzvah means that one is now responsible for observance of the *mitzvos* and can be relied on to observe them as an involved member of the community. Bar or bat mitzvah should be a rite of passage, but more often than not it's simply a farewell performance.

SZ: The problem transcends mere attitudes. Once when I was talking to our principal, I mentioned to her that one of the reasons I'd come to the temple was so that David and Julie would be around other Jewish children. She laughed and said, "But Sue, you have to realize that a lot of the kids in the school aren't even Jewish. I'm not sure that you would know who is or isn't."

Intermarriage was quite common among the congregants. In many cases, it was only the father of the child who was Jewish. Reform had made a decision to accept such children as Jewish, but according to traditional Jewish law, they weren't.

DK: There's a contradiction here. The principal said that the children weren't Jewish, but the synagogue did—or was it just the Reform movement?

SZ: The principal was Conservative and didn't hold personally by that Reform doctrine. She was speaking to me as a friend, not in her capacity as the principal. Until then, the whole matter had not occurred to me. I realized that she was right: My children were likely socializing with non-Jews, thinking that they were Jewish.

DK: How did you feel about that revelation, especially concerning your own situation?

SZ: I, of course, having had a "superior" Conservative conversion, was quite confident that my children were "kosher" Jews. It was the children of intermarriages and token conversions that we had to worry about.

DK: Ironic. But you see now why this is such a divisive issue. All else is rather easily correctable. Even if one doesn't keep kosher, accommodations can be made for those that do. Ultimately, the philosophies and affiliations don't matter, since Jewishness is expressed in observance. Even minimal observance can be a sufficient expression. The possibility of *teshuvah* preserves the Jewish connection.

But if there's no Jewishness to begin with, there's no connection, no matter how much observance. It's a fundamental divide that threatens the unity of the Jewish people.

Let's leave the speeches and situational irony aside for now. At the time, did this realization affect the way you did things?

SZ: Unfortunately, yes. A number of the children celebrated both Chanukah and Christmas, both Pesach and Easter. We teachers even had to be careful in class to not say things that might cause dissension in such families. Sometimes it was a fine line.

A couple of students came into my class who had spent the previous year attending Christian Sunday schools. Sometimes, class time had to be spent explaining that some things they had learned in those schools were just not Jewish.

I had another child who started doing poorly in class. The principal and I tried to find out the source of the problem. We discovered that the student felt that, by emphasizing his Jewishness, he was rejecting his father, a Christian. In order to gain his father's favor, the boy thought he had to reject his Jewishness and everything associated with it, including Hebrew school.

DK: The organized Jewish community is just waking up to the crisis of intermarriage, though statistics show that the rate among the non-observant is over 50 percent. (This doesn't take into account what you called "token" conversions, or redefinitions of status.)

SZ: Only a small percentage of those who intermarry actually try to raise their children as Jews, and even fewer have grandchildren who identify as Jews. What our enemies were not successful in doing to us, we are, sadly, doing to ourselves.

DK: One of the greatest challenges of Jewish outreach is to be sensitive to the individuals involved without compromising the standards of Judaism.

The basic rule, I think, is to treat everyone—including the non-Jewish spouse (or children)—with respect. Everything possible must be done to stop an intermarriage, of course. But even after the regrettable fact, we still have a responsibility to educate Jews and promote their observance of *mitzvos*. That often means educating non-Jews as well. It's a delicate situation that requires tact, firmness, empathy, conviction, and the strength to work with people in that situation. (For instance, I know of non-Jewish fathers who sent their children to Orthodox day schools; how they were treated helped them feel it was the right thing to do.)

SZ: I always thought that, strictly speaking, there was a communal responsibility to break up intermarriages. That's not so?

DK: Yes and no. What do we do when a non-Jewish man is married to a Jewish woman, they want to raise these halachically Jewish children in a Jewish environment, and the children identify themselves as Jews? Say that the non-Jewish husband is very supportive; in fact, both parents want the children to go to an Orthodox day school. Don't we have a responsibility to those Jewish children, even if it means "tolerating" an intermarriage?

How much is the non-Jewish spouse willing to learn? How far is the spouse willing to go? All we can do is to teach, be patient, be respectful, and be there. What our standards are, what Judaism says, they'll learn soon enough, if they don't already know. We can accept individuals without approving of their behavior. That's the essence of *ahavas yisroel* and its consequence, *ahavas habrios*, the love of all humanity.

Let's remember that we're talking about the community's responsibility. The family, while part of the community, has an internal dynamic; familial relationships involve strong emotions and past history. These affect how parents and siblings interact with and relate to an intermarried couple. While the family and the community to some extent mirror the response of each other, "the community" has no such emotional involvement or history; it can accept and disapprove at the same time. If "the community" couldn't stop the intermarriage—through a failure of education, observance, and the like—what makes it think that the happy couple will listen to it and break up?

I think that the communal responsibility is to help Jews live as Jews, and that means learning Torah and doing *mitzvos*. A Jew who observes *mitzvos* will face the dilemma on his or her own. A non-Jewish spouse who learns the importance of *mitzvos* for a Jew will also face the dilemma. We can only compel by example and education; we must ask ourselves, When the Jew does *teshuvah* and needs help, where will we be? Why should he or she come to us? We have to lay the groundwork for that *teshuvah*, but we also have to prepare it so that the *baal teshuvah* (who may even be the converted spouse) has a positive response to those questions.

The situation's not reducible to easy answers or formulas; the crisis requires both *Ahavas Yisroel* and an insistence on the observance of *mitzvos*. That it is a crisis, though, is an indictment of the Jewish leadership responsible for maintaining Jewish identity (read: observance). Feeling proud just isn't good enough. Despite all the facilitated discussions and "touchy-feely" programs, it never was.

Anyway, it seems that you became quite involved in this synagogue, unlike the others you'd joined. Of course, David and Julie had a lot to do with that. So for the children's sake you began doing more, while on your own part you were feeling spiritually emptied or lost?

SZ: It seemed to be going that way. Actually, I got a little ahead of myself. I'd like to go back to two events that occurred in 1992 and had a significant impact on my life.

The first event occurred on *erev* Pesach. We left early that Friday morning to head up to New York, where we planned to spend Pesach with Joe's family. It was quite foggy, and I was driving. Less than a mile from our home, we were broadsided by a car that ran a stop sign. Our minivan somersaulted and crashed on the side of the road. David was knocked unconscious (at first I thought he was dead), and a piece of flesh was ripped off Julie's leg to the bone. We were all taken to the hospital. Julie had to be operated on. I barely held myself together, in great part owing to the kindness of a neighbor who came to the hospital as soon as she heard about the accident. She stayed with us most of the day, reassuring us, helping us get through the bureaucratic red tape, and staying with Julie when Joe and I had to go for our own examinations. We will never forget her or her act of kindness.

DK: Thank God you all survived.

By the way, I notice that you didn't identify the neighbor. That's as it should be. Acts of goodness and kindness are the responsibility and prerogative of all humanity.

SZ: Needless to say, it was a frightening and difficult experience for all of us on many levels. It was hardest for Julie, who was then six years old. She had to remain in the hospital for a week. Joe or I were constantly with her, trying to answer her (and our) questions and deal with her (and our) anger.

"Why did I have to get hurt?" "Why didn't the man send me a get-well card or at least come say he was sorry?" "Why me?" "Why" questions are very hard to answer.

DK: "Why" questions—the ultimate "whys"—can't be answered. That's what Job learned. How do we reconcile Divine Providence, Divine Omnipotence, and Divine Justice, when we see so much that appears random or unjust? God answered Job from the whirlwind: Where were you when I was creating all existence? It seems an evasive answer, but it's not. We've all had experiences where something seemed unfair, but later turned out to be for the best. It's a matter of perspective. Lacking the Divine perspective, we can't answer these questions.

"Why did I have to get hurt?" There are a thousand possible explanations, but intellectual reasons don't respond to the pain. What Julie was asking for—and which you no doubt gave—was reassurance, the comfort of someone being there.

"Why me?" We ask this when we see no purpose behind the pain. But the purpose we're looking for is relational. A "worthy cause" simply means that someone needed the sacrifice we made. We are asking for the Divine Presence.

Children teach us that we have to have the relationship before the pain begins. If we're not there for the child before she falls, she won't look for us afterward. But if we are there, then, after a hug from us, she'll get up and take another step. The pain may still be there, but it's secondary.

Emunah, which we usually translate as "faith," actually comes from the Hebrew word for "craft." One has to work at having faith, and at being faithful. Like a skilled artisan, we have to practice the craft of faithfulness so that, when we need to "produce," we have the expertise and competence.

You obviously had that *emunah*, to be able to get through such an experience. And the fact that it occurred *erev* Pesach didn't help.

SZ: No. It really added to the difficulties. There was, of course, the internal rhetorical question: "What kind of a way to spend Pesach is this?"

DK: In a sense, the best way, since you were all alive after a life-threatening accident. Of course, you had other things on your mind as well.

SZ: The most immediate concerns were simple logistics. We asked the hospital to provide Julie with kosher meals, but when they came, they were not kosher for Pesach. We let her go back on a regular diet. Joe and I brought kosher-for-Pesach food from home for ourselves, much of it provided by Joe's folks, who came down from New York as soon as they could. We had no seder that year, but I sensed that we, too, had been spared from the Angel of Death. It was only by God's grace that we all had emerged alive from that accident.

DK: You had an actual exodus, a very personal redemption.

SZ: Yes, we did. There was a lesson there, too: Each day has to be appreciated and lived fully, because there are no guarantees of "tomorrow."

It could be that the accident and the lengthy aftermath (Julie needed to have three separate operations) changed me a little. I turned to God, praying for Julie's recovery, for my own strength and understanding, for a lot of things. Maybe that changed me, though it didn't seem obvious at the time.

DK: I guess that, just as it took Julie some time to recover from the trauma, it took some time for you to become cognizant of the personal significance of the events.

What was the second event?

SZ: The second event happened during the High Holiday services that autumn. The rabbi had challenged the congregation's members to take a look at their spiritual growth and, further, to come meet with him for a sort of spiritual checkup. He even provided us with "Spiritual Checkup Forms" to fill out and return to him when we made an appointment. He gave them back to us when we met, and I have kept mine. Would you like to read it?

DK: Need you ask?

SPIRITUAL CHECKUP FORM

PERSONAL

I am feeling positive/good about the following areas in my life:
My marriage, my kids, being involved in school.

I am having problems with/questions about the following areas in my life:
I wish I could become less shy in social relationships. I think I yell at my kids too much and would like to discipline them more gently.

INTERPERSONAL

The most important relationship(s) in my life is (are) (list key areas of satisfaction, dissatisfaction/problems, qualities you like or admire and those you dislike):
With Joe, who is thoughtful, tolerant and smart. I wish I felt more comfortable discussing religious issues with him.

TRANSPERSONAL

A time when I felt close to God was:
I always feel close to God when I confront the raw beauty in nature, the mountains, the night stars, and the songs of birds in the morning.

A time when I felt distant from God was:
I feel distant from God whenever I get so busy with everyday hassles that I don't take "time-outs." I feel distant from God when I am lonely.

The Jewish practices/teachings I especially value are:
I have always admired Micah's admonition, "To do justice, love mercy and walk humbly with God."

I have trouble with:
Managing my time. Initiating things—phone calls, etc.

My general feeling about coming to services is:
(a) I'd like to come more often. (b) I let my kids distract me too much when there.

I feel connected to our congregation/the Jewish community: true or false. Please explain.

*Half-true. I enjoy teaching because I get to spend more time at the Temple.
I would like to see something like a lunchtime Torah study so some of us
could be together while the kids are in school.*

And going out to meet Thee I found Thee coming toward me . . . by Judah
Halevi.

DK: Several things strike me about this checkup. You took your relationships quite seriously; you wanted perfection (don't we all!), and
saw the frailties of being finite as major problems; the spiritual remained abstract, and the physical a distraction from it.
   In many ways, it seems to be a typical response, almost cliched.
Alter a few items ("I enjoy volunteering" instead of "I enjoy teaching," for instance), and anyone could have written it.

SZ: I guess so, but at the time I felt very self-conscious, a little embarrassed even, opening myself up to the rabbi like that—especially discussing my feelings about God. I certainly wouldn't have felt that
"anyone" could have written it. In hindsight, though, I see that you're
right.

DK: Yet the fact that you filled it out also means that you gave some
serious thought to the questions, which probably puts you "ahead" of
the vast majority. But do you see what's missing from this "Spiritual
Checkup Form"?

SZ: I did give the questions serious thought. Some of the issues were
things I really wanted to talk about. As far as what was missing—
there were no questions about *mitzvos* or about learning. The real keys
to Jewish growth were conspicuously absent.

DK: How did filling it out affect you?

SZ: Just the act of filling out the form forced me to give some thought
to my spiritual health. I wasn't impressed with what I saw.

DK: Can you be more specific?

SZ: I realized that I wasn't growing. Increased ritual and involvement
hadn't brought a closer relationship to God or a stronger sense of

connection to the Jewish people. I looked over my journal and saw how much emotional energy I had once invested in desiring to become, and finally becoming, Jewish. It had faded. My involvement in the synagogue and Hebrew school helped to rekindle that need for connection, that hunger for more spirituality; but, in and of itself, the involvement presented no solution. Filling out the form was an attempt to ask for help.

DK: So how did you follow it up? Did you meet with the rabbi?

SZ: I met with the rabbi several weeks afterward. We talked about my answers a bit, but he wasn't able to offer much of the guidance I was looking for. He did sense my need for religious growth, and suggested that I read the book *God in Search of Man* by Abraham Heschel; in fact, he was kind enough to lend me his personal copy. The meeting also opened the door a little wider. I felt more comfortable approaching him a little later on.

I read the book, then read it again. Something clicked inside of me. Religion, Judaism, began to take on a great deal more significance. The need to move forward had been awakened, but there was no clear path.

I began to think that I had been escorted to the front door and told to "Go find it." I didn't know whether I was looking for a mountain or a valley, a river or an ocean. All I knew was that "it" was something Jewish, and that I didn't have "it."

DK: We've talked before about what "clicks" for a person, what moves one to grow. The "clicking point" depends as much on where you're at as on personality and content. I don't know that Heschel's work would have "clicked" for you before; I suspect that it wouldn't "click" for you now.

So how did you go about finding "it"?

SZ: I met with the rabbi again a few months later to try to resolve the difficulties I was experiencing. I expressed my distress at not being able to find the kind of fulfillment at the synagogue that I felt was possible. I remember him asking me, "So what do you want, to join Young Israel?" I gave him a blank look, and said I didn't know what that was.

"It's Orthodox," he replied. I told him that I didn't think I could really consider Orthodoxy because of its views on women.

DK: Little did you know. . . .

SZ: So true, and it seemed like such an innocent little exchange at the time.

The rabbi then related the story of the two travelers lost in the forest. One told the other, "I don't know the way out, but I can tell you the paths that don't lead out." It was not a satisfying response. To me, it meant that the rabbi was just as lost as I was. So, the questions I asked did not get answered in our meeting.

DK: I don't think a rabbi has to have all the answers, but he certainly should know the path (Torah and *mitzvos*). His metaphor I find poignant: The travelers are lost in the forest and need a path out. Why are they lost? Probably because they left the trail in the first place. They needed not to find a path out, but to get back to the path that took them through the forest in the first place. Then they could easily find their way home.

SZ: Perhaps I, too, recognized that the path home was the path of Torah and *mitzvos*. I remember asking the rabbi, "What is the difference between a good Jew and a good person?" I think the question caught him by surprise, and he gave me a vague reply to the effect that a Jew does more *mitzvos*, but with the Reform understanding of *mitzvos* that it is maybe a little unclear how much *mitzvos* define our Jewishness.

I was disturbed by the reply, and countered: "Okay, but if I observe only 10 percent of the *mitzvos*, and my children observe only 10 percent of what I do, then what will be left?" He didn't answer. The truth is, we both knew what the answer was.

Maybe it was burning frustration, but my fire was lit. I wanted to do something to help save what I was beginning to see as a sinking ship.

13
Reform, Part 2

DK: You said that you wanted to "do something." I sense the follow-up is "but. . . ."

SZ: . . . But I knew a little about a lot of Jewish things, and a lot about none of them. One problem was that I thought I knew more than I did, and often privately complained that the others weren't taking Judaism seriously enough.

DK: So, in the end, what did you do?

SZ: I took on a few special causes.

DK: Such as?

SZ: I wanted the kitchen at the temple to be kosher. Applying the same rationale that I had in my own life, I felt that it was only proper that any Jew, from any persuasion, should be able to come to our synagogue and eat with us. I also felt that the synagogue should set an example of what our goals of observance should be. This was defi-

nitely an uphill battle. The temple did have a policy of keeping "bib-
lically kosher," which meant not having pork, shellfish, or mixed meat
and dairy. The rabbi tried to keep that line drawn, at least.

DK: Your problem was that you assumed what the goals of observance
should be. If one accepts that the Torah was given to the Jewish people
on Mount Sinai and the accompanying process of application of its
laws and principles (*halacha*), the goal of observance is a given. If
not, there's really no basis, other than personal whim for any particular
goal of observance. There's no compulsion to move beyond the level
of intellectual identification.

SZ: There is the concept of Jewish unity, being family, doing something beyond our personal norm for the sake of those we care for. But
maybe that's my personal whim.

DK: Even if these concepts are more than a personal or collective whim,
they're still "only" nice ideals. Wanting a standard for goals of observance means that you want a standard of action; a way of measuring what people do, not what they feel. *Halacha* is a standard because
it sets criteria: This you may do, this you may not, this you must. Even
"Jewish unity," as a concept, doesn't require you to do anything.
Everyone's for unity; but what do we have to do to get a *Jewish* unity?

  Anyway, I take it that getting the synagogue's kitchen to be kosher was a losing battle?

SZ: The bottom line was that most of the congregation didn't want to
bother with it.

DK: If most of the congregation didn't want to bother with *kashrus*,
it's because they'd been taught they didn't have to, and shouldn't
want to.

SZ: What you say is true. The congregants didn't want to bother with
kashrus; most didn't know what it involved and didn't want to learn;
there was no official policy to motivate them "administratively"; and
there was no instruction in *halacha* to motivate them personally. If
one's view of "Jewish unity" is social events, congregational potluck
dinners, and Chanukah parties, then *kashrus* seems like something
to be avoided, not encouraged.

DK: Yes, that was my point about goals of observance. It's easy to be unified doing nothing. But if by Jewish unity you mean *Ahavas Yisroel*, then there are specific actions that meet the goal of observing *Ahavas Yisroel* (and these may include, in context, social events and the like).

SZ: In speaking with the parents of my students, I realized how many of the congregants didn't know a bit of Hebrew. I talked to the rabbi and the principal about it, and they suggested that I teach a beginning Hebrew class for adults, so I did. We had about nine students, and it went quite well. A few of the women were so inspired by their learning that they began to talk of having a "group bat mitzvah." We began a second session, but events were such that we only were able to have a few classes before the end of the school year.

DK: Still, completing that first session was quite an accomplishment. It shows that, contrary to the "experts" and the "leaders," people—regardless of synagogue affiliation—are willing to make sacrifices in order to learn and to observe the *mitzvos*, provided that the teacher accepts them as they are, respects their questions, doubts, and hesitations, and yet refuses to compromise the standards of observance.

That was one cause that wasn't lost, anyway. And the courage of your nine students should also be acknowledged.

SZ: Absolutely. Beginnings can be terribly difficult, and a real blow to the ego when we are already supposed to "know it all." I was also feeling the need to learn more, and approached the rabbi for ideas. "Maybe a lunchtime group, like the one I used to attend on the base," I suggested. The rabbi felt that it would be better to have a *Shabbos*-morning group once a month. We would have breakfast (bagels, juice, and coffee), then have a short service followed by a group study of the weekly Torah portion. Since there were only about a dozen of us, we met in the library rather than in the sanctuary.

I was also bothered by the fact that many of the adult social activities, like the "Fifties Sock Hop" and the "Square Dancing and Dinner Party," were devoid of Jewish themes. I wanted to organize something that would be fun and meaningful at the same time.

I proposed a *challah* workshop, and was given the green light to plan it as I saw fit. I sent out flyers, took reservations, prepared a workshop guide, purchased all the ingredients, and covered the tables with plastic.

DK: *Challah*-baking classes always seem to be popular. We do one with the students just about every year. Separating *challah*, which also represents keeping a kosher home, is one of the three special *mitzvos* for women. Interestingly, these three *mitzvos* preserve the sanctity of the home, which, as we've said, is far more important to the survival of Judaism than the sanctity of the synagogue.
Tell me about your *challah* class.

SZ: When it finally happened, there were twenty-three men and women up to their elbows in dough. With a couple of exceptions, this was the first time any of them had ever tried making *challah*. I asked how many of them had mothers who had made *challah* for Shabbat, and only a few raised their hands. I felt that I was providing a well-"kneaded" service.

DK: Don't start me on puns. But it's impressive that so many people came.

SZ: Especially so because I sensed that the people were there because they saw it as a way to forge another "connection" to Jewish life.

DK: Thus reaching a goal of observance.

SZ: The rabbi brought in a couple of "spectators" for a few minutes, another rabbi and his colleague who were teaching a community conversion class that was being held at the temple. They were amused at the sight, but were very impressed with the concept.

DK: That's more a comment on them than your workshop.

SZ: I had an ulterior motive in all this. I knew that while the loaves of bread were rising (under an electric blanket!) we would have some time to talk. I used as much of the "first rise" as possible to talk about spiritual issues. I used the Workshop Guide as a starting point.

DK: Let's take a look at the Guide.

SZ: Here it is:

SHABBAT CHALLOT

A WORKSHOP GUIDE BY SUE ZAKAR

There is something truly special about the loaves of challah that grace the Shabbat table. For many years I had been baking such loaves, varying the recipe this way or that, but it was only recently that I understood the "soul" of Shabbat Challot. I hope this workshop will help you understand it, too.

There is a recipe below that tells you the ingredients and mixing instructions for making challah. If you follow it you will likely come up with a good loaf of challah, but that is not the real point of this workshop. . . .

This workshop is also about *kavanah.*

Kavanah means attention, concentration and spirit of devotion, it involves the intention which lies behind our deeds. It can be the key which gives meaning to this (or any) experience. If you follow the recipe intending to receive compliments for your work, you will likely end up with two pretty loaves made of dough twisted and bound up in themselves. And you will find yourself being twisted and bound up similarly with the compliments you intended.

Yet, if you prepare the loaves with the intention of doing it for the sake of God, of doing it as a mitzvah that will help make the Shabbat meal a blessing, you will end up with Shabbat Challot. You will find yourself bound up in the twists of their meaning, and a greater sense of the power and holiness of Shabbat. The time you spend making challah is a good time to pray, to allow yourself to explore the "deeper meanings" hidden within the process, and to become more aware of God's presence.

DK: You've caught the essence of both the "spiritual dimension" of *mitzvos* and your own "spiritual dilemma" in dealing with it. The act hasn't changed, but the meanings hidden within have also become personalized.

SZ: Here's more of the Guide.

So, before you even begin to look at the recipe, think of *kavanah.* Take a break from the cleaning and chores to pray, read a psalm, sing a Hebrew song, read some Torah, or contemplate the meaning of Shabbat and its symbols. Don't worry about feeling "uncomfortable" or "too religious" about this.

DK: Exactly the point I made earlier: The teacher has to respect questions, doubts, and hesitations, and yet refuse to compromise the standards of observance.

SZ: That's true.

Most of us have learned all too well how to push our spiritual needs aside to accommodate the rest of our hectic lives. In the process, we have ignored our own need for ritual, for prayer and attachment to God. The time you spend making challah is a time you can rediscover some of those treasures. Set your intention on the Holy, and remember that your challot will provide the opportunity for a blessing to God as you recite the *hamotzi* at your Shabbat table.

DK: Beautifully said. The *Shabbos* table, of course, is compared to the altar in the Temple and our food to the sacrifices. I can't help but feeling, though, in light of your own searching and spiritual difficulties at this time, that this is addressed as much to your struggle to find (or accept) *mitzvos* as it is to your "class."

SZ: You're right.

As you prepare the Challot, let yourself find meaning in the process.

Perhaps you will see the analogy to a human life. As you mix the ingredients, you might see that the flour is like the dust from which we "were created." As you knead it, see how soft and smooth it becomes. It is like a baby's skin. As it rises, and is beaten down, it becomes stronger and tougher. After it has passed through the heat, the loaf is hard but at its most beautiful for all the experiences.

You will see that the dough must rest, if it is to rise and grow. Without that time, the loaves will be flat and formless. Is that, perhaps, part of the importance of Shabbat rest for us? Do we also need a time of quiet and rest to grow? Without it will our lives also be flat and less fulfilling than they might otherwise be?

DK: While this is a nice *drash* [homily], it also illustrates a danger I pointed out earlier. When we substitute symbolism for substance, the act itself loses significance. If the challah symbolizes only Sabbath rest, then anything else may do as well; we thus lose both the challah and the Sabbath rest. But if only the act of making challah—or more properly, making *hamotzi*—can sanctify, can give us Sabbath rest in actuality, then there can be no substitute. That is, if Sabbath rest is— as Torah tells us—act-specific, then it can be achieved only in the way defined by Torah.

SZ: That's a good point.

Before baking, you will remove a small piece of the dough and throw it into the oven as you say a blessing. This "separation" is a contemporary sacrifice that traditionally reminds us of our incomplete joy because of the destruction of the Temple. Perhaps it will bring to mind other thoughts: Can our joy be complete while others are hungry and homeless? Is our own happiness also incomplete when we shut God out of our lives? You will undoubtedly find more.

DK: A piece of dough is separated because a portion of dough—the first and best—was given to the *kohanim* who worked in the *Beis Hamikdash* [Temple]. Since the *Beis Hamikdash* has been destroyed, we can't give the dough to the *kohanim*; but we still separate it both in remembrance of the past and in anticipation of the future redemption, when the *Beis Hamikdash* will be rebuilt.

As I mentioned earlier, this is one of the three *mitzvos* special for women. Since the woman is the *akeres habayis*, the mainstay of the home, she prepares bread, the mainstay of the diet, the physical sustenance of the family. Observing the *mitzvah* of separating *challah*, she also prepares the spiritual sustenance, as well, for through the values she embodies and atmosphere she creates, she instills faith in God's Providence, the mainstay of our spiritual diet.

SZ: There's a bit more to the Guide.

As you form the dough into braids, consider the possible meaning of the three strands. Perhaps they are symbolic of how Israel is bound up with God and Torah. If any of the strands of dough are not present, the Challah will just be bread. If Israel is not bound up with God and Torah, it is just another people. Perhaps the three strands of dough represent the three things on which the world stands, ". . . on the Torah, and on worship, and on deeds of kindness." You may find other meanings. Be open to them. Or, you can also use this time in other special ways: Each time one strand is passed over another, say a prayer or read a line of a favorite psalm of praise.

The Shabbat Challot will bring all your senses into play. You will feel the dough, see it, hear it, smell it and finally, on Shabbat, taste it. Let each be a deliberate experience, and the Shabbat Challot will involve your whole, body, mind and soul in the service of the Holy. Once you have found the soul in the Challot, you will never want to make just plain bread for Shabbat again.

DK: Indeed, like *kashrus* in general, the physical becomes elevated to the spiritual.
A nice piece. What was the reaction to it? Have you used it since?

SZ: The reaction to it was positive. I followed the guide very closely during the first part of our *challah* workshop. I felt awkward at first, but when I realized that the participants *wanted* to talk about finding more spirituality in their lives, it got a lot easier.

DK: I've said it before, but it bears repetition. Leaders who ignore or underestimate people's desire for spirituality fail in their responsibility. I'll take a page from my college classroom experience. While some students simply go through the motions and others have their minds made up before the first day, most want to learn. They want to get it right and do it right. But they won't do any of it until it makes sense. So they keep asking and questioning and pushing until they "get it" (or until I've found a way to get the "Aha!" reaction). I've seen the truly interested students give up on teachers, but that's only because the teachers didn't respect where the students were "coming from," didn't earn their trust, and didn't make demands, pushing them (as a leader or coach must) beyond their own expectations.

SZ: The class itself was an unqualified success. Everyone was thrilled at having baked their first challahs. Many subsequently baked challahs at home and came back to tell me how much they enjoyed it.

DK: What more could a teacher want? Each *mitzvah* is significant in and of itself. We're taught that the effects of good are cumulative. The road to observance is built one *mitzvah* at a time.

SZ: I had given a copy of the Workshop Guide to my in-laws. I figured that it would probably end up in a family album somewhere. Instead, a couple of years later, my father-in-law informed me that he had sent it to *The Jewish Press* and that I should get a copy, because it was featured in the family section. Needless to say, I was surprised!

DK: *The Jewish Press* is a very "Orthodox" newspaper, yet it printed an article about *kavanah*, *Shabbos*, and *challah* written by a Reform Jew for a Reform synagogue. So, rhetorically, of what value are these labels? And who knows where the Guide may end up?

SZ: Who knows? It's still spinning out there in cyberspace on my home page.

DK: The Guide seemed to reflect your own spiritual condition at the time. Am I right? How closely did it express your search and its direction?

SZ: Very closely, as you guessed. Look at the themes: *kavanah*, *mitzvos*, blessings, connection to holiness. That "it" that I had begun searching for was starting to have a face. In earlier times, I might have written in my journal. This time, I felt a need to share, to reach out, to make the words mean something beyond myself. At the same time, in an environment where almost no one spoke of God or religion openly, it was a terribly difficult decision to "go public." At first I didn't even want to show it to Joe. I was embarrassed to admit that I felt the way I did.

DK: Well, your history of "going public" has a pretty successful track record.

SZ: The Guide was more than a creative essay. I actually had been making *challah* with that attitude and approach, that *kavanah* and striving for meaning. I was trying to wring drops of spirituality out of anything I could. I was thirsty.

DK: To put if better, to do *mitzvos* with anything you could, or reveal the spirituality within the physical through your acts.

These couple of years were obviously a time of great activity and struggle, reminiscent of your time in college. Between the car accident, the "Spiritual Checkup Form," and your involvement as a teacher of both children and adults, a lot happened in a short period of time. You were doing things; given the circumstances, you accomplished a lot. Yet I get the feeling from the way you're talking that, at least in hindsight, it was all preparation.

Does anything else stand out in your mind from this period?

SZ: Every year there was a special Sisterhood service. The women prepared and conducted the service. In 1993, I volunteered to organize the service. The president gave me a copy of the service that they wanted to use, which I newly typeset to produce small booklets that we used in place of the prayerbooks that night. I also was responsible for assigning the various parts of the service to all the women who would be participating. I asked if I could read the Torah that night. The rabbi said that that would be fine.

The rabbi provided me with a copy of the part I would read, both in standard Hebrew with *nikudos* [vowel marks] and in the form that it would appear in the Torah scroll. With a lot of practice, I learned the few paragraphs quite well. We didn't use *trop* [the musical notation for singing the Torah reading]—I didn't know it anyway—so I decided to read it just like I would read a story, trying to put meaning in the inflection of my voice. My goal was that the listeners should hear the Torah, not me. I remember praying for that. After the service, several people commented that they didn't know Hebrew, but could follow the translation from the way it was read. Others commented that it made the story seem "real." I felt that my goal had been reached.

DK: Well, the *trop* is also a grammatical tool, a way of reading the Torah so that the meaning comes across.

But how would you evaluate that experience today?

SZ: I'm glad, given the circumstances, that I did what I did, if for no other reason than to have been so close to the Torah—in terms of both the time I spent preparing, and the opportunity to touch the holy parchment. It is not an opportunity I have much anymore.

DK: Do you regret that?

SZ: Yes. I even miss the public part, reading the Torah at the service, *aliyos*, and such, despite the fact that I would be very uncomfortable doing that now. I'm a little embarrassed to admit how much I enjoyed the experience; I know that my ego was involved, despite my desires to the contrary. Ego is very hard to overcome.

DK: Ego is the hardest thing to overcome. Recognizing our feelings, the pull of our desires, doesn't mean that we have to act on them or even wrestle with them. The Talmud tells us that a person shouldn't say, "I don't want to eat *treif*," but rather one should say, "I want to eat *treif*, but what can I do? God has told me not to." In other words, only a *tzaddik* is above the struggle with the "good feelings." It seems that our actions and our intellect are more within our control than our feelings. But even fighting against the desire is a way of empowering it. Best, then, to acknowledge it and move on. (Complete *teshuva*, of course, means transforming the feelings and thoughts as well as the actions.)

However, there's another important issue here. In regard to women publicly participating in services, a lot has been written. We might even say that public prayer performance has become one of the two great divides in Jewish life today. As a woman who has "been there, done that," how do you explain to other women not only why you're "uncomfortable" reading the Torah or having an *aliyah*, but also why it's Jewishly wrong?

SZ: Well, we've already talked about women's obligations in *tefillah*. I'd just add that when a woman insists on assuming these roles *improperly*, she is, in a sense, thumbing her nose at the traditions, laws, and community of which she is a part.

That's also why I'd be uncomfortable in such roles now. It doesn't mean that I didn't enjoy doing those things at the time, but at the time I didn't know that Judaism saw them as wrong.

DK: Everyone encounters situations that, in retrospect, they wouldn't do now, but enjoyed at the time. Any "philosophy of the emotions" must resolve the struggle between current awareness and past experience. After all, *teshuvah* involves, among other things, a transformation of emotions. It's easy enough to acknowledge the wrongness of an action; but how do we return from a feeling (especially one that at the time and, thus, in remembrance, gave us joy)?

Perhaps we have to recognize that *teshuvah* requires a return from the feeling as well as from the act. We can all remember feelings that pleased us for the moment, but when we recollect those feelings now, we feel embarrassed or disgusted. Even as we re-experience the pleasure, we simultaneously reject it, because from where we are now the pleasure itself is repulsive.

SZ: I'm jumping ahead of my story, but even much later, I had internal struggles, not knowing by whom I've been "brainwashed." Is it a bunch of Jewish men who want the privileges of public service all to themselves and don't want their wives seen by other men? Or is it a secular society that tells me that women should have the same roles as men, and that if they don't, then there is something "wrong"? It isn't an easy question.

DK: The question is made harder than it needs to be. If one has accepted *halacha* as the enactment of God's will, then the answer is obvious. What's hard is putting the environment in perspective. (Yet we've all had to deal with "peer pressure," and secular society's expectations are just another form of it.) It's interesting that the substance of the attack on Judaism—*halacha* is a power play—is very old; every attempt to uproot the Jewish people's covenant, the exclusive relationship, with God, begins at the same point. Today, the form happens to be in "patriarchal" terms. But it's got the same source as Korach, Christianity, the Karaites, and so on—an ego-driven need to be a separate, independent power. (You recognized this above.) In Hebrew, it's called *ani v'efsi od*—"I and myself alone." Chassidus discusses this at length: the struggle between the animal soul and the Godly soul.

SZ: Well, it was hard for me to answer to myself, and it was even harder to ponder how I would explain to my daughter: "No, you won't be reading the Torah at your bat mitzvah, and Daddy won't be able to come hear you sing in your choir, and you won't get to dance with the Torah on Simchas Torah, or even have an *aliyah*."

DK: Yet that doesn't bother many women. It's easy to fool ourselves into thinking that what we want is why God needs us. Our animal soul instinctively hungers to feed itself; it wants to feed the ego as much as it wants to feed the body, so it hungers physically, emotionally, even intellectually. We rationalize this wanting, this taking, with idealism, with arguments about what we "need" to do. In so doing, we push aside what we're needed *for*. If what we're doing is for ourselves rather than for God, then even apparently good things can be wrong, even evil.

There's a story about a wealthy Chassid who had supported many families, particularly providing for the weddings of their children. A series of business losses left him a pauper. He imagined that he had to continue these philanthropic enterprises. However, his *avodah*, his personal relationship with God, needed refining; in his case, the wealth got in the way of the necessary personal introspection. Not knowing that his wealth had become a barrier to his own spiritual growth, he assumed that he should still be rich. He went to the Alter Rebbe and poured out his heart. "For me and my three daughters I'm not asking," he said. "We'll manage, and if they have to wait, they'll wait. But I need to take care of this one, and I need to provide that one something." The Alter Rebbe responded, "You tell me what you need, but what you're needed *for* you don't want to hear." At that point, the man realized he'd rationalized his situation in life—being rich—into his purpose in life. Once he internalized the reality of Divine Providence and recognized that being rich, even if it enabled him to help others, was not a purpose in life, he was able to move to the next spiritual level, so to speak, and from there regain his wealth.

It seems clear that so-called egalitarianism is one place where we're substituting what we need (i.e., want) in place of what we're needed for (why God predetermined certain things).

SZ: As a mother, I find it to be a special challenge. I try to teach my daughter according to *halacha* and what I have learned is the Jewish view of womanhood, but it is hard: I have to wrestle with these issues both intellectually and emotionally. I accept them, because I made a commitment to the whole of Jewish life, a life that is bounded by *halacha*. I realize that I can't just pick and choose: "This I accept, this I don't." I either accept *halacha* as valid and binding and live as a Jewish woman; or I don't, and I live however I please. The latter choice would be a lot easier, but I know that in doing so I would be turning my back on God, breaking promises I made to Him. I just can't do that.

Women's issues in Judaism are a challenge, and I know we'll be talking about them more because, at about this point in my life, I was beginning to focus on some of the same topics.

DK: I think we're approaching a climactic point in your story. Before we get to that, is there anything else from this time period that might be seen, either at the time or in hindsight, as relevant or preparatory?

SZ: Once in a while, the rabbi would be out of town and unable to lead the services. On one such occasion, he asked if our family would join with one other to conduct the services. We agreed. I again read the Torah that evening, and, taking a chance, took the opportunity to give a "sermon," too. Its theme was clearly an outgrowth of the same questions I had asked the rabbi. It went like this:

> When I learned that the Torah portion for this week dealt with dietary laws, I told the Rabbi that it was a great chance to give my schpiel why the kitchen in our new building should be kosher. But, in the end, another subject seemed to be far more important, and I found insights into it in the Holocaust, this week's Torah portion, the writings of several contemporary Jewish scholars and even last week's *Washington Post*.
>
> The horrors of the Holocaust savagely tore out the threads of many lives from the tapestry of Jewish existence, leaving a hole which can never be fully repaired. *We* Jews, however, remain—each a thread within the weave of that cloth of Israel. In the words of Abraham Heschel, "In this moment, we, the living, are Israel. The tasks begun by the patriarchs and prophets, and carried out by countless Jews of the past, are now entrusted to us. No other group has superseded them. We are the only channel of Jewish tradition, those who must save Judaism from oblivion, those who must hand over the entire past to the generations to come. We are either the last, the dying, Jews or else we are those who will give new life to our tradition . . . Unless being a Jew is of absolute significance how can we justify the ultimate price which our people was so often forced to pay throughout its history?"

DK: That the idea—not a new one—had to be phrased as a conditional question poignantly illustrates the destitute side of the Jewish situation. The absolute significance of being a Jew used to be (and, of course, by many still is) assumed. If we begin by asking, "Since being a Jew is of absolute significance" the nature of the inquiry and its response changes considerably. For one thing, it removes the desperation and assumes that there's a comfort for the despair.

SK: The sermon continues:

> Now, scarcely a half century after the Holocaust, I worry that our people now are confronted with a new enemy, faceless and subtle: the lack of a spiritual connection to our Jewishness. I wonder if our children will choose to remain committed to Judaism devoid of spirituality, where the importance of God and observance of even basic Jewish traditions as Shabbat take a back seat to soccer games, dances and other secular activities. Are we offering them a living, vital faith—or just a history learned in Hebrew school? As Rabbi Lawrence Hoffman, professor of liturgy at Hebrew Union College in New York, states: "One generation of baby boomers has come of age; either we will develop a Judaism with a sense of spirituality that provides authenticity for their lives and a connection to God or they will opt out."

DK: Here again, we see the importance of even a subtle difference in approach. Those people lost in the forest weren't suddenly transported there. They got lost by taking one step off the path. That's all it takes, one step in the wrong direction, and every other step takes you further from the path. When someone says, "We will develop a Judaism with a sense of spirituality that provides authenticity for their lives," I wonder what's wrong with the Judaism that's been around for over 3300 years. Maybe the problem isn't with Judaism, it's with the teachers. Judaism doesn't provide "authenticity"; it's a relationship. How much truer if he had said, "If we don't instill in them a sense of responsibility for the Jewish people's covenant with God, if we don't teach them that as with any relationship you have to do things and there's a right way to do them, then we will surely have taught them that spirituality has neither relevance nor reality. In that case, of course, they will opt out."

SZ: That's an excellent point. To continue:

> An article in last Sunday's *Washington Post*, titled "Twist of Faith," began like this:

Several years ago at my synagogue, the rabbi raised this question: "Why don't Jews come to services?" After listening to "Services are boring," "We're usually very tired at the end of the week" and the like, I hesitantly raised my hand, "I'm having a very strange experience here," I said, "I'm wondering if it's somehow inappropriate to mention God." Later, the author of this article expressed the fear that she would be regarded as the "weird one . . . who was always bringing God into the discussion."

Perhaps I will be regarded as the weird one at our Temple, and I wish I could say that I didn't identify with that woman, but in fact, I had made a very similar statement to the rabbi several months ago. I remember telling him how I felt uncomfortable discussing God, even with other Jews, even within the synagogue. How could I feel that way and at the same time be reciting "*v'dibartah bam, b'shivtcha b'veitecha*? . . . speak of them in your house and on your way, and when you lie down and when you rise up?" And I wonder: What does our temple have to offer to those who seek a deeper Jewish spirituality? While sock-hops, card games, sports, square dances and dinner dances allow us to socialize, what can we do that will emphasize our growth as Jews? Outside of Friday Night and Holiday services, what opportunities are there for our adult members to learn more about Torah, issues of faith and spirituality? As we look towards building a new edifice in which to worship, have we forgotten what it truly means to worship?

I also remember asking our Rabbi what I could tell my kids if they asked me what the difference was between being a good person and being a good Jew? I have since come to believe that a "good Jew" does what he or she does for the sake of God, the same way as we do what we do for those we love. What does our temple offer to help us as we seek to fulfill the commandment "*v'ahavtah et Adonai Elokeicha*? . . . And you shall love the Lord your God with all your heart, all your soul and all your might."

Even when there are opportunities at Temple S—— to strengthen our religious commitment, how many of us are present? Are we committed to our Jewishness only when it is convenient, we have nothing else to do, and we aren't too tired? Last fall only four people (including the Rabbi and his wife) showed up for Sukkot services, a MAJOR Jewish holiday. The good news and bad news is that I'm told that turnout was double last year's attendance! How many of us have come to a Shabbat morning discussion group? And I wonder if our children don't sometimes question why they learn the Shabbat morning service for bar/bat mitzvahs when Temple S—— is regularly empty and silent on the day of Shabbat. Who are we kidding?

DK: But why should they? After all, they can answer Heschel's question ("Unless being a Jew is of absolute significance") by saying, "But we've been taught that being a Jew isn't of absolute significance—of some significance, perhaps, but not absolute." Torah, though, starts with the assumption that being a Jew is and must be of absolute significance.

SZ: You're absolutely right.

In a 1992 article Dennis Prager wrote:

Non-Orthodox Jews must take Judaism as seriously as Orthodox Jews do. Most do not. For example when it comes to Jewish practices, the motto of many Reform Jews is, "I don't have to, I'm Reform"—an attitude that renders Reform Judaism an excuse rather than an affirmation. . . . and . . . "Non-Orthodox Jews must acknowledge the need for God and ritual in their lives. All Jews must affirm the centrality of ethics in Judaism—but it is one thing to acknowledge that Judaism emphasizes ethics and quite another to disregard all else. Judaism without the holy—without prayer, ritual, holy days—is no more than secular humanism with a rabbi."

DK: Once we acknowledge the need for ritual, we must also recognize that ritual can't be arbitrary, on the one hand, and must be sanctioned by history, on the other. And once we acknowledge the need for God, there has to be a way—literally, *halacha*—to express that need, a structure that is consistent over time and regardless of the variables of emotions and circumstances. Change the rules of the relationship (a covenant is a legal document), and you change the relationship. All humanity must acknowledge the need for God and ritual in their lives. Judaism without *halacha*—without Torah from Sinai, Torah from heaven, without the Oral Torah—is no more than secular humanism with a rabbi.

SZ: The sermon continues:

It goes without saying that Temple S—— should always be a center for *Tikun Olam,* repairing and transforming the world. Yet, our temple must address both our religious needs and our actions as Jews, and our actions *as* religious needs. It should remind us that, as Rabbi Lawrence Kushner says, "We are agents, instruments of God's presence. We are not at odds with the Self of the Universe; we are part of it. And to be aware of this is to give our lives ultimate meaning and purpose. To realize that we are servants, through everything we do, with or without our consent, is to be able to do anything; it is our empowerment and fulfillment. Spirituality is a dimension of living where we are aware of God's presence. It is being concerned with how what we do affects God and how what God does affects us."

And here at Temple S——, we should also learn to be unafraid of asking the kinds of questions Abraham Heschel posed:

"Is our religious attitude one of conviction or mere assertion? "Is the existence of God a probability to us or a certainty? "Is God a mere word to us, a name, a possibility, a hypothesis, or is He a living presence? "Is the claim of the prophets a figure of speech to us or a compelling belief?"

DK: Here might be a good place to ask the "why" question.

SZ: There's more:

In this week's Torah portion, we read of the sacrificial offerings made by Aaron and his sons, and by the congregation, the whole of Israel. The whole congregation brought what was required to the Tent of Meeting and stood before the Lord. But it is not until later, in the fulfillment of rituals that the "kavod Adonai" came upon them. Could this be a biblical reference to spirituality? Could it be that rituals provided a path to spirituality for our ancestors? And are rituals and spirituality still meaningful to us in modern times? Rabbi Lawrence Kushner offers this insight: "Religious rituals are a funny sequence of things we do to help us remember that we have forgotten why we have been created and gently provide us with the instruments of return. They are ancient techniques for sending us back to everyday life with a childlike sense of wonder." Elsewhere he writes: "Spiritual renewal for Jews includes unlocking the spiritual energy in the rituals and ethical traditions we have. It is doing what we do with a renewed sense of God's presence. You can start anywhere: Light Shabbat candles and imagine the preposterous possibility that God wants you to do this."

Ritual, spirituality, God . . .

If questions about these things belong anywhere, they belong in our synagogue. If our search for spirituality should begin anywhere it is here. If there is any place at all where ultimate questions and discussions of God and belief belong, it is here. Together, you and I, as Temple members and as family, need to help create and support new opportunities to increase Jewish learning and "ruchaniyut"—spirituality within our lives: Because if our members and our children and teens cannot find meaningful connections with our religion and our God here, where will they go to find them?

The last question was from my heart. I had to know the answer.

14

Internet

DK: You'd been a member of the Reform synagogue for nearly two and a half years, from September 1990 to April 1993. You'd become very active, teaching, giving sermons—some might say doing outreach work. Your life probably seemed to be quite fulfilled, didn't it?

SZ: In many ways, yes. I was active not only in the synagogue, but also in the public school that my children attended. I had been involved as a Cub Scout leader, a Brownie Leader, an Odyssey of the Mind coach, a substitute teacher, and more. The kids were active in sports activities and were doing well in school. I was happily married to a wonderful man who had a good job. In many ways, it was a wonderful life.

DK: Yet there were those nagging spiritual questions. Did these become an issue?

SZ: Yes, those questions remained. The rabbi didn't seem to have the answers, and I just didn't know whom else to ask.

DK: They obviously didn't interfere with your life, though. Do you think you would have just "gone on," with that vague uneasiness simply lurking in the background? Or, had Divine Providence not used your hobby once again, would something else have brought the "nagging questions" so forcefully forward?

SZ: There wasn't anything obvious that would have brought the questions to the fore. I suspect that I would have tried to push them out of my mind and just go on. Still, I had my children to consider. Was this the image of Judaism that I wanted to give them? It's one of those "what if" questions—very hard to answer.

DK: Very hard to answer, but also very revealing of decisions and goals—the way in which we wish to be led.

So what happened in April 1993?

SZ: Joe and I were both veteran computer hobbyists. Joe had begun using the Internet for technical information. One evening, I was looking over his shoulder in our basement as he meandered through a bunch of computer-related messages. I asked about them. He explained that he was reading a USENET newsgroup, a sort of public forum where topics related to the newsgroup title were discussed.

DK: This story reminds me of how you two met. Divine Providence works even through computers!

SZ: It certainly seems that way to me, too.

I asked Joe about other newsgroups, and whether there was anything Jewish. He said that there was: a group called "soc.culture.jewish"—"scj" for short. He located it for me and showed me how to follow a discussion topic from one message to another. He told me about "flames" and "flamebait," too. ("Flames" are messages that impolitely criticize what another person has posted; "flamebait" is a question posted with the sole intent of arousing argumentative discussions.)

I sat there for at least two hours, reading all kinds of messages from Jews of almost every persuasion. I was fascinated. I wanted to respond to some of the messages, but since I was using Joe's account, I couldn't; it would appear as though he, not I, sent the message. The only solution was for me to get my own account, which I did soon after.

The first message that I remember posting—I posted it to scj— may well have sounded like flamebait, but it wasn't. I was really interested in the answer.

I don't have a copy of that first question, but the gist of it was to ask why Orthodox Jews have the view of women that they do: not being allowed to read from the Torah, not being counted as equals in *minyans*, and so forth.

DK: Considering the range of questions spiritual, ritual, and social you'd been wrestling with, it's interesting that that would be the first one you'd ask in an open, yet anonymous, forum. As I recall, it was phrased in the form of an insistent, desperate why.

SZ: I asked that question because ever since I had made the comment to the rabbi about not being able to be Orthodox because of their views on women, I had been bothered by the fact that I really didn't *know* what Orthodox views on women really were.

DK: And that bothered you more than any of the other issues? Perhaps you suspected all along that in that answer you'd also find answers to the other questions—being spiritually aware, the role of ritual, the survival of Judaism and the Jewish people; in short, the subjects of your sermon and your challah Guide and the motivation for your involvement. If I were to guess at your unconscious, unarticulated reasoning, it might go like this: "The Orthodox seem to be spiritually aware, not worried about survival, and seem to have made ritual meaningful. Their method, *halacha*, should therefore be good. But they also seem not to allow women to have all these things. Their lack of egalitarianism is therefore bad. One of these impressions is wrong. My experience—and even my Reform rabbi—indicate that *halacha* is essentially good. So why do they exclude women from all the goodies?" Getting that question answered would provide the key to many others.

SZ: And it would tell me whether or not I could possibly consider becoming Orthodox. I wanted to know how any woman could remain Orthodox, if my perceptions of it were accurate.

DK: Why? There's an easy answer to what you wanted to know: Orthodox women are "brainwashed" into accepting their inferiority; they're trained from birth to accept a secondary role and isolation from the real world, so they don't realize they're being oppressed. It's a false answer, of course, but an easy one to digest, and certainly in accord with your perceptions of the time. There was no need to investigate further. So why did you need to know—then, and not before—whether there was any way you could accept Orthodoxy?

SZ: First, I regard womankind too highly to accept such a pat and condescending "easy" answer. It was obvious to me that there were Orthodox women who were highly intelligent and well-informed—hardly the type to be brainwashed.

Second, I had begun to suspect that if I had asked an Orthodox rabbi the same questions I had asked my Reform rabbi, the answers would have been clear. I wanted definite answers. At the same time, I knew that accepting such answers would mean a personal commitment, and that it would mean giving up much of what constituted spiritual expression in my life—particularly, participating in public prayer. With what I thought I knew about Orthodoxy, I wasn't convinced that it would be a worthwhile trade. I didn't want to sell myself into slavery just to live in the house of the sage.

DK: An interesting way of phrasing the conflict. Of course, if that had been your conclusion, then those highly intelligent and well-informed women would be living in slavery. That's obviously not the case.

Anyway, what was the response to your question?

SZ: My message was met with cautious skepticism. Similar messages in the past had sometimes been posted as flamebait in order to ignite a controversy aimed at deprecating Orthodox Judaism. Still, I did get answers, and tried to reply to those who wrote in a way that showed that the question was sincere. You were one of those who wrote to me. Do you remember that?

DK: Quite well. When I saw your question, I debated long and hard whether or not to respond. On the Internet, it's too easy to just dash off a response without regard to what you and the other person are actually saying. The strength of the Internet—its anonymity—is also its weakness. Also, I usually waited to see if someone else responded better.

Something about the way your post was written caught my attention. I saw something between the lines indicating that not only was the question from the heart, but that you would listen and take to heart an honest answer. "Words from the heart go to the heart."

I had, months earlier, adopted a policy of trying to respond objectively through e-mail to questions that seemed personal and emotionally laden. That, I found, kept the flames down and gave the questioner a chance to decide whether and how he or she wanted the conversation to proceed. So I answered you, suggesting some reading material. In fact, I think my first response was:

A few books I'd suggest you read on the subject:
  Jewish Woman in Jewish Law, Meiselman, Ktav
  To Be a Jew, Donin, Basic Books
  Aura (composite), Lubavitch Women's Organization
  The Modern Jewish Woman (composite), Lubavitch Women's Organization
  Doesn't Anyone Blush Anymore? Friedman, HarperCollins
  The Voice of Sarah, Frankiel, HarperCollins
  The Secret of Jewish Femininity, Abramov, Targum Press

Also, the Beis Chana Institute in St. Paul, MN produces some _excellent_ tapes on the subject of women in Judaism.

Not very profound, but practical.

I had no way of knowing who else you were corresponding with. Internet's scj wasn't the only avenue for Jewish networking. The mailing lists hadn't proliferated, but there were a few bulletin boards. I wasn't involved in any of those, but you had a lot more computer background than I.

SZ: Besides reading the scj newsgroup on the Internet, I also accessed a smaller network called "FIDOnet." There I participated in two forums, one called "Judaica," which was a broad-based discussion, and the other called "KesherNet," which followed a more Orthodox viewpoint.

After following the discussions for a while, I began to get to "know" the folks who posted, and began to think of them as friends—friends whom I hadn't met in person. I think that is a common phenomenon.

DK: Definitely.

SZ: I asked questions on those forums, too—often rather deep ones, like whether it made any sense to pray, since some modern Jewish theologians were saying that God doesn't do miracles and never did.

DK: How did hooking into the Internet make you feel?

SZ: Connected. What was really exciting was that I had found a group of people who were actually interested in talking about Jewish subjects, about God, and about religious topics. I felt more comfortable asking "hard" questions. I began to feel much less isolated and alone.

DK: That's important. I think a lot of people who "disconnect" from Judaism do so because they feel isolated historically; they don't have a sense of tradition as a vital part of their daily life. Isolated from the *mitzvos*, Judaism becomes irrelevant. Your Internet experience proves again what we said earlier, that the central institution in Judaism is the family—including the extended family. The innate spiritual interconnection between all Jews manifests itself even electronically across the Internet!

So in April you discovered the Internet, and by May had become a full-fledged participant. Let's get back to the question about women and Orthodoxy. You said that you were prompted to post it because you'd been bothered by the fact that you didn't *know* what Orthodox views on women really were.

I don't remember whether there was a certain urgency in the tone of your post, but I do recall wondering whether you wanted more than an intellectual explanation. I figured that if you wanted an experiential understanding, if the question was both academic and personal, I'd hear from you.

What else happened in May that made having an answer—an alternative—so important?

SZ: One Friday night in May, our family had gone to services at the temple. In the foyer were little ribbons that the congregation could wear—it had something to do with AIDS. During his sermon, the rabbi began to talk about homosexuality. (I was glad my children had gone to the library to read while the rabbi talked.) What I understood from his words was that even though the Torah said that it was a sin, that we shouldn't take that as true anymore, that times had changed and Judaism had to change with the times, so we shouldn't treat homosexual behavior as a sin anymore.

At the end of services, Joe and I stood up and looked at each other. I think that about all we said was: "That was just too much. This isn't the place for us." I don't think we even went to the *Oneg* Shabbat afterwards.

DK: Just like that?

SZ: Yes, just like that.

DK: Why? Granted, Joe had never fully adapted to the Reform approach, and you had some theological questions the rabbi couldn't answer. But you'd begun to make an impact. True, you'd noticed some problems with assimilation and intermarriage, but you'd become involved. Your children were comfortable. Why quit over a political disagreement?

SZ: It wasn't a political disagreement. It was the final unmasking of an attitude. It was clear to us that, in this synagogue, Torah didn't matter anymore. The new "torah" was the prevailing morality of the surrounding culture, the "torah" of political correctness. Whatever it was, it was not Judaism anymore.

DK: That's not what the Reform rabbi would have said. If the Torah requires interpretation in order to be relevant and the Reform rabbi is trained in Jewish interpretation, how can you say that his approach "was not Judaism any more"?

SZ: Well, I'm not in a position to judge whether or not the Reform rabbi was trained in interpretation, but I do know that there is a difference between interpreting the Torah and redefining it or declaring parts of it obsolete. If Torah is not absolutely true and valid, then nothing about Judaism is valid. Torah is the foundation for the whole structure of Judaism. Break away pieces of that foundation or weaken it, and everything that is built on it falls apart.

DK: Your last three sentences raise a critical, if not *the* critical, issue in the denominational debate. You're asserting the Orthodox position (and, I'd argue, one that is historically true), but is that what you thought and felt at the time?

SZ: It was what was becoming more and more obvious to me. What was not clear to me at that point was just what "Torah" really meant, what it encompassed. I still thought of it as just the words on the parchment scroll.

DK: Sounds like a case of knowing what it wasn't before knowing what it was. But I want to understand the basis for your decision. Was it just a snap decision, an emotional reaction to a politicized sermon with which you disagreed, or was there something more? You've recounted some of the theological and philosophical problems the Reform movement presented to you. But, for two and a half years, you'd managed to live with them.

SZ: The sermon was the straw that broke the camel's back. I was tired of not being able to progress spiritually. Every time I looked for a deeper connection to Judaism, for a stronger connection to tradition, I was met with an attitude of indifference.

DK: In other words, the search for spirituality, tradition—whatever we want to call the sense of Judaism as a living imperative, a controlling factor in one's life—led you either to a dead end or away from the teachings and experiences that had brought you thus far. No wonder you felt frustrated.

And yet, as one channel closed, another opened. Do you think that discovering the Jewish discussion groups on the Internet had any influence?

SZ: Absolutely. It gave me a chance to see how differently one's approach to Judaism affected the way one responded to various questions. I was struck by the fact that God and Torah seemed to be very real and very important to some folks.

DK: Did you and Joe discuss the decision further?

SZ: We discussed the decision to resign a little, mostly in terms of where David and Julie would attend Hebrew school the next year. We decided to put off that decision until the summer.

DK: So what happened next?

SZ: Soon afterward, I informed the principal that I would not be returning to teach at the Hebrew school the next year, though I did agree to finish the year. I wrote a letter of resignation and sent it off to the temple. We stopped going to services there. We assumed that we would rejoin the Conservative synagogue after David and Julie finished their year in Hebrew school.

DK: Was there any reaction to your resignation?

SZ: Almost none. One of my favorite students from the adult Hebrew class called to chastise me for leaving. I think she liked having someone who was pushing for a "higher level," encouraging folks to take Judaism more seriously.

DK: But was she willing to join you "out there"? A rhetorical question, but one that reflects the discouragement one feels when working from within a system that subverts its own goals.
     After the resignation was official, how did you feel?

SZ: Since most of my social contacts were through the temple by that point, I felt a little adrift.

DK: You'd hit another of those "transition times" when everything is in limbo and one just waits for time to pass or for something to happen.

SZ: Yes. We just tried to feel our way through. Friday nights seemed odd because we stopped going to services. On the positive side, we were no longer rushing through dinner just to get to services on time. We read from the *parsha* [the weekly Torah reading], or told stories or did family skits, instead.

DK: So then what did you do?

SZ: Shavuos was coming up. Now, without a synagogue, I posted a question on a local Jewish forum asking for suggestions of where I could go.

One man actually called me and tried to get me to arrange to stay in Baltimore and go to Orthodox services there. He even gave me the name of someone to contact. I didn't think our family was ready for that, but I thanked him, sincerely, for his trouble.

Most of the Conservative synagogues had confirmation ceremonies on Shavuos, and I didn't really want to watch a "graduation ceremony." I toyed with the idea of driving to an Orthodox synagogue just to see what it was like, but I didn't want to get caught in a potentially embarrassing question as to how I got there.

As it turned out, I was sick on Shavuos anyway. I stayed in bed the whole time and read a couple of books on women and Orthodox Judaism. One was a book that you and others had suggested: *Jewish Woman in Jewish Law*.

I have copies of many of the e-mail messages I sent back then.

DK: A good thing, or we probably wouldn't be having this conversation.

SZ: Maybe not. One of our early exchanges was this one:

> **SZ:** David, I just thought I'd get back to you. I got a nasty virus and spent a large part of Shavuot reading. I read "Jewish Woman in Jewish Law" and also a book called "The Invaluable Pearl" which takes virtually the same approach. I found the books to be very informative and, to be very honest, discovered that many of my *perceptions* of Orthodox attitudes towards women were flatout wrong. (Oops! Is admitting I'm wrong allowed on the Net?) Once I understood the basis of many of the Orthodox laws and practices pertaining to women, I found that most all of them made sense and were not, in any sense, demeaning. (Though I still have trouble accepting that women cannot come together as a "group" but only as individuals.)

DK: Just when I was wondering if staying on the Net is worthwhile, I get a message like this! Yes, one can admit making a mistake, but should be prepared for the worst flames imaginable. So much of what passes for discussion on the Net is only a reflection of a poor education and propaganda. I'm glad you were able to see through the misperceptions. (The question of women as a group versus individuals requires some explanation. But, as long as we're talking about perspectives, look at it this way: do women *need* to "come together" that way? Not *want* to, *need* to—in order to fulfill their obligations (and hence themselves).

(I'm not trying to smooth over your real concerns, just hopefully give you another way of looking at it.)

SZ: I think that I have come across some "poor role models" and based my perceptions on them. What I have learned from reading the books has given me a much better perspective of the whole matter. I learned a lot, and to be honest, feel that what I have learned will cause me to rethink many elements of my own Jewish lifestyle.

DK: Poor role models exist for all of us, unfortunately. The task is to learn what we can from them and gain the discretion to pick good ones. Your last sentence is very encouraging.

SZ: I sent another e-mail to a woman who had also been responding to my questions about Orthodoxy and women, and who had been encouraging me to speak to an Orthodox rabbi. She had even given me the name of a rabbi in the area who would be willing to talk to me. I told her pretty much the same thing that I told you, but added:

I have some big fears to overcome before I can progress much further in my own observance. My husband is concerned that if I "push it" (being more religious) I will alienate the kids, rather than reinforce their Jewishness. If I go off on my own seeking the help of an Orthodox Rabbi, I am afraid he would see it as trying to go behind his back. For now, I think I may need to take a slower path and seek counsel from the Rabbi of the Conservative synagogue we are re-joining. (He is in Israel for three months until August.) He has always tried very hard to get people to increase their levels of observance and I think will at least help get us started in the right direction. Then, maybe, we can talk about going further.

15
Realization

DK: Before you could talk about "going further" in your observance, something happened. You came to a realization.

SZ: That I did. A problem was beginning to rear its head—the result of reading those books over Shavuos.

I didn't tell you about it at first, maybe because I was too afraid of the consequences to face them myself, or perhaps because I didn't know whether you'd care. From your e-mail address, I had assumed that you were just a student at Tulane. I didn't realize until close to a month later that you were a *shaliach* there.

DK: I didn't know that. Anonymity has its disadvantages, as well.

SZ: But back to that "realization" . . . .

One unavoidable subject in any book on women's observance is that of *taharas mishpacha*, the laws of family purity, a subject I'd never even heard of. And central to *taharas mishpacha* is *mikvah*. It was the topic of *mikvah* that really caught my attention, since I knew that when I had converted, I had supposedly gone to a *mikvah*, but it was just a swimming pool; there was nothing especially "natural" about it. Then I read that a woman can have no intervening substance between her body and the water, not even so much as a loose strand of hair. At our "*mikvah*," we had been wearing swimsuits. Something clicked. I realized that there could be a very serious problem.

Up until this point, there was no imperative for me to move forward. In general, I wanted to be more observant, but there was nothing so uncomfortable or convincing that it could not be put off until the Conservative rabbi returned from Israel. Suddenly that changed. First, because this was potentially a matter of whether or not I was Jewish, it became urgent. Second, since the conversion had been done by a Conservative rabbi, I thought that maybe it would be best to get a second opinion outside that "cadre," meaning, of course, an Orthodox opinion.

I pondered this for a day or two, trying to decide what I should do. I was afraid to approach Joe. But one night, I couldn't sleep; I knew what I had to do. Joe was watching TV. I went down to talk to him, hoping that somehow I'd say the right thing. Joe turned off the television. The lights were out; I was glad it was dark, because I didn't want him to see the tears in my eyes or the fear on my face. I told Joe about the *mikvah*. I told him that I was afraid that my conversion wasn't kosher. I asked whether it would be okay for me to ask an Orthodox rabbi about it.

I remember Joe telling me that as far as he was concerned I was Jewish, that he had no questions about it. Still, he added, I should feel free to do whatever I needed to do in order to settle this in my own mind.

DK: It must have been a traumatic conversation for him as well as for you. I'm sure it took a lot of strength on his part to be able to give you both support and space.

SZ: I don't remember much else from that conversation. Afterward, I went up to bed and cried myself to sleep. I was afraid.

DK: Understandably so. Part of that fear came, I think, from realizing that, however much family and friends might be there for you, this dilemma you had to face by yourself.

One parlor game that used to be popular among the synagogue teenage youth groups was the question, What would you do if you woke up and discovered you weren't Jewish? It was meant to challenge and, presumably, reinforce the teenagers' fragile sense of Jewish identity. I never liked the game; it didn't confront the realities of Judaism. Now that I've met several adults who, unfortunately, have been in that position, I like it even less.

SZ: Like many such questions, this one really can't be answered unless it happens. And when it does. . . . I don't think anyone can imagine how it feels.

DK: No, we can never truly imagine such experiences. The impact of, and our reactions to, critical events, good or bad, almost always overwhelm us, even if we have time or knowledge enough to prepare for them.

So what did you do?

SZ: The next day I called Rabbi Zvi Teitelbaum. I didn't say exactly what the problem was, but asked if I could talk to him. He set up an appointment during his lunch break at the yeshiva where he taught.

DK: He must have sensed your distress. By the way, why did you go to him?

SZ: Internet again. Three different people had recommended Rabbi Teitelbaum when they sensed that I would benefit from a face-to-face meeting with an Orthodox rabbi. He was involved in outreach and, as I later learned, was extremely knowledgeable and understanding.

Knowing how easy it would be to fail to say what I needed to say in a situation like this, and realizing that Rabbi Teitelbaum knew nothing about me, I decided to write him a letter that would give him a clue as to why I wanted to talk to him. It was a long letter describing my life and my dilemma.

DK: In a lot of good stories, there's a recap before the climax. What did you write?

SZ: Here's the letter to Rabbi Teitelbaum:

First let me tell you a bit about myself:

I was born and raised in S———, Washington (the Jewish community there at the time was about 200 families). My parents were basically non-religious Christians, though my mother came from a strong Catholic background. In high school I began to recognize a need to have a spiritual base in my life. During a H.S. course in comparative philosophies, I realized that Judaism offered a path that was very attractive to me. Since my parents were not keen on the idea of me converting, they asked me to wait a year and if I still felt the same way, they would not interfere. And off I went to college in Bellingham. . . . While at college my need for a religious connection became even stronger and to make a long story short, I ended up being involved in very fundamentalist and Pentecostal Christian activities, including a Christian-freak coffeehouse commune which I almost dropped out of college to be with full time. It was a strange time—I won't bother with details here, but if you want to know them, it's no big deal to fill you in (I kept a journal of many of my thoughts during that time). In the end, it was all wrong. I knew it. I found it difficult to accept a religion where the world-to-come was more important than the world here and now. But even more important, there was simply no way I could ultimately reconcile the concept of Trinity with that of One God. I again looked to Judaism. About this time (Dec. '73) I graduated and returned to S———. At Expo '74 (a small world's fair) I became acquainted with some Jews and involved with them in an effort to gain release of Soviet Jews. Among them was the elderly but energetic Cantor (whom I will always remember as one of my most favorite people). I learned much from him, and through his invitation, began to come to Shabbat services. I spoke to the Rabbi about conversion. He questioned me thoroughly about my intentions and I began my studies in the fall of 1974. Rabbi G was ordained as an Orthodox rabbi, but served in S———'s only synagogue, which was Conservative.

Since S——— did not have a large number of people banging down the synagogue doors to become Jewish (there were only two or three of us), I studied Judaica with the confirmation class and also studied Hebrew with an adult ed class. We were expected to learn the fundamentals of Jewish laws, History, Holidays, theology, worship services, and customs, understand the Jewish Calendar and the importance of Torah. As I recall, we spent about 3 to 4 hours a week. At the completion of my studies, I was brought before a "Bet Din" in the Rabbi's office. It consisted of the Rabbi, the Cantor, and another man (the synagogue president, I think) who questioned me both on my studies and my intentions to follow the laws and practices of Torah and Judaism. We also went to a "*mikvah*," where we underwent immersion with the appropriate affirmations and blessings. This is the part that is giving me real problems, now. Since S——— did not have a mikveh, an indoor swimming pool was used for the immersion, and because of obvious modesty concerns, and lack of another solution, we had swimsuits on at the time. (At the time I didn't have any reason to question this, but as I have learned more, it has become clear that the mikvah could be a big problem. My choice now is to either ignore it or confront it. The only honest response is to confront it.) The final piece of the conversion was done in a naming ceremony where I was given the Hebrew name "Shoshana bat Avraham v'Sarah." Shortly thereafter, I was confirmed with the confirmation class.

The whole process took about 4–5 months. I did not consider it difficult, because I really wanted to learn what was being taught. Because I attended services regularly during that time, a lot of pieces fell into place easily. I think the most difficult part of conversion came well before any of the formal process began: Facing myself, my own beliefs and making the decision to convert knowing that my life would be irrevocably changed. For most converts, becoming Jewish means turning backs on family traditions and practices, dealing with parents' discomforts about the process, and in many cases, mine included, coming to terms with the denial of beliefs once held dear, and wondering if, this time, I was really finding truth or just fooling myself once again. It was only after I answered those questions with the most profound honesty possible, conversion could even begin.

I moved to Maryland about a year after converting. I tried to keep as much observance as I had learned. I met Joe a couple of years later, and when we got married I pretty much dropped down to his level of observance. As our children grew, we tried to bring a bit more Judaica into our lives, but, still, our family is only minimally observant, i.e. we try to keep a kosher home, celebrate Shabbat with kiddush & *hamotzi*, and have been attending Friday night services, send the kids to Hebrew school, and try to observe most holidays with at least some bit of tradition. That's about it. I am no longer satisfied with this situation, though, because I think it is really a thin veneer of "Judaica" that we are laying on a rather hollow commitment to God. It is a start, but I really feel the need for more. While I would really like to become more observant, my family seems reluctant to agree. When a few weeks ago I expressed a request that the family stop spending money on Shabbat, my son (11) accused me of going too far with "this religious thing," and my husband echoed a fear that I might end up alienating the kids if I pushed things "too hard." I am very discouraged. I love my family *very* deeply and am absolutely committed to my husband. I just don't know how I can resolve the conflict between observance and *shalom bayit*. It is even very difficult for me to discuss the issue with my husband, maybe because I don't want him to feel like I'm trying to push him into something he doesn't want. Sometimes I worry that even any new efforts on my part to become more observant will seem threatening to him, because most would inevitably affect other family members too.

I feel like I am being brought to this point where I find myself re-examining my level of Jewish commitment. I don't understand why me, why now, and I don't know what to do. So I guess that's why I'm here. It seems like a deep chasm separates me from where I am and where I know I should be. I need help to build a bridge or find a path around it. . . .

As you can see, I was troubled by both my own "status" (was I even Jewish?) and my desire to raise my level of observance. I was frustrated by my fears of how to "get there from here"—or if it would even be possible. I was torn between what I saw as a need—personal spiritual growth—and our survival as a family.

DK: Your letter didn't spend much time on your status. It's almost as if you were trying to make it secondary to your family conflict over observance, or hoping that it would be.

Just after your conversation with Joe, then, you posted a question about becoming newly observant with a family of children. The question didn't reflect your personal dilemma or indicate that there was an intrafamily conflict about observance. I'd thought you were talking about the whole family becoming observant. I remember being very curious about the question, considering our previous correspondence and your earlier posts.

SZ: It became a serious conflict only after that post. It all happened pretty suddenly. Shavuos fell at the end of May 1993. By the second week of June, I had begun to confront possibilities, and quickly reached out for some perspective from my "virtual community" on the Internet.

DK: It had actually been a few weeks since we'd talked about education and role models. All of a sudden, you posted to scj:

SZ: Has anyone out there had experience with becoming newly observant with a family that includes children of at least elementary age
(mine are 8 and 11)?

I would like to know what their experience was. Thanks in advance.

Remembering our earlier exchange, I replied (by e-mail; as I said,
I'd learned the dangers of trying to teach or deal with personal issues
in an open forum).

DK: My process began before marriage, continued through it (and continues now with several children), but I don't think I fit into the category
you're looking for. However, a friend of mine does, although his children were a bit younger when he started (2–3 and 4–5 range). He wanted
to move faster than his wife. (One problem of becoming observant with
a family is that one spouse may not want to do as much as the other as
quickly.)

Anyway, if you have some specific questions or problem areas, I'll
be glad to discuss them, or ask around and let you know what others
say they've gone through.

(Your family does have a "support family," doesn't it?)

I can tell you one other thing . . . with love and patience, it usually
works out.

Let me know.

I thought that you and your family were thinking about "moving
forward," and I wanted to provide an opening for discussion. Of
course, I had no idea that you were actually referring to a problem
with your conversion (since I didn't know that you had converted until
the next e-mail). What followed came as a bit of a shock.

SZ: I'm not surprised. When I wrote to you, I had already spoken to
Rabbi Teitelbaum. We met on June 14, 1993, in his office at the yeshiva high school where he was a teacher.

I gave him the letter I had written, and sat quietly while he read
through it. I felt nervous and embarrassed, and was wondering how
and why I'd gotten myself into this. I felt silly for having told him so
much that probably didn't matter anyway. But mostly I kept seeing
myself like a leper showing the High Priest my whitened skin and

having to ask, "Is it leprosy?" Only several minutes passed, but it seemed much longer.

The first thing Rabbi Teitelbaum said was, "It seems clear to me that you are not Jewish." It is one thing to suspect something; quite another to have it confirmed, to be forced to face it head-on. I knew that I had crossed a bridge and burned it behind me. Now my "secret" was no longer a secret. Every decision I would make from this point on was with the knowledge that, by Orthodox standards, I was no longer Jewish. But I wasn't "Orthodox," I tried to rationalize. Then why was I sitting there asking an Orthodox rabbi my question? Then that question came back again: "Whom do I trust?"

DK: It seems to me that, at that moment, you found—or accepted— the answer. Maybe later we'll talk about why. For now, what else did you discuss with him?

SZ: Rabbi Teitelbaum talked about our children, that they would also be affected. He talked about how this might affect our marriage. Of course he also talked about conversion. I had hoped that since I'd been living as a Jew for eighteen years that an Orthodox conversion would just be a formality. Repeat the *mikvah*, repeat the blessing, and that would be that. It soon became evident that such would not be the case. Just saying that I wanted to become more observant was not going to suffice. Rabbi Teitelbaum asked me about *kashrus*, and when I told him we were kosher only at home, he took the opportunity to begin teaching me, telling me that for a Jew, non-kosher foods are like poison; instead of poisoning the body, they poison the soul. He discussed the centrality of *mitzvos* and the importance of Oral Torah, and so much more. He spoke to me for over an hour. I mostly listened and said very little. By the time I left, I was beginning to understand how little I really knew about Judaism, and to sense that this would not be a "rubber-stamp" conversion.

DK: That's a tremendous amount to absorb and accept in a short period of time.

SZ: Yes, there was so much to consider. That's why I wrote to you about what I had done and why it meant so much to me to get your response—shocking though it may have been to you—I desperately needed someone to help me handle all the thoughts and emotions that I was dealing with.

DK: I'm still not sure why, of all your correspondents, you wrote to me.

SZ: It seemed like you wanted to help, and I needed help just then. I shared the story with a couple of other people, but I think that this e-mail exchange, where you responded to my message, tells the story best.

> **SZ:** Thanks for replying. My situation has become quite complicated, though I suspect that it is not unique. For one thing, as I began to explore moving to a more observant life, I started doing some reading along those lines. What I read in those books, especially the discussion of the *mikveh* in the family purity part, gave me cause for concern, to put it mildly. At that point a conference with an Orthodox Rabbi (whom I'll just call R' T) became critical.

When I made the appointment to speak with R' T, I knew that I would have to discuss an aspect of my conversion (the *mikveh* wasn't done properly) that I knew would mean that my conversion would be considered invalid by any Orthodox rabbi. I was basically presented with the choice of keeping this information to myself and remaining by anyone's consideration Jewish, or bringing the information out and thereby openly nullifying my Jewishness. I felt it would be dishonest to go to R' T without being willing to divulge this information.

> **DK:** I'm not sure exactly where to break in here, because some of what you wrote requires a specific response, and some a more general answer. Let me start by saying that as I read, I felt a tremendous sympathy for your situation. I have known, unfortunately, many people in a similar position, whether the problem began because of a problem with adoption or conversion.

I can only admire your fortitude, faith and will, and say I respect your husband tremendously for supporting you. You are quite fortunate. And yes, I do know of a couple in exactly the same situation as you. Things will work out.

> **SZ:** Yet, as there is nothing hidden from God's eyes, there was really only one choice to make. I passed on this information directly to R' T when I met with him Monday and he confirmed my fears. I now feel very confused, both Jewish and not at the same time: When I (at least thought I) converted 18 years ago, I made a promise, an oath to God in front of witnesses that I would live according to the laws and commandments of Torah, and accepted all the responsibilities of being

Jewish. I may not have done a very good job of keeping that promise, but I still consider it binding and something that I am obligated personally to strive to fulfill. The conversion may be void, but that oath can never be. I still accept those obligations, whether I am legally Jewish or not.

DK: What you have written above is the most eloquent testimony that you are doing the right thing. You might want to look at it this way, that you didn't convert 18 years ago, but that you have been converting that whole time. The process of conversion, like that of *teshuvah*, has no time limits, but one completes the process when one can and is supposed to. (Few of us do "a very good job of keeping" our promises/responsibilities.) Since you consider your oath binding, you know, as you've said, what you need to do.

Someone in this situation was once asked by the Beis Din why she wanted to be Jewish. Her tears were the answer. All I can tell you here is that the confusion, while very frustrating, painful, anxiety-ridden and anger-generating now, will be transformed into the joy that is, *midah kneged midah*, measure for measure (knowing that joy is always a thousandfold greater than its opposite). There will be a depth of *simcha*, awareness, closeness to God undreamt of now, as only one such as Ruth or a Baal Teshuvah can know. You'll get there—with your husband's love and support.

SZ: In regard to others, I feel very badly.

DK: Worry about your children and family, not "others."

SZ: I am concerned for my children, because they are of course affected by this and will also have to undergo conversion. They have only known being Jewish from birth. Though I can accept the laws for specific ritual requirements for conversion, I do not know how I will be able to explain this to them. I feel like I have betrayed them and in this sense failed in my responsibility as a mother and wife in the worst possible way.

DK: First, you must realize that far from betraying your children, you have proven how much you care for them, how deeply and safely they can trust you. Rather than hiding the truth, making excuses, finding a scapegoat, you are yourself honestly confronting the deeper spiritual truth behind the world, the holiness that informs our physical existence, and connecting yourself to it despite all obstacles, including deceit, that have been put in your path. This, despite personal turmoil, you have committed yourself to accomplishing. Don't you see that you are teaching your children the most basic message of the first convert, Avraham, namely, mesiros nefesh, self-sacrifice? Even to the point not just of b'chol nafshecha, with one's life, but with *b'chol m'odecha*, with all one's "veriness," one's sense of self, you have committed to the principle of the *Shema*. You have not failed in your responsibility. You are just beginning to fulfill it.

Now, to the practical question of explaining it. They are, I think you said, 8 and 11. I have a 9 and an 11 year old, so I can relate to the thought processes. First, what you need to do, must be done _with_ your husband. Your children need to see that their parents support each other; from this, they will know that you support them. Do they know that you are a convert? If so, then you and your husband can explain that, unbeknownst to you, there was a problem with the conversion. You should explain that the problem is both technical and practical: a Jew is supposed to keep God's commandments; not keeping them doesn't stop that person from being Jewish. But if someone wants to _become_ Jewish, they have to "prove" their sincerity by being observant, which is the right thing to do anyway. Because of the technical problem, you and your husband have decided to examine Judaism further and make that commitment, which, as you've taught them at least theoretically, is the way to live anyway. Once the family (always emphasize family unity) understands and starts practicing what you've taught them is the way God wants it anyway, the technicality can be dealt with.

They may even ask at some point if this means they are not Jewish. Either way, you can say that what affects you, affects them, and that you want to do this as a family, knowing that it will bring you all closer to each other, because you will be living the way God wants and the way you've raised them.

You'll have to find your own words, of course, and it may be traumatic for them (although, if you're as upset as your post indicates, I'm sure they suspect something's wrong and probably have an idea of what. Children are very critical and astute observers, especially of their parents).

The main points to emphasize, I think, are that the problem is newly discovered, that the technicality is tied to some real, practical changes, that had you and your husband known then, it would have been done right the first time, that you and your husband support each other, that once the process is complete no one can ever question their Jewishness, and that this is something you all need to do as a family.

And of course, make use of support groups/people (be it R' T, the local Chabad rabbi, family, or whoever).

SZ: I am concerned, too, that because my conversion was not legal, I may have caused others to say *brachot* regarding my children and me (e.g., wedding, brit milah, etc.) which were improper. I feel sick inside to think that I may have been the cause of such empty blessings.

DK: Actually, this is something that you don't have to worry about, because you are not the cause, but rather the individual is who misled you. The case is similar to a kosher butcher who sells treif meat. While those who eat it or are served it must do *teshuvah* for themselves, the butcher is the one to blame for their eating treif. This is why one who causes others to sin is in the worst category and those in a position of communal responsibility must be very careful.

Also, bear in mind that nothing happens without God's consent. *Hashgacha pratis*, Divine Providence, allowed this situation to occur. I assume a rabbi officiated at your wedding and the brit milah of your son(s)—did he know? If so, he should have said something.

SZ: Yes, I can convert Orthodox, and R' T has offered to have me come to some of his classes to learn from him. If I am to convert, then he will of course require me to abide by the laws of Torah as Orthodox see them, i.e., to be observant. In truth, that is all I wanted to move toward, in the first place, but now the nature of the decision has changed dramatically.

DK: Yes, because now it's not an "If I want to," but an "I have to." And yet, that imperative is still a function of your will and desire. You could, after all, choose what others have done—to reject halacha. That you can't/won't means _you_ have chosen to do what you wanted to not just "move toward" but actually be in the first place.

SZ: How strange it is—I often worried whether my kids would end up intermarried. I never dreamed I would. I have to trust that there is a reason for this. For 18 years I have only known myself to be Jewish though not very observant, and as I complete my 40th year of life, I suddenly find myself facing the decision to commit myself to becoming a fully observant Jewess or face the consequences of not doing so. With such choices, perhaps it is more than a coincidence that the Torah portion immediately following my birthday this year is *Nitzavim/ Vayelech*. The right choice seems clear.

DK: I will point out two facts: 18 is *Chai*, life, and 40 is the number of *Binah*, Understanding. Why it had to be this way and take so long, I, of course, can't answer. No one can. But as you say, the right choice IS clear.

I can only repeat, that with the love and support of your husband, the patience and understanding of your rabbi, your own determination and strength of will—you and your family will succeed in unimaginable ways.

SZ: I guess I worry about how to deal with the kids, helping them to understand the meaning behind all the "new" rules that will be changing their lives. How do I approach this so that they will understand how mitzvot fulfill our lives, not imprison us. My husband will, he has said, do whatever is necessary to help me resolve this situation, but he also has major concerns about the kids in this respect. I guess I'm just looking to learn from someone else's experience.

DK: The best way to deal with the kids is to be honest, patient and loving, and to let them experience your joy (and anticipation) and the meaningfulness of the rules.

Please let me know how things are going and if I can be of any help. I would also suggest you think about writing the Lubavitcher Rebbe and asking for his advice or a brocha. (I will tell you an incident: an "older" couple (in their fifties—and I'm in my forties!) were determined to become Jewish. Without all the details, they went to NY for their conversion and, because they had become involved with Chabad here, went to see the Rebbe, when he was giving out dollars on Sundays (may he do so again soon). The wife, taking the opportunity to ask for a brocha, as was customary, asked the Rebbe for a *brocha* for all the Jews of Louisiana (this was when David Duke was running for governor) for their safety. The Rebbe responded amen, and said, now you are Jewish, just like me (pointing to himself) and the others (pointing to some of the rabbis and his attendants).
Stay in touch.

SZ: It was a relief to hear from you. After that meeting with Rabbi Teitelbaum, I was really in need of some reassurance that I was doing the right thing—that things could work out.

16
A New Path

DK: Reassurance I could give you. I'm reminded of a story about the Mitteler Rebbe, a renowned scholar, noted for his powers of concentration. Once, when deeply immersed in his studies, his young child began crying in the next room. He didn't hear the infant, but his father, the Alter Rebbe, who lived in a room upstairs, did. Although also immersed in his studies, he gave the child his immediate attention. After comforting his grandson, he told the Mitteler Rebbe, "No matter how busy or important you are, you should always hear the cry of a child." Even as adults, we can be emotionally, intellectually—and most often spiritually—children.

But I could only "be there" virtually; I could offer support, advice, and some guidance. Whether or not you (and your family) took the path I knew God had given the Jewish people was up to you. And while I was confident that you would, I was also worried for you, concerned about all the "little" obstacles in the way.

SZ: That e-mail made a big difference. I felt that it offered hope, and, even more important, you made it clear that you were willing to listen. You were right. I was crying out. I felt helpless, lost. There were so many unknowns. I needed to know that someone understood. Your response convinced me that you did.

SZ: I can't thank you enough for all your wisdom, encouragement and comments. Your letter was the first thing I saw after sharing *havdalah* with my husband.

What a beautiful way to start a week!

DK: Thanks. "Words from the heart go to the heart," as the Rebbe says. . . .

SZ: Your comments on dealing with the children were especially welcome. One thing I don't want to do is have this situation cause negative feelings about Orthodox Judaism, i.e., blaming the wrong party for it. You have some good and helpful suggestions. We haven't discussed any of this with them yet, and probably won't until we get a better understanding from R' T of what their conversions will need to entail. We need to figure out what to do about Hebrew school too. Oh well—one thing at a time.

DK: A smart approach—finding out first what they're going to need to do. I'd think as far as school, though, you'd want to get them into an Orthodox day school as soon as possible.

SZ: I am already beginning to see light within this difficult situation. Before, I was always hesitant to bring up the subject of religion with Joe. Now I find that we have had a few good talks about being Jewish and even why he has not chosen to be observant. We had a good discussion with our son after Shabbat dinner on a lot of questions about living Jewishly, things like whether he would like to live in a Jewish neighborhood, how he perceives Orthodox kids, and a number of related topics, many of which I have learned from asking questions on KesherNet. Joe even went upstairs to find his tefillin—it was the first time I'd seen tefillin up close. Anyway it's nice to be talking about the subject. We even touched briefly the idea of moving (the public schools here have a problem anyway) and I'm sure if we do, a Jewish community would be a lot higher on the priorities than when we moved here.

DK: Good, deep discussions are a good way to start. That Joe expressed willingness, on his own, to start putting on tefillin again is in itself proof all of you are doing the right thing and that it will bring you closer together. (By the way, if he hasn't used them in a while, he should have them checked by a competent sofer as soon as possible. Ask R' T.)

SZ: [In the last message you said] "Also, bear in mind that nothing happens without God's consent. *Hashgocha pratis*, Divine Providence, allowed this situation to occur."

This knowledge, above all else, is what gives me hope.

[You also asked] "I assume a rabbi officiated at your wedding and the brit milah of your son(s)—did he know? If so, he should have said something."

Actually they looked at the conversion document. It looks very proper and says all the right things. Others converted by this rabbi had even done aliyah successfully based on the same documentation. My father-in-law took the paper to his Orthodox rabbi, even. They wouldn't have had any way to know.

Thanks again, David (by the way, my son's name is David Michael). I will stay in touch. I need understanding friends.

DK: I'll be glad to listen, advise, or whatever. I look forward to hearing from you soon.

DK: Several things stand out in that exchange. We'd already assumed that the decision has been made. You and your children were going to have a halachic conversion. Joe would support you, difficult as it would be for him, on both a family and a personal level. You recognized the difficulties involved: the changes in the children's lives, the family upheavals, the questions and accusations the revelation and decision would bring, and so on. At least you had your Internet friends.

SZ: Yes, but I was beginning to realize just how difficult this journey might be. I wasn't making a decision that affected only me. That would have been easy. As you said, I was making choices that had to involve the entire family, and that was an awesome responsibility.

DK: And you couldn't make them alone.

SZ: No, each one of us had to be willing to make changes. The impact of my decision on David and Julie was uppermost in my mind. Living in a decidedly non-Jewish suburban community, virtually all social interaction happened on Saturdays: swim meets, tennis tournaments, soccer games, scout outings and camping trips, birthday parties, overnights, family nights at the pool. . . . You get the idea. Life for the children in the community revolved around Saturdays and non-kosher food.

Now I was considering telling my children that all of these things had to fall by the wayside so that their mother could "get religion." What could I offer to replace all of that? I couldn't even offer them a synagogue and a group of Jewish friends! What if they saw it as some sort of punishment? What if it made them despise what precious little grasp of Judaism they had? What if, God forbid, it made them reject God? What if it made them reject me?

DK: All your fears were real possibilities. We talked about this. I felt then, and still feel, that children want the truth. We have to be careful and considerate in how we approach them with it. It's easier to see from the outside just how desperately children want to trust their parents (and vice versa) and how much they're willing to accept, if dealt with honestly.

You felt as if you were taking something away from them, be it the social life, the "sense of identity," or the family security. In truth, however, you had actually determined to give all that to them.

SZ: That's what I hoped. Yet there was always that question lingering in the back of my mind: "What if I'm wrong?"

I was afraid of how my decision would affect our marriage, how it would affect Joe. He wasn't the one asking for this. I would be asking him to allow changes in our marriage and relationship that neither of us would have imagined. What if the demands made him miserable? What right did I have to take away his happiness simply to seek my own? What if . . . what if he decided that this path was just too much? The possibility that choosing Judaism would result in the breakup of our family was terrifying.

DK: Rightfully so. I don't know how your other e-mail correspondents responded, but I knew that you *had* to have Joe's support. That meant that you had to do everything possible—without compromising your decision—to accommodate Joe's feelings. He had to know what you were doing, thinking, feeling; and he had to agree with, or at least accept, your decisions. That might mean a delay, a compromise, who knows what. But even though you had to have a kosher conversion, you also had to keep your family together.

SZ: In hindsight, I talked to Joe far less about my thoughts and feelings than I should have. I was afraid to risk saying anything for fear that it would come out wrong and destroy the one chance I had to find my way "home." It seemed to me that God was presenting me with my own personal *Akedah* [the classic term for the sacrifice of Isaac]. Was I being too dramatic? I'm not sure. I also shared my dilemma with another Jew on the Net. Part of his response was:

Unfortunately, it is time for me to pack up my computer and move. Fortunately, I am about to get married (God willing).

I wish I had more time to talk with you as I am aware of how much you feel in need of support. . . .

I don't have time to say this gracefully, but I'm sure you will want to hear it. If you are truly to become a Jew, it will be necessary for your husband to walk in the ways of our Torah if you hope to remain with him, which I'm sure you do. I don't think that this is a halachic requirement, but it is just my feeling that a marriage where only one person's essence is consciously rooted in accepting the kingship of Hashem is doomed to fail. I do not envy the anxiety you are going through, but you have the opportunity to make tremendous improvements in your and your family's lives.

I know that your greatest fear is that your path could end up not being theirs. It is a valid concern, and it would be dishonest for me to say that everything will work out as you hope. It is always true that "It'll all work out in the end" because it is Hashem who is in charge. You will now be called on to have complete faith in him. You were quite right to wonder whether you have the same courage as Avraham Avinu, because you will certainly be called on to perform the same test. Isaac was given back to Avraham in the end, but we have no guarantees that the same will be for you. I do feel for you, but it would be dishonest for me to put this any more lightly.

May Hashem give you the strength to fulfill His will and the confidence that as long as you do so, He will decide where you are supposed to be and with whom.

DK: What an arrogant message! First, since he doesn't know the *halacha*, how can he make demands on your husband? The truth is, there are many families where only one spouse is observant. Certain laws would, of course, require your husband's cooperation (*taharas mishpacha*; *kashrus* in the home), but in other areas (even *Shabbos* observance), his observance of *mitzvos* might not affect yours. That's why the "instant expertise" of the Internet can be so dangerous. Second, he should have realized that if he didn't "have time to say this gracefully," he shouldn't have said it at all. This message is a poor example of how an observant person should approach anyone else, let alone someone in your position.

SZ: This message only added fuel to the fire. He may have thought I would "want" to hear it, but I didn't! I resented his very pessimistic view. I thought it unkind of him to have the *chutzpah* to be so blunt. Here he was, going off to begin a marriage, and telling me that mine could be in danger.

DK: Exactly. He didn't know what he was talking about.

SZ: I tried to ignore what he'd written, but it was sometimes difficult. I explained my situation to a couple of Jewish friends, hoping to find some encouragement and understanding. I described, late in June, the responses I got to Sheldon, a friend and observant Jew with whom I frequently corresponded by e-mail.

> **SZ:** What I've been finding is that most of the folks that I've talked with about the mikveh problem have, in effect, been telling me that I was crazy to bring it up to the Rabbi. In a way, I guess I expected to hear that from a few folks, but it still distresses me. One person suggested that it was wrong (from even a Jewish perspective) to bring trouble on myself; another, that it was a rather severe thing to do to the kids; and more than once, questioning why I was trying to please the "fanatics." Somehow I end up feeling guilty for doing what seemed (and still does) the only right thing to do.
>
> I've also been confronted with the suggestion that maybe the reason I wanted to become observant (and have a kosher conversion) was that I was trying to prove something to somebody; that I had to "justify" my

Jewishness out of guilt for something that wasn't my fault. I don't know how to really respond to that: particularly since I don't even fully understand the inner need that drove me to want to become observant. I just know that it is there and it is real just as love is real. . . .

In the end, there is nothing to prove, to myself or anyone else. I realize that if right now, I were to find that I was "really" Jewish by birth, I would proceed in exactly the same direction I am now.

DK: You were already experiencing the difficulties and pressures—the self-sacrifice—necessary to live according to the covenant of Abraham. You, of course, know the famous story about Rabbi Akiva, who continued to teach Torah even when the Romans decreed the death penalty for anyone doing so. When his disciples urged him to stop, he said that one time a fox saw some fish swimming desperately upstream. The fox asked the fish why they were in such a hurry and so worried. The fish replied that they were fleeing the fisherman's net. The fox then told them to come on shore with him and he would protect them. The fish answered by saying that the supposedly clever fox was surely a fool. If in the water, which was their life, the fish were in danger, how much more so on dry land. So, too, Rabbi Akiva explained, the Torah is our water, our life. Even when in danger, we must "swim" in it.

Often, those who choose to be observant must swim against the tide of popular culture, public opinion, materialism's hardening of our spiritual arteries, pseudointellectualism, and ignorance.

SZ: I remember one way I looked at my situation. I felt that I had been given a wondrously valuable gift (to be Jewish), but, as it turned out, it had been given in error, and now I had to decide whether I was willing to "return" it. On the one hand, I could say, "It wasn't my fault that things weren't done right, so why should I suffer the consequences?" On the other hand, I had come to the realization that this gift was not, had never been, mine at all. To try to keep it would be dishonest. I felt as if I was being asked to return my very soul. It wasn't easy, but it had to be done.

DK: What impresses me even now is the depth of your commitment—even before you fully understood what was involved. When the Jewish people received the Torah—when they 'converted,' so to speak—

their response was, *Naaseh v'nishmah* (first we will do [observe the *mitzvos*], then we'll understand).

SZ: Perhaps they responded that way because, above all, they trusted God. They were willing to do what they were instructed, knowing that the understanding, if needed, would come. I didn't have the benefit of hearing God's voice, but I did feel that I could trust Rabbi Teitelbaum as a teacher, and you and a few other observant Jews as friends.

DK: I know. At times, I felt like a cheering section—unable to do more than encourage and watch and hope.

Let's get back to what you were doing. All the talk on the Internet probably helped your soul's first two "garments"—thought and speech. But what about action? What steps were you taking toward the conversion itself?

SZ: We had begun to take small steps toward becoming observant. The first decision was to stop shopping on Saturday. I sensed that I was being branded as a religious fanatic, but somehow we got used to it. I talked about the challenge of becoming observant in a message I wrote to you a short while later:

> On the home front, I've been discussing our goal to become observant with the kids whenever the opportunity arises. So far they seem remarkably understanding and willing to cooperate. It really is interesting to see how even this amount of "extra" discussion is causing them to bring "Jewishness" into their own conversations. I also realize how important it is becoming to move into a Jewish community. It could provide a sort of demarcation, a point at which we can "really" begin to be observant. I asked them today, too, if, as of right now, they were free to "not be Jewish," and to be whatever they wanted, what would they do? They thought about it for a bit and decided that they would be Jewish. (exit one relieved, but not surprised, mom :-))

You replied, "I told you to have confidence in them! And, yes, the community will make a big difference."

DK: What was the children's reaction to the changes?

SZ: At times, it was very difficult for them. As I mentioned earlier, their peer group's social calendar was anything but compatible with Jewish observance. Still, though they often had disappointments because of the "new rules," I don't recall them ever saying that we "shouldn't" be doing these things. Both David and Julie seemed to accept "Jews are not supposed to do this" as a sufficient answer.

DK: Most Jews know instinctively that, in fact, the answer is sufficient. But the arrogance of the intellect, the mockery from outsiders, and the impulses and cravings of the animal soul excuse and conceal our failure to accept and act on that answer.

SZ: I hadn't told the children about the problem with the conversion. As far as they were concerned, we were just becoming more observant, "doing what is really the Jewish thing to do." Only Joe, Rabbi Teitelbaum, and I knew the facts—well, outside of who-knows-how-many folks on the Net.

We knew that we would have to move to a community where there were other observant Jews, and Jewish schools. Baltimore was a possibility. I had corresponded with a couple of people in the Baltimore area who had suggested calling a certain Rabbi Porter, which I did a few days later. When I spoke with Rabbi Porter, I didn't give him the whole story. I just told him that we were trying to become more observant and possibly looking to move to Baltimore, and asked if he could tell me something about it.

Rabbi Porter was very friendly and helpful. Besides sharing information about the community with me, he also sent me some information about classes that were available at Etz Chaim, a learning and outreach center for adults. I began to seriously entertain the possibility that some major hurdles might yet be surmountable, as I concluded when I wrote to you:

I really am hopeful of finding a better community to live in. God willing, I think all will turn out well in the end. I know it is the right thing to do.

Even knowing what was the right thing to do, I was still very much aware of what this decision meant. The problem with my conversion and what to do about it had become a subject of conversation on FIDO–Judaica. One participant in the thread wrote:

Like I said, what does she have to lose??? By going to the strictest authority (a) she guarantees acceptance by all Jews and (b) she is sure she's done her best before God.

DK: In its own way, that participant is being as shallow and callous as the correspondent who signed off with some pompous preaching. "What do you have to lose?" is hardly a sufficient reason for having a kosher conversion, a conversion according to *halacha*. This "cover your bases" attitude demeans *halacha* and Torah. Rather than confronting the issue of Divine revelation and Jewish response and responsibility to it, "What does she have to lose?" ignores the issues of absolutes and spirituality and focuses on social convenience.

SZ: I needed to respond to that message. I knew that the writer meant well, but I felt compelled to explain that this was no simple matter. It is so easy to think, "Just convert," but there is no "just." I tried to make that point when I replied:

I really want to respond to this discussion from a personal perspective. It's long-winded so those who would "rather not" read on can save themselves time. The rest of you can indulge my soul-purging.

What does she have to lose? She does have a lot to lose.

By going the Orthodox way, the first thing she loses is her identity as a Jew, and her children lose their identity as Jews. Some might counter that "it's only a technicality," but such an "out" is not available to her. If she accepts *halacha*, she denies her Jewishness. If she continues to accept herself as a Jew, she denies *halacha*. There is no halfway position.

Next, say that she accepts *halacha*, and denies her Jewishness. Now she finds herself in the odd position of being unqualified to perform the very mitzvot that she originally wanted to learn and observe. In fact, even those mitzvot which she did observe for many years, she can only perform, at best, as "shadows," as a "learning experience." Though she had begun her "search" to learn to observe Shabbat, she is now forbidden to do so. Again she cannot be both Jewish and not at the same time.

This might not be a problem for someone who just converted for convenience or to get married, and did not carry their commitment beyond the act of conversion, but such was not her case. Her identity for almost two decades was, completely and without reservation, Jewish (albeit from a Reform/Conservative perspective). Now it is gone. She can only ask that you try to imagine yourself, how you would feel if, God forbid, you suddenly discovered that you were no longer a Jew.

If life weren't complicated enough, she now is faced with the fact that the _only_ way she can become Jewish (by the standards she now accepts) is to go through an Orthodox conversion. This requires, naturally, becoming observant, but not really with the luxury of time that baalei teshuvah might have to do it _gradually_, but in a far more urgent sense. Of course, she soon realizes that learning to be and being observant is all but impossible in a community devoid of observant Jews. That means she must be serious enough to move, uprooting the entire family, if that's what it takes.

Of course, aside from moving, the whole family becomes deeply affected by many other aspects of being observant. All the while she _knows_ that it was not _their_ decision that prompted all this, but hers. It is a frightening position to be in, because she knows, if she's not doing the "right thing" then her family will have sacrificed a lot, needlessly, because of her "folly." And there are plenty of people suggesting that she _is_ wrong. Fortunately, there are a few who tell her she's right, too.

There are, in the end, many things that "she's got to lose." But the most valuable thing is the first thing given up: Her Jewishness, her soul.

DK: You have expressed the dilemma eloquently from the heart. It all makes sense, except that it prompts a question: *Why* does she now accept these standards? What is it about a life committed to complete observance that rings so true?

SZ: I concluded with a bit of poetry that I hoped would express my feelings. A little later I wrote a preface to that poem, completing, as best I could, my thoughts on the whole matter. In them, I think, lies the answer to your questions.

Why do I want to be Jewish? Right now, if I chose, I could declare myself halachically free of all the mitzvot beyond the 7 Noachide laws. I could eat anything, have no restrictions on my time, dress and act however I pleased, not pay synagogue dues or pay for Hebrew school, not keep two sets of dishes, and on and on. I could walk away but I would find myself stranded in a world full of questions for which I would have no answers. I would have no standard by which to judge my actions. I would be walking away from the awareness that every moment and every action can be holy.

DK: Yes. That's the answer: To make every moment and every action holy. To make the world a dwelling place for Godliness. That can be done only through a life of Torah and *mitzvos*.

SZ: The preface continues, followed by the poem.

For 18 years I have travelled life with the Jewish people, albeit (it has turned out) as a stowaway. For me to walk away now would be as inconceivable as ripping off my right arm. I have come to love the Creator, the God of Israel. I have grown to love His chosen people as I love my family. And I have learned that Torah is truth that can only be truly understood when it is lived. To walk away would be to abandon hope of ever really participating in tikkun olam. To walk away would be a denial of everything I hold dear.

Still it is not easy. Admitting that I was not ever really Jewish is almost like experiencing a death. There is shock, and fear and pain, and the realization that something in life has been shattered and can never be fully restored. I feel alone with a great loss, afraid and confused.

> What does it feel like
> To have your soul ripped out
> from within you?
> Cast aside, as if it meant nothing.
> How does it feel
> To have no identity,
> Belonging neither here,
> Nor there.
> I was a stranger among you,
> But I did not know it.
> I was a stranger among you,
> But you were my brothers and sisters
> I thought—
> I was as one of you.
> But I am cast out.
> And I feel alone,
> Like a child shivering in the dark,
> Unable to find her family,
> Not knowing if she abandoned
> or was abandoned.
> There is nothing here for me.
> The world here is dark and cold and uninviting.
> I cannot find hope here.
> You are my family.
> Your God is my God.

Teach me the path that I must go,
So that I may find you and return.
How does it feel here?
It feels like tears.

DK: I remember that poem. My reaction was:

I don't think the last stanza has been written. That, though, will have to wait. (I suspect that there will be another one in between as part of the journey.)

SZ: I'm still waiting for the last stanza, when we *all* finally return, but certainly I have found my family and my God.

17
A New Path, Part 2

DK: I remember the end of July and August 1993 as a time of particularly intense exchanges between us. Reading between the lines, I gathered that you'd plunged into what a friend of mine calls the ocean of Judaism.

SZ: It is an apt way of looking at it. I think that the enormity of what I was facing was starting to hit. I was trying to move, but was in serious need of some regular spiritual direction. Rabbi Teitelbaum was away, and I was just hanging. I realized, too, that there were different approaches within observant Judaism. A couple of people had recommended a certain hasidic rabbi in Baltimore. I mentioned it to you:

> **SZ:** I think I will try to get in touch with this rabbi and find out a little more. I admit that I have ambivalent feelings about the hasidic expression of Judaism, but I'm not sure why. I honestly remember my only real contact with it (the Chabad House in Seattle) to be very warm and positive. Perhaps I'm just a little afraid of culture shock.

> **DK:** I think the "culture shock" is more imagination than real. Anyway, I know the two Shluchim in the area and they are both fine people. Give them a call and tell them you know me.

(If I can put in a plug, I think you'll find Chassidus will help answer a lot of your _why_ questions concerning the conversion, etc., in a very positive way.)

You might tell your husband that you are both very fortunate for having each other—he for having someone as both honest and determined and committed as yourself, you for having someone as supportive and understanding and patient as himself.

And your children must therefore also be blessed.

Thanks for keeping in touch. (And I'll reiterate what I said earlier: I think you should write the Lubavitcher Rebbe as soon as possible and ask for blessing and advice.)

May you and your family be counted among the Jewish people when we greet Moshiach—today!

All the best, and let me know if I can be of any help at all.

DK: It seemed to me at the time that you needed help to "straighten things out" in three areas of your life:

1. Work toward the conversion itself, which meant learning with a competent Orthodox rabbi, perhaps Rabbi Teitelbaum, and observing the *mitzvos* and following *halacha*. I was pleased that you'd already begun to do this.
2. Work things out with Joe. Only the two of you could do that, and it seemed that you were doing so. I wasn't too worried about your children; I felt that they'd handle it all right, if the changes and revelations were presented with sensitivity and understanding.
3. Get the "why" questions answered. To bring "deep spirituality" into the everyday, Chassidus is invaluable.

SZ: I recognized the first two items as areas of challenge. The last one, getting "why" questions answered, wasn't obvious to me at the time. In retrospect, part of the challenge was to get me to *ask* such questions and get answers, instead of dwelling on them and letting them drag me down. Of course, I had only a little idea of what Chassidus was, or of how it would benefit me. That took quite some time, though I was certainly open to exploring it.

At about the same time that correspondence took place, the children headed off for summer camp up in the Poconos. Joe and I, wanting to give them an opportunity to have a strong, positive, Jewish experience, had chosen this camp, run by a well-known international Jewish organization, back in February, before all these changes took place. They attended a four-week session beginning at the end of July 1993.

While the children frolicked in camp, I was still trying to put the pieces of the puzzle together, and to catch up on some e-mail. In our last e-mail exchange, you had suggested calling the *shluchim*. The term was unfamiliar to me. I asked you about it, and in the process found out more than I'd expected.

SZ: What are "Shluchim"? (I'm guessing the term is from the Hebrew *shalach*, but what's the context?) My hesitation to phone comes mostly from not having any idea what I'm calling about: "Hello, Rabbi. I want to tell you my problems" just doesn't seem right, somehow.

DK: Sorry, I assumed since you had had contact with Chabad, you knew what a Shliach (pl. Shluchim) is. A Shliach (and Shlucha, as we always work in pairs) is an emissary (literally), sent by the Rebbe to establish Chabad centers around the country and world, to be lamplighters of Yiddishkeit. As for your hesitation: A Lubavitch Shliach _wants_ a call like "Hello, Rabbi, I want to tell you my problem" (not at 2 AM, obviously, and not from someone with a problem out of his field). Seriously, the very reason Lubavitchers are sent around the world is to help—and often the best help is being able to listen, to accept the other person completely while still maintaining the highest standards.

SZ: The phrase "we always work in pairs" took me a little by surprise. I had assumed that you were a religious student at Tulane. Now I realized that you were a *shaliach*. I had a mixed reaction to that revelation. Normally, the Internet is a great equalizer. Most correspondence is on a first-name or alias basis; titles are rarely used. While you were a "student" in my mind, I had no qualms about disputing anything you'd say, because my opinion was just as valid as yours. Now you had a title, *shaliach*. I suddenly gave a lot more weight to your opinion because you obviously had experience in that of which you spoke.

In my mind, the relationship suddenly changed from peer–peer to student–teacher. I felt a little embarrassed, too.

DK: Funny, I had always thought of it as teacher–student. (I never imagined being mistaken for a student.) But then, I didn't consider the Internet an equalizer in the sense that it made all opinions equally valid.

Why were you embarrassed?

SZ: It's hard to pinpoint. I was probably afraid I'd said something stupid, or bothered you too much. If I'd known I was speaking with a "professional," I might have couched my words more carefully. In hindsight, it's better that I didn't know. Remember, I was still very "rabbi-shy" at that point.

Even so, I decided that it was too late to let this new situation frighten me off, and plunged ahead, sharing my thoughts and fears with you. In fact, the knowledge that you were a *shaliach* now had a positive effect. I could approach you as someone in a position whose guidance I would take more seriously than that coming from an unknown peer.

> **SZ:** [You had said] "If I can put in a plug, I think you'll find Chassidus will help answer a lot of your _why_ questions concerning the conversion, etc., in a very positive way."
>
> Deep down inside, I think you may be right. There is probably a good reason why I have so often felt drawn to Chassidus, even though as I look at it "intellectually," it seems strange to me.

> **DK:** Interesting, since Chabad is the intellectual branch of Chassidus. It can explain the concepts of conversion and the feminine role in the most spiritual, positive manner.

DK: Well, I'm glad I didn't frighten you off.

SZ: I am, too. As we continued our conversation, I related the story of the auto accident we had been in the year before. I told you that one reason I wanted to get the conversion done soon was that I now understood that:

. . . we are promised no tomorrows. I wouldn't want to spend my last day as a gentile.

DK: I felt strongly about that, too.

SZ: You told me to make it a priority, to push as hard as possible. And you encouraged me to write to the Rebbe to ask for a blessing and advice. It seemed a little strange to ask such things of someone whom I'd never met. Also, I had no idea how one would write to someone like the Lubavitcher Rebbe. I hinted at that, and you gave me the address and even protocol guidelines. Awkward as I felt, I told you:

> I guess I'd be willing to write, and just have to trust God to help me with what to say. Still the Rebbe must at times feel like Moshe Rabbeinu, what with all the folks beating on him for advice and such. I hate to add to the burden.

> **DK:** Interesting you should compare the Rebbe to Moshe Rabbeinu! But, again, if you could help someone but needed them to ask, wouldn't it be more of a burden not to be asked? If you feel you want/should write the letter, then do so. You'll get an answer (even if you don't get one in writing or by phone or by e-mail—since a letter read is a letter answered).

SZ: I wasn't sure what you meant by that.

DK: What I meant was that, having established a spiritual connection (by writing), there would be a spiritual answer. What you'd been reaching for is what Judaism maintains, namely, that there is a spiritual reality within the physical world. Observance of *mitzvos* reveals it; connecting to one who lives spiritually enables us to see and understand it.

SZ: I didn't understand much at that point, but I was beginning to see that there were different perspectives, even among observant Jews. There seemed to be a running discussion on the Internet about Chabad, and sometimes the messages weren't terribly friendly. I found it a little disturbing. I discussed it with another "netter" who echoed a concern about Lubavitch. I figured that the best way to understand the other side was to ask, so I wrote to you, explaining the controversy I was seeing and expressing my concerns that:

We had a rather frank discussion on the specific issues involved. The details aren't so critical right now, but the discussion was important, because of the degree of trust I was beginning to put in you as I turned to you for advice. The last thing I wanted was to be pulled down another false path. In time I realized that we weren't going to agree on everything, but that there was a common ground of commitment to *mitzvos* and Torah, and *Ahavas Yisroel.*

DK: What's interesting here, by the way, is that although we'd never met and hadn't even spoken on the phone, you had discerned that I was trustworthy. In fact, you'd been quite discriminating about whom on the Internet you trusted. It seems that the ancient question that had caused you so much trouble and anguish had found a way to be answered. You'd found a method for proving trustworthiness, even if you didn't recognize it or couldn't articulate it yet.

To put it into your words, "It's the common ground of commitment to *mitzvos* and Torah, and *Ahavas Yisroel.*" And that's enough, isn't it?

SZ: Yes, I hope so. I also related my less-than-successful attempts to contact one of the *shluchim* you had suggested. August wasn't the best time for contacting rabbis; they were either out of town or busy covering for those who were. Because of that, I hadn't had much opportunity to go further toward formal conversion, but I was trying to make progress in other areas.

Keeping kosher had become one of my major concerns. We had stopped eating out, but I was concerned about how to handle longer trips, especially our trip back from picking up the kids. I had written to Sheldon, whom I knew traveled on business on occasion, and asked how he handled it. He gave me some practical suggestions, and I wrote back:

Thanks for your comments on how you manage to keep kosher out. Joe and I were discussing this a little at dinner tonight, but more from a perspective of how it would affect our interaction with my side of the family and with old (non-Jewish) friends. No doubt it will be difficult. I told Joe that I thought my family, especially my mother, would understand, even though they would think I was "overdoing it." My mom is sensitive to my need to keep my religious faith strong.

In any case, I said that I didn't think I could let a week every couple of years be the deciding factor in whether I should keep kosher or not. As for friends, I guess if they are real friends (and I think they are) they'll manage to accept it. We would miss eating out—dinner theaters and such. It will take some adjustment, but hey, we haven't eaten out together since I was "re-educated" by Rabbi Teitelbaum, and we seem to be surviving just fine.

In case it appears that way, I don't mean to give the impression that Joe is trying to talk me out of becoming observant. He is just trying to make sure that I am really thinking the whole thing through. It probably goes back to what I said before about him not thinking very highly of religious commitments that aren't consistent. He has made it very clear to me that he will support me as long as I don't get _weird_ on him. I asked if that meant like leaving home to go to Israel to study Kabbalah. He said that would be a start. ;-) He definitely doesn't see being observant as weird, though, and has told me it simply would not be in his character to tell me or anyone else to be "less Jewish."

We do sometimes get into rather energetic conversations about one aspect or another of observant Judaism. All it usually ends up doing is to make both of us realize how little we either really know.

I was thinking afterwards, that I could draw a parallel between what's happening to us and the story of the spies. I can look at all the "giants" (restrictions and possible problems) and say that I can't possibly deal with them; or I can just trust Hashem, and go where I'm supposed to go, and do what must be right to do, in spite of them. I think the Torah was pretty clear on the right choice in such matters.

I did talk to Rabbi Teitelbaum tonight. He asked Joe and I to meet with him on Tuesday evening. I feel nervous about it—but then I always feel nervous around Rabbis. (It always gives me the feeling like I'm going to the principal's office. ;-)) Anyway, God willing, we will be talking to him then, and hopefully have a little better idea where we go from here.

As planned, Joe and I met with Rabbi Teitelbaum that Tuesday evening. I related the experience to Sheldon:

Okay, here's how it went with Rabbi Teitelbaum (R' T) last evening.

I enjoyed the session. I learned a bit and I left feeling very comfortable with staying with R' T as a teacher and Rabbi to oversee my and my kids' conversions.

I don't know that Joe is personally any more or less comfortable with R' T after meeting with him, _but_ he does seem to agree that R' T's motives are good ones. As long as I am comfortable with R' T as a Rabbi, Joe has no objections to him overseeing my studies and conversion.

Joe and I talked afterwards for a couple of hours. What was most interesting about that conversation was how differently we each understood some of the things that Rabbi Teitelbaum had to say. I guess we come at the situation from such different perspectives that it is inevitable. Joe will need to find his own pace and approach to being religious. In any case he is absolutely honest in his promise to support my efforts both to become observant and to have an observant household. Enough about Joe.

We talked with R' T a little about observance right now, but I really need to talk with him a little more about it. It's something I have to organize my thoughts on and ask some specific questions. He offered to come help kasher our kitchen. He talked about the sink and stove. I forgot to ask about dishwashers. At first, I thought that, considering the effort it would take, we might as well wait until we move, but today I'm having second thoughts. Funny how things get turned around: Used to be I worried about the kitchen but not at which restaurant I ate at. Now I worry about the restaurants, but my kitchen isn't as kosher as it should be. When will I ever learn to do things right the first time?

We talked about the kids. Rabbi Teitelbaum seemed very sensitive to addressing the problem and agreed that it should be minimized. He offered to talk to them himself, if that would make things go easier. I have to give that some thought. There's no rush, since R' T seems disinclined to convert the children before I go through my conversion.

I asked how long the process for conversion would take. R' T really couldn't give me a specific answer. I understand that he needs to know me better, make sure that I understand my commitments, etc. I'm sure that he has a responsibility to the Beis Din, too. Mostly I think he wants to ensure that when I do convert, it will be to Torah-true Judaism, with a full and deep commitment to Halacha. I want that too.

I am _really_ looking forward to going to R' T's classes. It's an opportunity that (a) I wouldn't have found out about and (b) probably have denied myself, had it not become a necessity. I fully expect that learning will be my favorite part of the process.

Rabbi Teitelbaum seems to be a man who finds great pleasure in studying Torah and doing mitzvot, and who wants others to know that kind of pleasure. I think I will do well to learn from him.

DK: It sounds like you were making progress. What happened next?

SZ: Joe and I decided to take a vacation together when we went to pick up the kids from camp. We traveled up to Niagara Falls, an awesome and amazing sight, then went on to Toronto. This was the first trip we made keeping kosher the whole way. It really changed the nature of "vacationing." Leaving behind the ability to go into just any restaurant and eat, or to taste local cuisine as the mood hit—that was difficult. Also, we had to pick David and Julie up at camp on Sunday as early as possible. In order to keep what *Shabbos* observance we had progressed to by that point, we decided to stay at one of the kosher resort hotels in the Poconos on Friday and Saturday night. It was a costly stay, but I had absolutely no other idea how to handle *Shabbos*.

We lit candles in a dining room somewhere on a lower level, then went up to dinner, where we joined another couple who had been at the resort for some time. At this point I didn't know about washing before eating, and I didn't know the Grace After Meals except for maybe the first paragraph (because I had taught that in my Hebrew-school class). I did wear a hat, and tried to dress according to what guidelines I knew.

It was extremely awkward. On the one hand, we didn't want to tell the whole world that we were uneducated in Jewish observance; on the other hand, one can only "fake" so much. I summed up the experience in a message to Sheldon:

JB had at one point suggested that (since we had been in a reform environment) we probably ought to avoid the Shomer Shabbat lodges. I'm very glad I didn't take his advice. Not only was the day extremely restful, but we had the opportunity to hear a couple of excellent lectures (one on Haredi separatism and another on saving the Jewish family) and attend services, and shiurim. I have never had the opportunity to spend a Shabbat like that. It was deeply rewarding, but also troubling—one thing I learned was how little I know. I felt very awkward among all those who seem so comfortable in the environment, and discouraged a bit, by the thought that so much of the knowledge that made that comfort possible was really only/best learned by growing up in the traditions of a family.

We left Sunday morning to pick up the kids at camp. They had fun, but in retrospect the camp program left a _lot_ to be desired from a Jewish perspective. David reported a general lack of control, some rather questionable activities (including middle of the night bunk raids and letting kids as young as 8 watch *Terminator 2*—fortunately my kids opted for crafts. They know how I feel about such movies.) They will definitely not be going to that camp again. David's comments were to the effect of, "if somebody who wasn't Jewish saw how a lot of the campers were behaving, they would get a pretty bad opinion about Jews. There wasn't much Jewish about the camp except saying Hamotzi and Birkat Hamazon, and the Shabbat services were more Reform than Reform."

I learned that sometimes there's more to a "Jewish" experience than a name.

18
On the Way

DK: Although you had made your decision, you weren't exactly in the ideal situation. There was no observant community nearby and no support group. What were some of the steps you took to begin the process?

SZ: Both before and after David and Julie went to camp, we had been trying to "grow" as a family. Up to this point we'd had very little guidance on how to go about that task. There was *kashrus*, of course, and by the time camp was finished, we were observing *kashrus* inside the home and out.

DK: That probably felt like a natural move. After all, your home had been kosher, after a fashion, for a while. What else?

SZ: When it came to *Shabbos*, it was a lot trickier. Friday nights were nice. Of course, Julie and I lit candles, and Joe said Kiddush, and we almost always had fresh-baked *challah* and a nice meal. Often we did a skit about the Torah portion for that week (the *parsha*), or I took other ideas from a resource book for Hebrew-school teachers. Sometimes we actually read through the *parsha*. It was nice spending time together as a family and not worrying about finishing in time to get to the synagogue for services.

We no longer drove on *Shabbos*, but were still turning lights on and off and using electricity. We soon stopped watching television on *Shabbos*, and I stopped using the computer; that was a tough one for me.

DK: There are always little personal conflicts, a "small" pleasure that's a big challenge to give up. But *mesiras nefesh*, self-sacrifice, often focuses on the apparently insignificant details that have a depth of meaning for the individual.

SZ: The details—and the inconsistencies—didn't escape the children's attention, either. Julie asked why we didn't have the lights on a timer. I said that we weren't that far along yet, but that she was right, we ought to be. We told her that, starting on Yom Kippur, we would use timers, and we would not flip lights on and off anymore.

DK: It seems like your children didn't have much of a problem adjusting; at the least, a lot of the fears you shared with me apparently were groundless. I'd bet that, in some things, they were ahead of you.

SZ: Perhaps. I think there was a a turning point where my children began to see that observance was part and parcel of being Jewish. There was a fine line at this point between encouraging the seeds of enthusiasm for taking on a stronger, more observant Jewish identity, and at the same time not letting them take on a "superior" attitude.

DK: That's a not-so-fine line that even some adults have trouble with. Once, in an Introduction to Judaism class I taught, a student asked, quite sincerely, whether "Orthodox" Jews considered "Reform" Jews heretics. The question arose from an encounter she'd had in her hometown. I tried to explain to her the importance of *Ahavas Yisroel*, which meant loving a fellow Jew even if—or even because—he or she had a different level of observance. A lower level of observance doesn't mean that someone is less of a Jew. There are many hasidic stories about the spiritual importance of even a simple, unlearned, or non-observant Jew. We have to remember that an increase in our observance of God's commandments, in order to become closer to Him, also means an increase in our humility and respect for our fellow Jews, regardless of their "*mitzvah* counts." Being observant, like being Jewish, means being more responsible—and more responsive.

But we were talking about your children. How did Julie and David feel about the changes, in general? This is also a good place to ask how they reacted to the camp experience, what questions they had.

SZ: Other than what I described before, they didn't react to the camp experience very strongly. They had had fun for the most part, but the camp wasn't very "Jewish." It was the first time, though, that Julie had seen someone put on *tefillin*; one counselor had put them on on the bus during a day trip. The rest of the story was telling, however: Some of the other counselors made jokes about him doing it.

DK: A condescending attitude does not confine itself to one lifestyle. At any rate, the *mitzvah* of *Ahavas Yisroel* applies across the board.

SZ: Interestingly, David and Julie were already a few steps ahead of the rest of the campers in terms of observance. In fact, Julie told me that there were times that she had to make compromises in order to fit in.

DK: That's an uncomfortable feeling, I know. But had you told them yet what the full situation entailed? If not, how did you explain this sudden increase in observance?

SZ: As I'd mentioned before, they knew nothing of the conversion problem. When I first began pushing *Shabbos* observance, *kashrus*, and such, they chided me that I was having a mid-life crisis. Maybe they hoped it would blow over, and meanwhile would just humor me.

They didn't ask many questions, but when they did, I tried to explain as truthfully as possible: I had been learning more what it really means to be Jewish, and how special Torah is, and how important it is to observe the *mitzvos*. That sometimes when we learn new things, they are important enough to require us to change the way we have been living our lives, and that that was what was happening to us.

DK: You made a lot of changes in two months, all without rabbinic guidance or a strong support group. That took a lot of courage. Of course, you made these changes together, as a family. Was there anything you did personally, though, on an individual basis?

SZ: One decision I made at this point was to start covering my hair.

DK: That was quite a decision. That's often one of the hardest *mitzvos* for a woman to accept. How did that come about?

SZ: The fear that "culture shock" might yet prove to be the one insurmountable hurdle to becoming observant was still very real. I remember when we took a family trip to the Baltimore Zoo one weekend in early summer, and I saw a number of women wearing snoods that covered all their hair. I wondered whether it was embarrassing to them, and couldn't imagine myself with my hair so blatantly covered in such a public setting. Still, I understood that this was part of the "package deal." Married women are halachically required to cover their hair, and if I was going to accept *halacha* as part of conversion, then I needed to cover my hair, too. I decided to take on the challenge. It became a test of my own personal religious commitment. I wanted to know whether I could "handle" this: If covering my hair was going to stop me, then we might as well know it up front, give up this whole notion of ever becoming Orthodox, and head back to the Conservative synagogue.

That sounds pretty strange, doesn't it?

DK: No, actually it makes a lot of sense. When becoming observant, some parts are easy; they come naturally and seem to fit comfortably into one's lifestyle. (Obviously, which *mitzvos* these are varies, but *kashrus*, *tefillin*, and *Shabbos* candles seem to be early ones for a lot of *baalei teshuvah* and converts.) Some just have to be put off for a while. But some, like covering the hair, in your case, become a personal challenge, a test of—or focal point for—one's faith, commitment, and strength. Actually, I think that "grabbing a *mitzvah*" helps solidify and intensify the what and why of the journey, giving substance to the struggle. The idea of being scrupulous and exacting about a particular *mitzvah* is the subject of a talmudic dialogue.

Given that you felt a certain discomfort with the *mitzvah* of covering your hair, how did you meet the challenge?

SZ: I started gradually. I bought a couple of hats and berets and started
wearing them. I began by wearing hats when it seemed not inappropriate, and going bareheaded when it seemed out of place. Over several months I wore hats more and more of the time. I felt very self-
conscious, even though in Bowie it wasn't likely that anyone would
associate a hat with being a religious Jew. Mostly I just felt "different" from everyone else, an oddball. Later, when we started going
to Baltimore, it was wonderful to see so many other women covering their hair. At least I knew that when we finally moved, I would
"fit in."

You commented that this is one of the hardest *mitzvos* for many
women to observe. I agree. We live in a society where neither men
nor women cover their heads. Wearing hats or wigs or *yarmulkas* sets
us apart and makes us feel different. While for a Jew that should be a
good reason to cover one's head, many of us have also bought into
the idea that being different, being special, is "bad." It's not easy to
overcome that attitude after decades of exposure to it.

DK: You mentioned that if you couldn't handle keeping your hair covered, you thought that you might as well "give up this whole notion
of ever becoming Orthodox, and head back to the Conservative synagogue." Why didn't you go back to the Conservative synagogue
and at least talk to the rabbi there about your situation? Why did
you almost automatically—and exclusively—go to the Orthodox
synagogue?

SZ: Actually, we had planned to go back to the Conservative synagogue
in Bowie right after we left the Reform synagogue. We were just going
to hold off until the rabbi returned from his trip to Israel at the end of
the summer. We also wanted to get a feel for the Hebrew-school situation. Obviously, as you noticed, that meeting didn't happen. The
conversion issue was the biggest reason for this.

I considered the options.

If I went to the Conservative synagogue, I could effectively increase
my level of observance and ignore the possible problems with the con-

version. Since my conversion was done under a Conservative rabbi, it was unlikely that anyone would have questioned it further. I couldn't live with this; I needed to know whether or not the conversion was valid.

A second option was to ask the Conservative rabbi about the *mikvah*–conversion issue and let him deal with it as he saw fit. Part of my hesitation stemmed from the fact that a rabbi affiliated with the Conservative branch already had done things that caused problems. Even though this rabbi might not (and probably wouldn't) make the same errors in judgment, how would I know? If one rabbi could bend the rules so far that things broke, why not the next?

DK: A good argument, by the way, for being careful with how we represent ourselves and our affiliations. Of course, the "guilt by association" may be logically flawed, but it's often emotionally irrefutable.

SZ: When the stakes are as high as I perceived them to be, even emotional arguments are persuasive. I wanted to set my life aright again, to become certain beyond doubt that I was Jewish.

I had read enough on the Internet to realize that Orthodox Jews might not consider me a Jew after a Conservative conversion, even a "redone" one. What if they were right in their assessment? What if neither they nor God considered me Jewish?

DK: Of course, the real question comes from the source of all the political disputes—the so-called OCR (Orthodox–Conservative–Reform) "flame wars": If the "Orthodox" position is correct, then God would not consider you Jewish. It takes a lot of intellectual integrity, theological honesty, and emotional courage to recognize, and accept, that truth.

This goes back to your earlier question of whether or not the conversion was valid. You had to know, however, that the Conservative and Reform movements considered it valid. It comes down to the question of authority—particularly religious authority—that's been so central a theme in our discussion, doesn't it?

SZ: Yes. I was back to dealing with the issue of "Whom do I trust?" I needed to decide somehow whether to trust the Conservative views on Judaism or the Orthodox ones.

DK: How did you decide?

SZ: In the end, I looked at the way that Jews lived, both those who called themselves Orthodox and those who called themselves Conservative. How much did Judaism matter? Was God a central part of their lives, a priority, or was He an afterthought? Did Judaism influence their lives more than secular society? How much were they willing to give up in order to live "Jewishly"? If there was a conflict between religious observance and a secular demand, which won out?

DK: Of course, many members of Conservative and Reform synagogues might claim that they, too, choose religious observance over secular demands, that they keep kosher, and so forth. But you were looking for a consistency of significance: What took priority in their lives? When did they pay attention to details and minutiae? We're meticulous with what's meaningful, and any successful professional knows that dedication is measured in the details.

SZ: I'm not sure I recognized it as "details and minutiae," but, in fact, that may well have been what I was seeing. At the time, my reasoning was simply that if one was confronted with the truth, with God, that it would indelibly change their lives on a daily basis, not just at *shul* or when it came to educating their children.

DK: This means that the encounter has to be concretized if it's to be real. Actions make it real, and Jewish actions are *mitzvos*.

You're saying, in effect, that if experiencing Godliness is more than a transitory feeling, there has to be some practical expression of that relationship.

SZ: Right. It seemed to me that I saw those "practical expressions" far more often in the lives of Orthodox Jews than in the members of the Conservative synagogue.

I guess it's selfish, but I wanted to know that, after going through all this, I would have gained something worthwhile.

DK: I don't think it's selfish. Of course, the leaders and philosophers of the various movements marshal a multitude of arguments to support their contentions concerning the spiritual validity of their approach. You found a different—although equally intellectually sound—

solution. Who are living as if God is central to their lives, and does that way of life, if followed assiduously, lead to the emotional, social, and spiritual ideals? That's not so different a standard than the one used in the Torah itself.

So far, it seems that you didn't hit any truly rough spots. But I'm sure you did at some point.

SZ: Difficulties are inevitable. The first one I remember happened when David volunteered to help the teachers at the elementary school get ready for the new school year. These older students were put to work for the day, and in return were treated to a pizza lunch. I told David that he had to bring his own lunch because, as we both knew, the pizza wasn't kosher. He felt awkward and out of place, about the worst thing that can happen to an adolescent.

This was only the beginning of a series of personal and social conflicts that faced both Julie and David because of the fact that they were trying to "do the right thing."

DK: That's one aspect of *mesiras nefesh*: doing the right thing even if it makes you uncomfortable. I'm reminded of the story about the father over in Russia who took his young son to a lake the village used as a *mikvah*. It was in the middle of the winter, and so the lake was frozen over. After cutting a hole in the ice, the father plunged his son into the freezing water. Quickly pulling him out, the father wrapped his son in a thick fur, one designed to provide warmth and comfort. Back home, he asked his son to describe what he felt, first when plunged into the water, then when wrapped in the fur. The boy said that it went from "Oy!" to "Ah!" That's the difference between a sin and a *mitzvah*, the father explained; a sin leads from "Ah!" to "Oy!"; a *mitzvah* from "Oy!" to "Ah!"

Still, doing the right thing isn't easy, particularly for children, especially when they're asked to make a sudden change without an obvious reason. Can you give me another example or two? How did they handle it? How did you and Joe handle it?

SZ: The elementary school made a big deal out of Halloween. The students dressed in costumes, and there were class parties and a costume parade for the whole school. Parents came to take pictures. Classrooms were decorated with pumpkins, ghosts, and witches. I had to think long and hard about this one. In the past, we had always "done" Halloween like everyone else in the community: trick-or-treating, fun costumes, sometimes even parties. Now I had to deal with the question of whether that was proper. On the one hand, Halloween, as it is celebrated now, is little but a "dress-up-and-have-fun" event. Few folks know or admit to its pagan and religious origins.

I remember reading some discussion about it on the Internet. Even though the messages had a broad range of opinions, I picked up enough to come to the conclusion that celebrating Halloween was inappropriate. Joe let me call the shots on this one. His main concern was safety, not religion. I talked to David and Julie about it. Eliminating the trick-or-treating wasn't hard, since most of the candy wasn't kosher anyway. I did offer to provide them some favorite candy in exchange for what they'd be "losing out on." The school activities took a bit more planning. It would have been awkward for them to remain at school and sit out all the activities. We decided that I would pick them up after lunch and that we would all go out for ice cream while their classmates paraded and partied on.

It helped, but both of the children took some flak for it. They were marked as "different," and I was beginning to earn a reputation as a fanatic.

DK: Rightfully so. But there are different kinds of fanatics. Rabbi Akiva, for instance, was also a fanatic. Remember the story about the fish and the fox?

SZ: Of course. But, unlike the fish, we weren't yet so sure of our element. In December, the holiday dilemma hit again. Art projects became Christmas-oriented: Christmas trees, Santa Claus faces, reindeer. The chorus went caroling in the halls. The school did try to recognize Chanukah as well, but a few decorations and a "*dreidel* song" cannot compensate for the Christmas "overload" that was inevitable in that community. The students sang "secular" Christmas songs in music class. These were mandatory, although David and Julie asked, and were permitted, to sit in the library when the choir and band presented the Winter (a.k.a. Christmas) Concert.

I was proud of the kids for standing up for their principles, but I recognized that they were paying a heavy price socially for doing so.

David's class had two overnight field trips, which of course meant making special arrangements for his food. I did my best to give him his favorite foods and lots of treats, but no delicacy compensated for the teasing that inevitably resulted from being "different." David was near tears after one of these trips. He told me that the ones who teased him the most about eating kosher were the two other Jewish students in his grade. I'm not sure I understood any better than he did why that was so.

DK: That one's almost too easy. David's "fanaticism" made them face their own Jewishness. They felt uncomfortable and, frankly, uneducated. Nobody likes to feel that way. Here they were, fitting in, assimilating nicely, and along comes your son. The other non-Jews turn to them and say, "Are you like him? Do you follow all those rules? What do they mean?" All of a sudden, the social circle changes—and they can't even turn to "those rules" as compensation, because they don't know what they are or what principles they follow.

SZ: I wonder if fifth-graders are that sophisticated, or whether these kids simply echoed the attitudes of their parents. In any case, whenever I saw my children hurting, I cried too. Every time, I asked myself, and God, "Am I really doing the right thing?"

DK: Where did you find the answer—or did you leave it in abeyance?

SZ: More than anything, it was the process of elimination. Every other choice seemed "more wrong." What bothered me the most was whether I had the right to demand that others (my children and my husband) make sacrifices just because I was on a religious quest of sorts. Perhaps I was just being selfish. Was my search for religious fulfillment and truth so important that I should make others suffer? I felt very much alone with those questions.

DK: Any *baal teshuvah* has similar feelings. They're certainly most intense within a family setting. One always has to try to balance one's spiritual needs with respect for others whose awareness isn't there yet. Of course, every Jew needs to observe the *mitzvos*, but all we can do is provide situations for Jews to realize why on their own.

What other obstacles did you face?

SZ: At this point, I had no experiential knowledge. I was trying to do everything "by the book." There have been science-fiction stories where an alien civilization obtains a book from Earth and decides to structure its society based on the descriptions in the text. The results are both humorous and bizarre. That's how I felt I was approaching observant Judaism. I had never spent a *Shabbos* in an observant home. Everything I knew about *kashrus* was from books. Family dynamics, community, dress: It was all pictures painted from things I'd read.

DK: Judaism was never meant to be a "cookbook" religion, one where you do it on your own (even if you have the "recipes"). In the Torah itself, Moses tells the Jewish people to listen to the leaders of their generation. Without the Oral Law—the chain of tradition from Sinai through the prophets to the rabbis, even to present-day "legal experts"—there could be no Judaism. The Oral Law, the corpus of commentary, legal discussions, Jewish law, mysticism, and so on, explains the Written Law, the Torah, gives it context and currency. Furthermore, Judaism looks not just to the text but to the *tzaddik*, an individual who is a living Torah. Judaism, as we discussed much earlier, demands experiential knowledge—*daas*.

SZ: As much as I agree with you, at that point I had no way to obtain that "experiential knowledge."

DK: Anyway, you accomplished a lot that summer. But you still didn't have a regular learning program or a schedule for conversion. And your children needed some sort of Jewish schooling. Come September and the start of a new school year, how did you proceed?

SZ: I was always on the lookout for Jewish activities in the area. On Labor Day there was a Jewish-American festival being held in Baltimore. We decided to go. In order to make the trip more productive, we also arranged with a realtor to show us around the area. He told us that his *shul*, Shomrei Emunah, was having a barbecue that afternoon, so we added that to our plans, too.

DK: Did you choose an observant realtor deliberately?

SZ: No. I got his name from an ad in the Baltimore *Jewish Times*. It was *hashgocha pratis* [Divine Providence] that he was also observant.

There were a lot of booths at the festival. I remember three of them quite well. One was a display of calligraphic art in which the artist created a picture by writing out entire books from the Torah. I had seen his work before and admired it a lot. Joe bought me a lithograph of the book of Shemos [Exodus] as a birthday gift.

DK: I'm sure you remember the other two booths, because they also became significant in your journey.

SZ: They certainly did! As a former fundamentalist Christian, I was rather interested in the Jews for Judaism booth. I was too shy to strike up a conversation with the volunteers, though, so I just took a brochure and moved on.

Since I had already talked to Rabbi Porter on the phone, I wanted to stop by the Etz Chaim Center's booth and see what it was all about. I also was looking for ideas as to where to send my children for Hebrew school, and hoped that someone there could give me a lead.

While Joe, David, and Julie took a lunch break, I walked over to the booth and looked around. The volunteer came over to talk to me. We chatted a bit, mostly about where I was from and whether I would like to sign up for the mailing list. Then I asked about Hebrew schools. The volunteer suggested that I call a friend of his who taught at one local Hebrew school where most of the teachers were *frum*. He gave me a brochure with the teacher's name and telephone number, and wrote his name on it as well. He seemed very nice.

After the festival, we went to the barbecue. This event turned out to be a lot of fun for the children. There were lots of games and activities. And it was a big crowd, hundreds of people. Our realtor also caught up with us there and introduced us to the rabbi and a lot of other congregants. It was a bit overwhelming.

DK: But at least you'd come into contact with an observant community. You'd "networked."

SZ: I couldn't have realized at the time the import that a couple of these connections would have in my future.

DK: Let me guess. The first booth—well, you had a present from there. Jews for Judaism didn't enter the picture right away, did it? The third booth must have had an immediate impact.

SZ: It did. The brochure that I received from the volunteer at the booth was the Etz Chaim schedule for classes centered on Rosh Hashanah and Yom Kippur. I decided to drive up to attend one of them. Rabbi Porter was teaching the class, and, afterwards, I approached him and introduced myself. He invited me to come into his office to talk. When we had spoken on the phone a few weeks earlier, I hadn't mentioned the problem with the conversion. Now I did. I again felt like a leper yelling, "Unclean! Unclean!"

DK: Still? After all the e-mail support? It's hard for those who haven't undergone such a transformation to realize not only how traumatic it is—on that we can find analogies—but also how insecure the process makes one feel. Essentially, you were back in that limbo.

SZ: Yes, and every time I had to relive the pain of facing the fact that I and my children were not—never had been—Jewish. It was embarrassing to talk about my past "Jewish" experiences. And I never knew just how the next person—or rabbi—would react.

DK: It is to be hoped that the observant community reacts with understanding, support, and encouragement. Otherwise, it would be like blaming a child for falling down while learning to walk.

SZ: Rabbi Porter dealt with the issue very forthrightly and compassionately and went on to offer assistance. He suggested the same Hebrew-school program that the volunteer at the booth had, and gave me the name of the principal there. He inquired where we would be spending the holidays. I told him that we would be in New York for Rosh Hashanah and Yom Kippur, but as yet had no plans for Sukkos. He offered to arrange for us to stay in Baltimore. The idea sounded nice, but I needed to ask Joe.

I was pleasantly surprised when Joe agreed to the stay. At Rabbi Porter's suggestion, I called Cindy, the woman who arranged for hospitality for Etz Chaim, and left the matter in her capable hands while we headed to New York for the High Holy Days. We went to my father-in-law's *shul*. It was the same *shul* and the same *mechitza* that had so upset me before, but now, somehow, the *mechitza* was less imposing and insulting than it had been. It hadn't changed. I had.

DK: How true. Too often we blame the Torah for our own lack of understanding or commitment. Determining whether the fault lies with ourselves or with the text or situation requires humility, self-awareness, and a breadth of knowledge. One pretty sure guide is the decision of those wiser and more experienced who have gone before us. History and truth are closely related.

SZ: It wasn't the *mechitza* that I remember most clearly about Rosh Hashanah and Yom Kippur that year, but how much it hurt to go through those days. Almost every blessing, every prayer and supplication, contains phrases such as: "our Father," "our King," "our God," "Your people, *am Yisroel*." I tried to reframe the prayers, to reword, to do anything. Mostly I just tried to hold back the tears and hope that no one but God would notice. I prayed very hard. I prayed that things would work out, and for forgiveness for the mistakes I had made that had brought me to this point. I hoped that God would listen. I knew that He was pretty busy listening to His people right then. I wondered whether I mattered.

DK: Of course you mattered. Everything that God creates matters.
  The more I talk with converts, the more I see that the tears and yearning are a sort of necessary prerequisite. It's as if the convert has to turn herself inside out, intellectually and emotionally.
  A convert is compared to a newborn, so it seems fair to compare the process of conversion with the process of giving birth. The difference is that a woman in labor gives birth to a child, while a convert gives birth, so to speak, to his or her own soul.

SZ: You've described it well. The intensity and difficulty of the process is not generally known or understood. Few converts discuss it publicly. While that is understandable, this absence of communication leads each convert to conclude that he or she is "alone" in the experience, alone in the emotional traumas that are a normal part of the journey.

DK: But we, the community, can help. There's going to be a certain sense of 'aloneness' in such a journey, but there should also be a feeling that there's support along the way and that the door is open at the other end.

SZ: But, back to Sukkos:

After we returned from New York, Cindy called to give us the arrangements for our stay in Baltimore. In 1993 the first two days of Sukkos were Thursday and Friday; *Shabbos* followed, making this a three-day event. We would be staying at the Heiligmans' and eating meals with several other families, including the Porters and the Fields. Cindy said that I had met Binyomin Field, and after a bit of mental backtracking I remembered that he was the volunteer at the Etz Chaim booth at the Jewish Festival.

Our first taste of Baltimore Orthodox hospitality was an incredible experience. We were taken aback by the friendliness and generosity of all of the families, folks who opened their homes to a family of total strangers and shared their time, their food (invariably delicious), and their families with us. I began to understand what "community" really meant. Each family, in its own way, was emulating the hospitality of Abraham.

It was hard to know whether to try to "blend in" and act as though we were already observant, or to be open about our situation and take advantage of learning what could be learned. Joe leaned toward the former choice; I leaned toward the latter, although I did not discuss the conversion issue.

DK: In my experience, both approaches work, depending on the individual. Usually those who "act observant" give themselves away, through either some surprise, uneasiness, or question. The main thing is for the host not to embarrass or be condescending, but to make the guests feel comfortable.

A three-day Sukkos must have been quite an experience for you. How did the family like it?

SZ: This was our first real Sukkos experience. We were all a bit overwhelmed by it. David and Julie found the services a little tedious. And there was a certain stress; it's hard to relax completely when you are not in your own home. There was so much to take in. It reminded me of Pesach: the family gathering; the songs; the words of Torah; the blessings; the wine. Especially at night, when the *sukkahs* were only dimly lit and the air was chilly, I felt like I was reliving a piece of history.

Our first meal at the Fields' was lunch on Friday, the second day of Sukkos. In the *sukkah* we were greeted by eight young men, all dressed in suits and ties, several wearing black hats. I had guessed that a couple of their sons had brought home friends from yeshiva. Not so. All eight were their sons; their ninth son was in Israel with his wife. (I was amazed!) The meal was filled with *zemiros* [songs] and discussions about Torah topics. It felt good to me to be in a place where people talked about God without a veiled embarrassment. I thought sometimes that rabbis were lucky; people *expected* them to talk about God. For the rest of us. . . . Well, in my experience, it had always seemed out of place somehow.

DK: That's one of the myths so many Jews get in their miseducation. God belongs at the cemetery; perhaps He'll be under the *chupah* [wedding canopy]; He's invited to the bar or bat mitzvah, but is not expected to show up. Rabbis talk about God, but aside from a few fanatics who think they're *tzaddikim*, no one really lives with God (except for the prophets and a *tzaddik* or two nowadays).

And yet, we never get away from the reality of God. At some level, even the sciences have to confront it.

Is talking about God "out of place" or uncomfortable? If we talk about our families, for instance, that automatically implies responsibilities, duties, obligations—as well as joys and triumphs. Talking about God means that we recognize His relevance—eternal and immediate—within our lives. But then we have to do something.

SZ: Maybe that is why the conversations centering around God in these families seemed so genuine. They were doing, living the responsibilities. We encountered the same environment when we went to Rabbi Porter's home.

I was convinced that even if the lights had gone out, the glow from the rabbi's personality—and from his wife Shoshana's smiles and kindness—would have kept the *sukkah* brightly lit all night. We had a wonderful time. I was beginning to understand what *Shabbos* could really be like: not a day filled with stultifying limitations, but a time of freedom from the shackles of everyday existence.

On *Shabbos*, we ate lunch with the Fields again. It wasn't until then that I realized that Binyomin Field was a rabbi, though not a congregational rabbi.

DK: Did this new knowledge affect your attitude about him?

SZ: It was an honest mistake. I had expected that a rabbi would introduce himself as "Rabbi Field," not as "Binyomin." We saw so many men dressed in dark suits and black hats in Baltimore that I simply didn't realize that he was a rabbi. The biggest effect that that knowledge had on me was to put him into the category of "authority": Someone of whom I could ask questions and be reasonably confident of the answer.

DK: Why? If he didn't have the title "Rabbi," would that mean that his answers would be any less correct? What about others with the same title? They were also called "Rabbi"; why weren't their answers correct?

If the so-called communications revolution in general and the Internet in particular have blurred the lines of authority, titles have less significance, and perhaps less truth. Why do we rely on a title or on an authority? What are the limits of logic here?

This is perhaps not the place to answer these questions, though clearly you'd found—or had begun to find—a reliable theology-to-philosophy barometer. Let's get through the holidays.

SZ: Rabbi Field and his wife, Helene, spent a lot of time talking to us, learning about our backgrounds, and so forth. I still didn't talk about the conversion problem.

As they walked us back toward the Heiligmans', Rabbi Field tried very hard to convince us to return to Baltimore for Shmini Atzeres and Simchas Torah. I wanted to come back, but wasn't sure about the rest of the family. As nice as it had been, it was an intense three days.

In the end, Rabbi Field prevailed. We would spend the last days of Yom Tov with them. Cindy again arranged for some meals at other folks' homes.

I don't know how Rabbi and Mrs. Field managed to fit our family, themselves, and their sons into their modest home, but there we were. It was either a miracle or an example of *mesiras nefesh* on their part. Maybe both.

We had *Shabbos* lunch at their home again. Afterward, Joe went upstairs for a *Shabbos* nap while Rabbi Field and I sat out on the front steps and talked—and talked. He was like a skilled surgeon, probing, examining, and finally exposing the disease. I admitted that there had been a problem with my conversion. He told me later that he had surmised the situation almost immediately when we had been there the first days of Sukkos. He had wanted me to open up, but it had to be my choice. I needed to trust him enough to talk about it.

DK: The who and how of "trust" is something we've searched for since the beginning. Look at how many religious titles you trusted. Did they share any similarities?

SZ: It goes back to what you asked a little earlier about the title "Rabbi." When it comes right down to it, these people didn't share much but their title, and a perception on my part that if they had a title, then they must know more than I did. I looked at the "title"—minister, elder, rabbi, cantor—and not the person. In so doing, I ascribed a legitimacy (and trust) that, in many cases, was undeserved.

In Rabbi Field's case, time proved my trust to have been well-placed.

DK: Once you opened up to him, were you glad?

SZ: Yes. It felt good to be able to talk about what I was going through after hiding it so much. And it was nice to feel that I had someone I could confide in and ask advice of if it came to that.

And it did come to that.

I was becoming frustrated with the difficulty of trying to schedule time to learn with Rabbi Teitelbaum, in Silver Spring. We were able to meet only a couple of times, and for reasons I don't remember, the other classes he taught weren't really appropriate to what I needed. I understood that he was doing his best with an unrelentingly busy schedule; besides, I didn't know what kind of progress to expect in an Orthodox conversion. Maybe my expectations were not realistic.

I called Rabbi Field and arranged to visit him. I saw him foremost as a friend, but also as a knowledgeable rabbi whose counsel I could trust. I explained the situation to him and asked his advice. He suggested that none of the difficulties I had encountered were insurmountable, but that it might work out better for me to transfer the auspices of my conversion to a Baltimore *Bais Din*, since we were planning to move there anyway. He promised to discuss the matter with Rabbi Porter and get back to me.

A few days later, I heard from Rabbi Teitelbaum that Rabbi Porter had arranged to "carry the ball" in Baltimore. We both felt confident that it would work out much better that way.

Maybe it was the changes, but I was feeling really stressed out. I wanted to talk to someone. I turned to Rabbi Field again. He set aside some time on a Wednesday morning in mid-November. The evening before, I left an envelope in his door. One of the papers in it was the piece I showed you earlier: "Why do I want to be Jewish?" I just wanted him to understand how important this was to me.

Wednesday morning, I knocked on Rabbi Field's door and he invited me in, motioning to me to have a seat on the sofa. He said almost nothing, then brought out the papers I had left for him. His face was very tight, and I was sure that I had done or written something terrible and that he was upset with me.

It wasn't that. In fact, it turned out that he was almost feeling the emotions I was expressing; he was empathizing.

DK: You seem to have that effect on your readers.

SZ: We talked a long time about that piece, and about why I wanted to convert, and what commitments would be involved, and more. At the end, he had a surprise for me: "I spoke with Rabbi Feldman, the head of the *Bais Din*, and he asked whether I would sponsor you for conversion." Rabbi Field told me that at first he wasn't sure, but after seeing the letter and talking to me, he was ready to supervise my conversion if I wanted him to do so.

It wasn't a complete surprise; in fact, I'd wondered whether that would happen. I had mixed feelings about it. On the one hand, I certainly knew that I was in good hands, but on the other, I was afraid that the "rabbi–convert" relationship would erode the openness and trust that I was able to have with him as just a friend.

Nonetheless, I readily agreed.

Trust was definitely an issue. Rabbi Field emphasized that I would need to trust him through this process. He promised to never lead me in any path that was contrary to Torah. It was enough. I resolved from that moment to trust him completely.

DK: So, where did the trust come from?

SZ: First, he had "references": Rabbi Porter and the *Av Bais Din* [head of the rabbinical court] had confidence in him. Second, he was making Torah the foundation of the relationship. Third, I had seen first-hand his commitment to observant Judaism when we had spent time with his family. I had seen that "practical expression of the experience of Godliness" that we discussed earlier.

DK: Now you were at last on the final stage of the journey. One way or the other, this had to be it. How did you feel?

SZ: I felt like a child just beginning to learn, needing a lot of guidance—not just intellectually, but also emotionally. And I had a sense of wonderment about so much of what I was learning and seeing. I wanted to ask, to question, to understand, but. . . .

I was also aware of how much was at stake. I knew that a convert had to be willing to accept the entire Torah, without exception. I was afraid that my questions might be interpreted as doubts, and that the *Bais Din* would refuse to convert me.

I also had promised Rabbi Field that I would trust him. I was afraid that if I asked too many questions, or disagreed with him, it might mean that I didn't trust him after all.

Finally, I realized that, like a child, I really didn't know anything. What right did I have to disagree? What did I know?

DK: Isn't that one of the measurements of trust? If you can question—disagree—and still walk the same path, there must be some standard of trust.

SZ: It took a while before I understood that. Getting me to stop "yessing" him, as he called it, turned out to be one of Rabbi Field's more difficult tasks. Eventually I did start questioning more, asking more, even disagreeing on occasion. Always we would talk about it, and almost always he would bring me around to seeing things his way. He was a good teacher because he didn't want me to settle for "accepting" when he knew that I was capable of understanding and knowing.

19
On the Way, Part 2

DK: Although you'd entered a formal program for conversion, there were still obstacles other than the course of study itself. Let's talk about some of the difficulties you encountered in the fall of 1993.

SZ: By then we had registered our children in the Hebrew school, and I was bringing them up to Baltimore—about 45 miles from Bowie—three days a week: twice after their public-school classes, and again on Sundays. It made for very long Tuesdays and Thursdays, for we didn't get back until after seven at night. It also destroyed virtually all of the social life that our kids had left. To their credit, the kids seldom complained. Both adjusted to the Hebrew school, loved their teachers, and learned a lot.

The long commute to Hebrew school was one of two factors that forced a decision on whether and when to move. The other was that the *Av Bais Din* for my conversion was resolute in his decision that we had to move into a community with an Orthodox infrastructure: proximity to an Orthodox *shul*, Jewish day schools, and so on. We put up our house for sale and began the long wait.

DK: The necessity of such a move must have been obvious, though I'm sure it added to your frustration. Here it was, some four or five months after you realized that you had to convert all over again; you'd finally started the process, but didn't know when it would end. That was contingent on when you sold your house.

SZ: Obviously, trying to become observant while living where we were was a nearly impossible task. Still, I didn't completely understand why, after we listed our house for sale, the *Bais Din* wouldn't see that as a promise of good intentions and go ahead with the conversion. It was more than frustrating—it didn't seem "fair."

DK: That sounds like something children say! You know now, of course, that what's true isn't always "fair." When I hear someone say that something doesn't seem fair, it usually means, "It's not happening the way I want it to." But just because the ego wants something doesn't mean that it should be that way. An inherent flaw of secularism is the measuring of rightness by personal desire.

As I'm sure you realized even then, the issue wasn't your good intentions (you'd had those all along), but your actions. Unless we are *tzaddikim*, we're constantly at war with ourselves, with our feelings. I think that you understood why; you just didn't like it. That's understandable. Feelings are important, but they have to be guided (as you did yours) by the mind. As the Alter Rebbe says, the mind rules the heart.

Anyway, you still had those long commutes. What did you do with the time?

SZ: Because of the length of the trip, I stayed in Baltimore while the children were in Hebrew school. On Sunday mornings, I met with Rabbi Field. On Tuesday and Thursday afternoons, I volunteered at the Jews for Judaism office. Jews for Judaism is an organization that tries to teach Jews why Christianity and Judaism are incompatible, to educate Jews about the efforts of Christian missionaries to convert Jews, and to provide support to those who seek a way back after having been involved in either Christianity or cults.

DK: It's an organization that needs more publicity and more support. It's fighting a bottom-line issue.

SZ: Indeed. I had some personal motives in wanting to volunteer for Jews for Judaism. I was in the midst of a major re-evaluation of religious truth, making major changes in the way I lived, whom I trusted, and what sources I relied on as authoritative. Even though I felt that I was making the right choices, I kept thinking back to events over two decades earlier, when I had become a fundamentalist Christian because it "felt" right. When I left Christianity, I did so because it didn't "feel" right. I never questioned the correctness of my decision, but had anyone asked, I wouldn't have been able to articulate a very solid intellectual, historical, or factual basis for it, either.

So here I was, twenty-odd years later, needing to address the issue on a different level. You see, when I left Christianity, I left something that I once believed in quite strongly, something to which I had made a "lifelong" commitment. At some level I was asking myself: "If I could leave that behind, why should I think that I won't at some point leave observant Judaism behind?" One does not make a commitment to God and still believe that she can walk away from it. I considered that my conversion would be an absolute and irreversible act. That is why the question was so important.

DK: Exactly. Emotionally and theologically, you had the answer, but intellectually. . . .

SZ: I needed to know that my "gut decision" to leave Christianity was, in fact, a sound decision supportable by facts and evidence, even if, at the time, I knew them only at a subconscious level. Then I would have an answer—that I had left Christianity because it *was* wrong, not just because it *seemed* wrong.

DK: Even if you didn't know it at the time, you wanted to prove your instincts correct.

SZ: Right. I was no longer satisfied with an emotional understanding of truth; I needed an intellectual one.

In fact, I learned a lot from helping at the Jews for Judaism office. A staggering amount of evidence and scriptural proof clearly demonstrates that Christianity and Judaism are theological opposites on many fundamental religious issues, including who is qualified to be the Messiah and what he will accomplish. Unfortunately, I also

became aware of the staggeringly intense (and all-too-often successful) efforts of missionaries to target Jews. They have lured away hundreds of thousands of Jewish souls, who, in almost every case, were
ignorant of or indifferent to their own rich spiritual heritage.

Mark Powers (the Director of Jews for Judaism) and Melody
Weiscott (the office manager), both observant Jews, were wonderfully supportive of my choice to have an Orthodox conversion. I often
talked to them about my hopes and frustrations, my plans and progress.
In time, they became—and remain—two of my closest friends.

DK: It must have felt strange to be involved in outreach when you were,
in a sense, the "subject" of outreach, now more than ever.

SZ: Yes, especially since I wasn't even Jewish! What I did understand
was how special it was to be Jewish, and how important it was to
be meticulous in observing *halacha*. I had learned first-hand what
can happen when *halacha* takes a back seat to convenience. When
I saw Jews who were taking their Jewishness for granted, or—
worse—abandoning it, I wanted to shake them and scream at them,
"Don't you know what a precious gift your heritage is? Don't you
understand that the Torah you pass off as "obsolete" is a source of
far greater wisdom than the secular world will ever understand? Do
you have any idea how much it hurts to be unable to be a part of
that heritage and wisdom?" (Of course, I never shook or screamed
at anyone.)

DK: It's the "We don't realize the value of what we have" syndrome.
The only way to make people realize it is by helping them to see it
themselves—show it to them, enable them to live Judaism—daily,
halachically.

SZ: I did share my thoughts with others on the Internet. It was awkward; even though I was echoing Orthodox opinions, I knew full well
that those to whom my comments were directed had every right to
tell me that, as a non-Jew, I had no business to say anything regarding what was important about being Jewish.

DK: I'm not sure about that. One should accept the truth from which-
ever messenger delivers it. "Who is wise?" *Pirkei Avos* asks; "He who

learns from everyone." Because of your learning and commitment, you had every right to speak, and every obligation to teach.

Let's talk about your conversion itself. What did you do, and how did it differ from your earlier experience?

SZ: On Sunday mornings, while the children were in school, and again on Wednesday mornings, I met with Rabbi Field to study for the conversion. I sometimes wondered whether he was one of the thirty-six secret *tzaddikim*, because of his patience with me in filling a role that was rabbi, counselor, teacher, father-figure, and friend.

At first, Rabbi Field had laid out a well-organized syllabus for us to cover. He asked me to highlight the subjects that I felt I knew the least about, and we would go from there. That lasted about two sessions. Then we became a lot more flexible.

More and more, our sessions became driven by my questions. Many difficult issues came up, and I dropped almost every one of them into Rabbi Field's lap. Sometimes this was hard.

DK: What was hard? Asking the questions or resolving them?

SZ: Asking them. I saw one of Rabbi Field's roles as "gatekeeper." He was the one who could approve me for conversion, and also the one who could keep it from me. As a result, it was difficult, especially at first, to discuss subjects that might seem to betray doubts or second thoughts on my part.

DK: I can understand that, but the doubts and second thoughts had to be dealt with. You wouldn't have been fair (if I may use that term) to yourself or to anyone else if they weren't confronted.

SZ: Yes, and I realized that quite early on. I decided that this whole process was in God's hands, anyway. If, for whatever reason, some circumstance in my life meant that I couldn't become Jewish, then I had to accept that, too. After that, every issue was fair game. While I didn't ask every question right away, I did know that eventually I would have to ask.

Often, learning was itself the source of more questions.

DK: That's usually the case. What were some of the questions, the difficult issues that drove your sessions?

SZ: I learned that a halachic marriage can occur only between a Jewish man and a Jewish woman. We would have to have a kosher wedding after the conversion. Obviously, that meant that we weren't married in the Jewish sense of the word. Was I allowed to have relations with Joe? Did I, as one book suggested, drive the *Shechina* [Divine Presence] from the world every time I did? Should I be using a *mikvah*? Is a non-Jew ever in a state of purity?

DK: These questions, and I'm sure a lot of your others, probably seemed rather demeaning or restrictive, especially at first glance. Although the specific answers to your particular questions aren't important right now, we do need to discuss the source of the questions. They came not from your discussions, but from your reading. Obviously if something came up as you were learning with Rabbi Field, you'd deal with it then and there. But these "difficult-issue" questions that lingered from session to session came from your own thoughts and study.

Yet books don't always create a context, explain a nuance, or deal with "extenuating circumstances" that modify a flat pronouncement. And even with the best of books, we can't do it ourselves. That's why the Torah emphasizes the importance—and responsibility—of leaders. There must be a Moses in every generation. And the Talmud directs each of us to "acquire a teacher."

While your questions have yes-and-no answers, that yes or no may on occasion itself be contingent (a "yes" for you might be a "no" for someone else, and vice versa). And the acceptance of it depends upon how it's presented.

SZ: Sometimes questions had "yes-and-no" answers. Rabbi Field would explain that one opinion held one way and another opinion held a different way. I found that very frustrating, because I had somehow come to believe that for every situation there must be a "right way," and that the Torah would be very clear as to what that "right way" was. I wanted a black-and-white world. I wanted things to be clear so that I would never make a mistake again. I didn't plan on the possibility that God might want us to think for ourselves.

DK: If not, why make man? Free will—choosing to do *mitzvos*—is what creates a dwelling place for God in the physical world. Making a home isn't always about yes or no, though there are right ways and wrong ways to do it; we make a home when we build a relationship. The analogy, I trust, is obvious.

SZ: It is. Still, it was clear to me that some things were black-and-white—for instance, there is no "almost" to being Jewish. I wondered about what would happen if I died before I became a Jew. And I read one source that felt that only Jews would be part of the bodily resurrection. So Joe would be back and I wouldn't? Maybe it sounds silly, but it was a very serious concern.

I learned that every day we expect *Moshiach* to come, but that when he does, there will be no more conversions. What if he came before my conversion was completed?

DK: We discussed these subjects in our e-mail. Your concerns revealed a depth of feeling and an earnestness of thought that demonstrated an unquestionable sincerity, a true desire for and appreciation of the covenant.

I'm sure that you had other types of questions, as well.

SZ: Sure. I asked plenty of general questions about *kashrus* and *Shabbos* observance, and what I should learn and read. Some of the questions were more immediate and practical. Once, for example, I asked how much I should tell our hosts when we were visiting for a Jewish holiday or for *Shabbos*. Rabbi Field told me that it generally was unnecessary and probably inadvisable to discuss the conversion, so usually we just said that we were becoming observant, and let it go at that.

Sometimes that resulted in rather odd situations. One such time occurred when an administrator at the Hebrew school invited us to come to her home for *Shabbos*. Her husband was a congregational rabbi. I never told her that I was converting; if she knew, she didn't let on. I went to the women's *shiur* [class] on *Shabbos* and what I remember most was that a question came up about a convert's position in such and such a case. The gentleman giving the lecture brushed the question off, saying, "Most conversions are just for convenience, not very sincere or serious. Once a *goy*, always a *goy*. They were a *goy* before the conversion and after—still a *goy*. So what difference does it make?" I kept quiet, but inside felt very hurt by the comment. I wondered if that was why Rabbi Field had advised me to keep the conversion to myself.

DK: I don't think so, but now we know why watching what we say is so important. The Torah is very harsh regarding *lashon hara*—gossip, slanderous speech—because it's so easy to do and so devastating. The Talmud says that *lashon hara* "kills" three people: the one speaking it, the one hearing it, and the subject of it.

There's a famous hasidic story about the village gossip. No matter what anyone said, he continued to engage in *lashon hara.* "What's the problem?" he would say. "It doesn't do any harm; besides, I'm only speaking the truth." Desperate, the villagers asked the rabbi to do something. He agreed, and asked the gossiper to come to his house and bring a pillow. The man didn't understand the strange request, but felt honored to be asked to the rabbi's home. When he arrived, the rabbi greeted him at the door. Before letting him in, the rabbi conveyed to him the concerns of his fellow villagers and asked him to stop. The gossip politely dismissed the rabbi's request, repeating his justifications. The rabbi then asked if the man had brought the pillow. The man said yes and held it up for the rabbi. Suddenly, the rabbi pulled out a knife and ripped through the lining of the pillow. Feathers flew everywhere. "What am I to do for a pillow?" the man asked. "Gather the feathers," the rabbi replied. "I can't," the gossip said, "the wind has carried them away to I know not where." "The same is true," the rabbi said, "of your words. They are carried you know not where with you know not what effect. Once spoken, they are harder to gather than those scattered feathers."

And, of course, the Torah cautions us repeatedly about shaming a convert. In fact, because every Jew was a "stranger" [*ger*] in Egypt, we need to be extra sensitive about the situation of a convert [*ger*].

SZ: I mentioned it to the administrator later that *Shabbos.* She said that there really is a big problem. When a convert fails to live up to the promises he or she has made, or goes back to another religion, it is a very serious matter. She told me that her husband no longer supervised conversions because of a couple that "went bad." Her husband took the failures very personally, and very seriously. I respected him a lot for that, because I knew that he understood the importance of the act.

DK: Yes, it's a very serious responsibility. I know several rabbis who will only teach a potential convert; they won't supervise the actual conversion—that is, sit on the *Bais Din*. Rather, they'll take the "candidate" to a well-respected *Rav*. This not only ensures that there are no questions, but also helps the "candidate" understand and accept the seriousness of the commitment.

So when did you put up your house for sale, and how did that go?

SZ: We listed the house right after Sukkos. The real-estate market was terrible. Almost nobody came to look at the house. It seemed likely that we would be living there quite a while longer.

About that same time, Rabbi Field asked me if I would help him set up an outreach group in Bowie. He suggested that I invite a few couples to get together and that he would come and talk to them. It would be informal. They could ask questions that might be on their minds. He would encourage them to think a little more deeply about what is important in life.

I agreed to give it a try, and invited a few couples that I knew from the Reform synagogue. I put out a few refreshments and we got things started by talking about educating our children, what we wanted for them. What was conspicuously absent from our conversation was any real sense of Jewish values. Awkward as it was that first evening, we did agree to meet again. I spoke to Rabbi Field the next day. He commented that he had expected a group that was Jewishly unconnected, but never imagined just how unconnected these folks were.

DK: It's always a shock to realize how Jewishly ignorant our generation has become. Torah knowledge is more accessible than ever, but the "forces of society"—secularism, political ideologies, assimilation—create a false image, an idol of Jewish irrelevance.

SZ: Yet all these couples were quite involved in the synagogue. There, at least, they still found it relevant to be Jewish. Beyond that. . . .

Rabbi Field also asked me about a possible subject for the next session: "Is there a difference between being a Jew and being Jewish?" Or, "Can a non-Jew be Jewish?"

I think that he was just throwing out ideas, but somehow this hit me really hard, triggering emotions that I had managed to push deep into my soul. I sat down at my computer and wrote the following piece. Feelings and questions, thoughts and memories, came rushing out at me. Most of it was written while I was actually in tears. It was addressed to Rabbi Field. So many of the questions and doubts that I had kept inside were suddenly coming to the fore. I gave him the essay, knowing that it was now time to deal with them.

HOME

Once I lived in that house: The really big one. The one where Uncle Abe is tending to everyone's needs. The one where Aunt Sarah is giving the just-baked cookies to all the little and not-so-little members of the family.

Once I lived in that house—Where David is singing songs. Aunt Miriam is weaving her wondrous stories. Grandpa Moshe, beloved and revered Grandpa, reminds everyone of who they are, and how they should behave, and to Whom they are answerable.

It was a great place to live. I moved in when I was already a little older—there were some folks who arranged the adoption and told me to pack up and move on in. It was very nice in that house. I came in through a back door. I found room in one of the wings. I was there many years. It became the only family I knew. I found my husband there. My children were born there and came to know the family as their own.

Every year there was a great family reunion. We came together as family like never before. It was just for family. A big sign on the door announced: "Out of respect for the elders of the family, out of respect for who we are and to Whom we answer, please be welcome if you are family, but please, don't enter if you are not." Every year the family was together at the big reunion.

This year there was a reunion. This year I was not there. This year I stood outside the window and peered in like a hungry child. This year I did not celebrate. This year I cried.

I found out about the adoption. It was never official. I had to move out. Out of respect for the elders of the family, out of respect for who the family is, and to Whom they answer: I had to leave. But I couldn't go far.

I had nowhere to go.

So, I stood on tiptoes peering into the open window. I listened, whispering along with the hopes and dreams of those inside. It was not much of a connection, but I treasured it, believing that somehow I was still a part of it.

Then you asked that question:

"Can a non-Jew be Jewish?" Why did you ask me that question? How did you expect me to react? Did you expect it to affect me as it did? Did you know how painful it would be to deal with it? Did you know that after answering without thought, I would be forced to roll it over and over in my mind, to deal with it at a level that tore at my very soul? Why did you ask me that question?

With that question, the window has slammed shut on my hand. I pull back in pain and find myself out on the street. There are so many houses out there with welcome mats. I desire only this one. Yet I know I cannot enter until the door is opened for me. Life seems uncertain. I feel frightened, not knowing if I will live to see the time when I can come home.

Listen to my heart:

Everything that I must learn, every prayer, every action done or not done, every bracha, every tradition observed—to you they bring joy, to me, along with hope, they bring confusion and pain.

How could I pray as a Jew? Had I every *Siddur* ever written, I could not do so.

With every "... *v'elokei avoteinu* ... ," I am reminded that I am not part of this family. How I wish that I were. On Yom Kippur, I've always imagined that as each Jew approaches Hashem in judgement, behind him stand Avraham, Yitzchak and Yaakov, that Hashem thus remembers the merits of the Avos as He passes judgement. This year there was no reason to look behind me. I felt so alone, so small—nothingness in the face of the Judge of all living things. And there could be no plea to look beyond me, to remember the Promise—for it was not made to me. I remember crying. I cannot say where the tears fell. . . .

"... *She lo asani goy*." I don't even know whether I should be saying that blessing. And if I do, do I take the name of Hashem in vain? Do I lie? Or do I say it with a vision of hope for what, God willing, may someday be?

In almost every prayer are painful reminders of who I am not. How can I observe mitzvot? Would that it were possible. . . .

The mitzvot that make one truly Jewish are commanded only to Jews. I cannot fulfill a command that has not been given to me. I can do (or abstain from) the physical action, but at the deeper level, the spiritual level, it is not effective. It is like a child playing with dolls. She can do every motherly act, but she is still not a mother.

I am not even permitted to keep Shabbat in its entirety. Am I allowed to be at a Seder? Is the wine cooked—or do I have to somehow manage to avoid touching it as the glass is passed to the end of the table? I could not help light the Chanukkah candles this year.

I say a *brocha* and separate out a piece of challah, knowing that this bread should be forbidden to Jews, for I baked it. My husband will eat it. Am I doing him wrong by offering it to him?

And I don't even know if I can call him my husband: Are we even married? I know we must marry again when, please God, I have converted for real. Is he my husband? I love him as deeply and closely as I ever have. Two precious children have grown out of that love, but now I am told that the marriage was not valid, and I don't know—what does that mean? Rather than being his partner, am I causing his downfall? Have I kept him from growing as a Jew? Is it wrong for us to be together, to have a physical relationship?

I took a class in *kashrus*. I understand, enough, how to do it. I also know that dishes must be immersed in a mikvah—and I know that I can't do that. And the books tell me that I am not permitted to do the cooking alone, anyway, lest the kitchen be considered treif again. Perhaps there is a way around it, but the fact remains that it would be at best a concession. Kashrus is for Jews. It is, in part, meant to keep Jews and non-Jews separate. I can do everything "right," but, in the final analysis, I can only come close. My kitchen cannot be really kosher until I am.

But all these are the little things.

The most difficult thing of all is not knowing what Hashem expects of me. How do I, as a non-Jew, express my love for Him? You have prayers, mitzvot. You have Shabbat, and Kashrus and times and seasons. You have a covenant and a promise. Without these, how does one approach their Creator? I shake in silence and tears at my inability to come any nearer to Hashem. And my heart pleas in that silence to be allowed to come back home. And I pray that He will hear.

I look at my life. I have been blessed with so much, and I am very thankful for it all. The blessings have come, unearned on my part. I do not believe that things just "happen," but that Hashem directs everything for His purpose.

I don't understand this path, why I have—or have been—chosen to travel it, but for all the pain, all the confusion, and all the tears, I consider myself blessed beyond measure to know where, ultimately, "home" is, to be given the chance to learn what this "family" truly is, and to have someone who is, at once, a friend, and a teacher, and a trusted guide, to bring me, God willing, in through the front door as a real member of the family.

That I will truly understand. . . .

Respect for the elders of the family, respect for who the family is, and to Whom we all must answer.

DK: Three are forgiven all their sins, are considered as newborns: the one appointed to high office, the bride and groom, and the convert. You've just explained why: To enter this new condition, this new state of being, one must stare into one's soul and accept its transformation.

I remember how well, in your e-mail, you transmitted your pain and longing and confusion. I remember trying to make you see, by force of will and a few well-chosen (I hoped) words, not only that you were on the right path, that everyone inside was waiting to welcome you back home (for our sages tell us that a convert possesses a Jewish soul that, for some necessary spiritual reason, got lost among the nations of the world), but also that, in some things, you were making the process more difficult—and it was certainly difficult enough.

In the essay you asked, "How can I observe *mitzvot*?" You asked me a similar question back then; the answer still applies. How does a child observe *mitzvot*? How does a child make a *brocha*? A child is not responsible for his or her actions. The *mitzvah*, the *brocha*—they don't count. Why do children do it? Practice. They are in training, learning to be a bar or bas mitzvah—meaning one responsible, one under the yoke of the commandments. How should you have done them? Like a child.

In our prayers, we say "our God and God of our fathers." But, you protested, your fathers and mothers weren't Jewish. And what, I would have answered you, will you say after your conversion? Biologically, your ancestors still aren't Jewish. But every convert is a child of Abraham, as is every Jew, because Abraham was the first convert and every Jew is a descendant of converts.

You talked about *kashrus* and wine and other things, *mitzvos* and activities in which you could have limited participation. Just like a child.

What matter our age, our wisdom? When we come before God, when we change who we are, whether weekly on *Shabbos*, yearly on Yom Kippur, or once in a lifetime, we are, we must be, like children.

Like children, we sometimes wonder whether we belong. We have to figure out the rules, we have to wait, we have to practice. We need approval. But, for children, however they come to be members of the family and even as they are becoming members of the family, the door is always open.

That's how I would have answered you then, had I seen this.

But I'm sure that Rabbi Field answered the questions and helped you through the feelings.

SZ: He certainly spent many hours trying. So many of the questions I had left unasked were suddenly and forcefully unearthed. When I gave the essay to Rabbi Field, I was looking for understanding as much as for answers.

We talked about the answers to the "simpler" questions, about *brachos* and wine and *mitzvos*. In much the same way that you would have answered me, Rabbi Field explained that while it was true that I did not do the *mitzvos* for the same reason as Jews do (because they are commanded to do them), I was doing them because it was my task to *learn* to do them. The best way to learn is to do. My responsibility was to learn to do these *mitzvos* so that they became almost second-nature; after the *mikvah*, I would be responsible for all of them. A person cannot go from 0 to 613 in an instant. It was essential that when the moment came, when I once and forever joined the Jewish people, I be prepared.

DK: Did that satisfy you, dispel some of the confusion, relieve some of the pain?

SZ: Recognizing that the learning and training was my assigned task for the moment helped the confusion. Still, the child learns at home, with her family, and I was not home and had no Jewish family—not yet. But the pain was deeper, beyond words. It was as if the soul that linked me to God had been ripped in half. The inner agony—the need to reconnect—was intense. So while I understood, intellectually, that the training—the "doing like a child"—was the key to repairing that connection, it only made the pain meaningful; it did not ease it.

DK: Well, the intellectual and the emotional are two different realms; they interact, influencing each other, but ultimately pain or pleasure in one is not transferable to the other. Each has its own way of being healed, elevated, sanctified, or redeemed. That which requires thought cannot be satisfied by feelings or actions, and so with the other combinations. That's why we have to live through things we know. There's no substitute for experience—*daas*. Only the removal of the source of pain can ease the pain.

SZ: As for the rest of the thoughts, it was evident that Rabbi Field understood what I was trying to tell him: how important the conversion was to me, and how special a teacher I knew him to be.

It was already almost March 1994. While waiting to sell our house, we had to keep making plans for the future. Pesach was approaching and we had to make a difficult decision. Every Pesach we had gone to New York to have the first seder with Joe's extended family. In terms of family, it was a significant event. There was a bit of a problem, though: The only way to get to where the seders were was to drive on Pesach. I knew that driving on Yom Tov was forbidden by *halacha*. We had a choice: We could backtrack on our observance for the sake of peace in the family, or we could choose to not join the family this year.

I discussed the matter with Rabbi Field, hoping that he might give us some way out of it. He didn't—observing the *halacha* was paramount—but he did offer to make arrangements for us in Baltimore. We accepted the offer. When Joe's folks visited the next time, he explained the situation to them. His father later told me that even though he didn't like the consequences (that we wouldn't be at the seders), he knew that we were doing the right thing. I was happy that he understood.

20
Baltimore

DK: Before we discuss the last stages of your journey, we ought to confront an issue that's been pretty much "running in the background," to use a computer metaphor. You must have been sensitive to the charge that you had an "extremist" personality, that you simply took twenty years to exchange one form of religious extremism for another. I suspect that you had encountered it, both on the Net and in daily interactions.

SZ: Yes. Sometimes the accusations were quite direct. "Fanatic" and "zealot" are words that come to mind. Other people were more subtle. It should be obvious by now that I harbored some of the same fears.

DK: Then I have two questions, one in each direction. Externally, how did you answer the charges, what responses satisfied your "critics," both on the Internet and in person? Internally, how did you deal with your fears?

SZ: To a great extent, I answered myself and others the same way. The term "zealot" connotes someone who has a single-minded desire to

261

achieve certain objectives. So, it might be true that I was—and am—a zealot of sorts. But zealotry is not automatically "wrong." It is not the intensity with which we seek our goals that matters so much as the goodness of the goals and the means we employ to achieve them. In fact, given good goals and good ways to achieve them, zealotry is probably an admirable trait.

DK: Indeed, being called "zealous" is usually considered a compliment. Sales and motivational seminars stress the importance of zeal—energetic enthusiasm—in being successful. The current term is "focused," I think, but it means the same thing. People don't object to determination per se; rather, they feel uncomfortable when the persistence and tenacity is directed toward something they personally can and should pay more attention to. That's why being "zealous" in the abstract is good, but being a "zealot" is bad. Everyone has a cause that arouses within him or her a passionate intensity. ("Fan," as in sports fan, is shorthand for "fanatic.") People protest the objective, not the process.

  That also explains, by the way, why many who are non-observant, or only partially so, admire and even support the "zealots." Either they're comfortable where they are but respect the need for the "tradition" to continue, or they want to increase their own observance, to whatever degree, and look on the observant as role models. (Although they may never reach, or want to reach, the role model's level, they want and need to have a role model.)

SZ: With all that in mind, the question was turned on its side, and I could ask whether the goals I was pursuing were good goals, goals of truth; whether the path I was taking was a good path. So, whether I was accusing myself or someone else was accusing me, I found that the best way to answer a charge of zealotry was to ask another question.

Charge: You make yourself different from everyone else and don't "fit in" anymore.

Response: Is it better to assimilate or to have a strong Jewish identity?

Charge: You're crazy for following all those silly customs and rules.

Response: If I keep the *mitzvos*, will Jewish identity be strengthened for me and my children?

Charge: You never "chill out." Religion runs your life. Take a break.

Response: Is a commitment "only when I feel like it" a true commitment at all?

Charge: You let your rabbis do all your thinking for you.

Response: Is it reasonable to ask a knowledgeable teacher when questions regarding religious observance arise?

Charge: You're messing up your family's life by adopting this lifestyle.

Response: What is the community that follows these "extremist" guidelines like? Are the families stable? Are there solid moral values? Do the children grow into upstanding people? How does it compare to society at large?

DK: You've done an admirable job of summarizing the arguments. Of course, the debate isn't won so easily, if only because it's not easy to get everyone to agree to reduce it to the simple, lowest-common-denominator form you present. A counter-question always lurks in the background. And even if everyone concurs with your responses, many would still ask how to apply them or question the traditional implementation.

Still, you've distilled the essence of the problem. Other people may still object, but you have, at the least, proved the reasonableness of observance, even "fanatical" observance.

SZ: I was satisfied by my own answers to these questions. Others? I don't know. I was sure of the goodness of my path. What others thought mattered far less. (How different than before when in college I had to convince others in order to convince myself!)

DK: That, of course, answers another question. But let's get back to the point where you had decided to spend Pesach in Baltimore.

SZ: Pesach did indeed come, as it is wont to do every year. We still had no idea when we would be able to sell the house. I did my best to get our house ready for Pesach while still keeping it in shape for potential buyers. Joe met with Rabbi Field to take care of selling the *chometz.* I was feeling overwhelmed. There were so many details to attend to. Shopping, getting out Pesach dishes, cleaning, cleaning, cleaning. . . .

DK: It can be overwhelming even to seasoned veterans. It's probably the most labor-intensive holiday. That means it's also spiritually intensive.

Was this the first time you'd made Pesach?

SZ: Actually, since our marriage, we had always prepared for Pesach—cleaning, putting away dishes, taking out the *Pesachdik* ones, covering the counters. There is no denying, though, that there was something special about this Pesach.

DK: Pesach, which celebrates redemption and the beginning of the Jewish people, a going out from limitations, had a lot of personal meaning for you in that regard. Some important redemptions-along-the-way and personal beginnings are connected with Pesach, aren't they? There's the Pesach you spent alone in Washington State, the seder at the Chabad House, and the first sederim with your in-laws. Each came at a significant time and marked a transition.

Now here you were, preparing for a different type of Pesach, but still preparing as Jewish women had been doing for over 3300 years, since the first one.

SZ: The physical preparations may have been similar, but emotionally, mentally, I had to face one overwhelming fact: I was not Jewish and didn't have a real part in the celebration of Pesach. I was well aware that my efforts to kasher things for Pesach were ultimately futile. I was a non-Jew, and a non-Jew cannot be trusted with *kashrus*. It hurt to realize that I was not trusted and that there was nothing I could do to change that. I made my effort for Joe's sake, that *his* house would be free of *chometz*, that as much as possible I would make *his* Pesach kosher.

DK: I think that you were being unfair to yourself and even overly judgmental. If you were simply "not Jewish," then, yes, you didn't have a real part in the celebration of Pesach. But as someone in a transition stage, as someone learning to be Jewish, you had to have a part in Pesach. Otherwise, how could you cross that threshhold? Why not say, rather, that you were *not yet* Jewish? Don't forget that before the revelation at Sinai the Jewish people were not yet the Jewish people.

Spiritually, your soul was in Egypt; your soul stood at Sinai. As a child in Jewishness, if not yet a Jewish child, surely the four questions applied, on some level, to you as well.

And I object to the assertion that your efforts to kasher things for Pesach were "ultimately futile." Does that mean that when a child, who also cannot kasher utensils, spends hours and hours scrubbing them clean, his efforts are futile? Has he contributed nothing? I don't think so.

Of course, emotionally it must have been very difficult to do what you had done for eighteen years, but now feeling as if you were someone else. Still, I hope that you felt something positive as well; in fighting the depression, a tool of the *yetzer hara*, was there not the expectation of an irrevocable peace of mind and the determination that nothing would stop you from your personal Exodus from your own *mitzrayim* (which means both "Egypt" and "limitations")? Remind me to tell you the story about *cholent* and *Moshiach*.

SZ: That sounds intriguing. When should I remind you?

DK: Now, I guess. One Rosh Hashanah, an ignorant, illiterate peasant decided to go to services. Not having any idea what was going on, he could only watch and guess the reason behind the action. He was deeply moved by the cantor's beautiful voice and the intensity of the people, though of course he had no idea what the cantor was singing about or what aroused such depths of fervor in the people. At one point, without warning, everyone began to cry and beat their chests. Our visiting peasant was surprised and wondered what had entered their heads, for nothing had happened to cause such a change. As it was already late morning, he decided that they must be hungry and were crying for the *cholent* [a hot, stew-like *Shabbos* dish] that was even now cooking in their homes. Suddenly, feeling his own hunger, he also began to cry. Then, just as suddenly, everyone stopped crying; the singing became almost joyous. The peasant was really confused now. What did they realize that he hadn't? Ah, he thought, the longer a *cholent* cooks, the better it tastes; the anticipation of the delicious meal had excited them. Satisfied, he was beginning to enjoy the service again, when they all began to cry again, this time more than ever. What now? he thought. He could think of only one reason for their renewed, intensified brokenheartedness. True, *cholent* tastes better the longer it cooks, but how long can one wait? And he began to cry bitterly over the uneaten *cholent.*

We are the peasant and Redemption is the *cholent.*

I think that this story makes a good point about longing and determination.

SZ: Yes, it does. I also had a sense of hope and determination. The whole theme of Pesach is that God is in charge of history, and I trusted that, however small, I was a part of that, too.

DK: That's important to a process that can seem like an "all-day *cholent.*"

But you said that a non-Jew cannot be trusted with *kashrus.* Is it really an issue of trust? Many companies that manufacture kosher food have non-Jews working there, and they aren't necessarily supervised twenty-four hours a day.

Rather, it's a matter of responsibility and accountability. Kashrus doesn't affect a non-Jew. So, no matter how knowledgeable and meticulous and trustworthy, a non-Jew can't be held accountable, spiritually, for *kashrus.* Notice, though, that the same applies to a child. You could be trusted; you just weren't yet in a position to be held responsible. There's a big difference.

Obviously, you weren't reacting logically; you were justifying a sense of distance, a feeling of being left out when you wanted to be included, when you felt that you deserved to "be there" already.

Judaism—and, I'll bet, Rabbi Field—never said that you weren't to be trusted. The issue was a mask for your real feelings. When you say that it hurt to realize that you were not trusted and that there was nothing you could do to change that, what you really meant was that it hurt to realize that you weren't Jewish and that there was nothing you could do to change that.

Of course, I can understand why you didn't want to confront that feeling directly. It's uncomfortable being in transition, especially when you feel that you've already done it, or shouldn't have to do it. It's like passing a qualifying exam, then finding out that there was something wrong with the test or the teacher. You must take the test over, but you feel, "It's not my fault; why should I suffer?"

As long as the issues are theoretical, part of a formal learning process, the feelings can be pretty much contained. But when the issues become practical, an unavoidable reality, that's when the feelings erupt—more powerfully than they can be handled. So whatever can be shifted or projected elsewhere, is.

SZ: Until someone comes along and points out the emotionally driven deceit that I was foisting on myself. It underscores the need to have someone to whom we can turn for an objective perspective when our emotions begin to overpower our logic and intellect.

DK: Of course. It's the idea of having a *Rav* or a *mashpia*. But I'm sure that all the holidays must have been quite difficult.

SZ: Holidays were always the hardest. Every holiday I was back to standing outside that "window," trying to be part of the "family gathering," but ultimately realizing that at the deepest spiritual level I and my children were still "on the street."

Cindy had once again made hospitality arrangements for us. I made a map of the area and wrote our "itinerary" on it. I've kept that map and the other lists of our host families as a reminder of all those who exemplified Abraham's trait of hospitality to strangers. I scan the list—so many names, each bringing a bit of warmth, a fond memory of a kindness done; in several cases, the beginning of a lasting friendship.

The Fields invited us to join them for both sederim. A family they knew was going to be out of town for Pesach, and they were generously letting us stay in their home in their absence. Once again, I was seeing the message played out: Kindness and hospitality are not just philosophical ideals in the observant community, but a very important part of everyday life.

DK: Here may be the answer to all charges of "fanaticism," at least those with negative connotations.

SZ: If such kindheartedness is "fanaticism," then may we all be blessed with it!

The first seder fell out on Saturday night. We arrived at the Fields' home late in the evening. After dark, we took our places at the seder table. I wondered whether Joe missed being with his family. For me, it was very special to sit at my teacher's table at the sederim. I had been looking forward to the experience, and was not disappointed. The sederim lasted into the early hours of the morning. I remember the care that Rabbi Field took to ensure that we had all eaten the proper measures of *matzoh* and *maror*, and that we ate the *afikomen* at just the right time.

I realized just how much I had learned during the seven months that had passed since Sukkos. I felt comfortable here in the midst of *mitzvos* and *minhagim* [customs]. Without the awkwardness and confusion that had afflicted me then, I was able to truly absorb the sanctity and spirituality that pervaded the atmosphere.

DK: Isn't it amazing how far we can go in a short time, once we begin? As you noted, the hardest part about doing a *mitzvah* is being comfortable with it. And isn't learning to be "comfortable" (comfortable with others, comfortable with delayed gratification, comfortable with truth) part of the task of childhood?

SZ: And the task of a convert or *baal teshuvah*? The "doing" makes it part of us. No amount of planning, imagining, or contemplating is as effective in making us comfortable with a *mitzvah* as "doing" it.

DK: The main thing is the action.

SZ: While we were at the Fields', we encountered some new *minhagim*, among them *gebrokts*. Some Jews don't allow matzoh to come in contact with liquids (*gebrokts*), because it might result in some accidental leavening. This *chumrah* [stringency] was one I did not adopt. In other areas, too, sometimes the right path for me, with my situation and my family, was *not* the strictest one.

One thing most converts believe is that they have to be perfect Jews by the day they convert. They are different in this way from *baalei teshuvah*. While a *baal teshuvah* can take on *mitzvos* one at a time, step by step, if the convert refuses even a single *mitzvah*, he or she will not be accepted for conversion.

DK: There's a difference between perfection and acceptance of responsibilities. I'd say, rather, that a *baal teshuvah* ends where a convert begins, namely, with full acceptance of the yoke of *mitzvos*. No one reasonably expects a *baal teshuvah* or a convert to be perfect in the sense that a pot won't, on occasion, accidentally become *treif*. What is expected—and rightfully so—is that a convert has prepared himself or herself so that at the moment of conversion he or she willingly accepts responsibility to fulfill all the *mitzvos*. A *baal teshuvah*, at some point, makes the same decision. This doesn't mean that along the way there won't be detours, roadblocks, and pitfalls.

But, to continue. . . . At the time, did this Pesach have the same transformative or transitional value that some of the earlier ones did?

SZ: It was mostly an inner transformation. I visualized myself as coming out of Egypt. I was still on my way to the *Yam Suf* [Sea of Reeds]. In a way, this Pesach was echoing and portending my own spiritual quest. The waters of the *mikvah* would be my "sea," and the acceptance of the *mitzvos* my affirmation at Sinai.

DK: That's what I thought. And your inner image was most appropriate, for that's how it actually was at Sinai. Now, if only the knowing and the feeling could have been on the same wavelength. . . .

Anyway, what happened after Pesach?

SZ: After Pesach, we started planning for what was still an uncertain future. On Rabbi Field's recommendation, we enrolled David and Julie in Camp Shoresh, a summer day camp in Frederick, Maryland. Staffed by observant Jews and attended by campers of every level of observance, it offered our children the chance to learn without feeling out of place. At the Reform synagogue, they had been among the most religious of their peers. In Baltimore, it was obvious that they would suddenly be at the bottom of that spectrum. We were aware of the self-esteem problems that that might cause, and tried to make every effort to alleviate it. Camp Shoresh looked like a good bet.

We also needed to enroll David and Julie in day schools for the coming school year. I spoke with Rabbi Field about this. Joe and I had learned enough about the schools in the area that we had pretty much settled on Bais Yaakov for Julie and Chofetz Chaim Talmudical Academy for David. My greatest concern was whether the schools would accept our enrollment before the conversions were *fait accompli*. Rabbi Field urged me to go ahead and register them. If there were any problems, he assured me, Rabbi Feldman (the

Av Beis Din) would intercede on our behalf. He emphasized that the schools were heavily attended, so it was important to register as early as possible.

Of course, the process meant having to describe, yet again, the details of my situation.

DK: I suppose that one never gets used to or comfortable with that.

SZ: It's always awkward. Thankfully, the principals—both rabbis—were quite understanding, and, knowing that we were pursuing an appropriate course, did not hesitate to let us continue the enrollment process. The principal at Bais Yaakov, however, made a point of talking about one particular difficulty that we would face when Julie became bat mitzvah. He reiterated what I already knew: At that point Julie would have the freedom to decide whether she wanted to continue to be Jewish. He said that parents often find this to be a very difficult time, and that the school didn't have the resources to deal with trying to resolve the issue, that it had to be a family issue. I wondered why he brought it up, but didn't ask.

DK: Of course, the same applied to David. Maybe he was just sensitive to the issue. Speaking of which, did the children know yet about the conversion?

SZ: No, they still didn't know. Since they were both minors, it didn't have any great affect on what they could or should be doing. We decided to put off the explanation as long as possible.

DK: That must have been an additional burden. Did you ever wonder at some point whether you should tell them? Would it have made any easier the many adjustments they were being asked to make?

SZ: Joe and I talked about it a number of times. In retrospect, I think we did the right thing. Telling them would only have added to the confusion and stress. They were learning to make adjustments in a way that could serve them for the rest of their lives. "We will do this because the Torah says it's right, and that's what Jews should do."

I also wondered, at times, whether someone in our situation could have "faked it"—simply enrolled their children as if they were

Jewish, without explaining anything. The forms made it obvious that, short of lying, such an attempt would likely fail. The forms asked for Hebrew names—not just of the children, but of the parents and even grandparents. The forms stated that if the mother was a convert, then a copy of the conversion certificate must be provided. Whether any of this information is checked out I don't know, but it is asked for. It must be an increasingly sensitive issue in the observant community.

DK: It's an issue that threatens to divide the Jewish people, God forbid. As far back as the 1950s, the danger was recognized even by secularists such as David ben Gurion.

At this point, it had been about a year since you'd discovered the problem. There had been a lot of changes and a lot of progress. But you weren't there yet, in more ways than one. You were still living in Bowie, which meant that you still couldn't complete the conversion.

SZ: No, and I was starting to feel a little discouraged. Then, in the beginning of May 1994, we received some news: Someone had made a very unfavorable offer on our house. I was getting nervous about day schools and camp, not to mention the conversion, so we agreed (though far from enthusiastically) to accept the contract. We had to go to settlement within forty-five days, which meant finding a house in Baltimore very quickly. We finally found an acceptable house that we would be able to move into very quickly. In the end, we concluded the contracts, but the deal cost us tens of thousands of dollars, and we ended up with a smaller and older house.

DK: We've talked a lot about *mesiras nefesh* [self-sacrifice], its importance within the framework of Jewish life and thought. Here you provide a living example. Surely you and your family followed in the footsteps of Abraham, to whom God said, "Get yourself out," and Ruth, who said, "Where you go, I shall go." It's no coincidence that both were converts, that from Abraham descends every Jew and from Ruth's offspring will come *Moshiach*, the descendant of King David.

It took courage and conviction to lose tens of thousands of dollars to become Jewish.

SZ: In my mind, the real hero was Joe. Had I not had his love and support, his self-sacrifice. . . . Like I said, he's a hero.

DK: I agree. In a sense, you had to do all this; he didn't. He did it vol-
untarily—for the reasons you name. The true heroes are usually the
"silent spouses."

SZ: We came very close to a test of *mesiras nefesh* right after settlement. Originally the closing was scheduled for Monday, June 13, but
a last-minute problem forced us to move it up to Friday, June 10. This
was also the *Shabbos* that Mark Powers (of Jews for Judaism) and
his family had invited us to spend with them in Harrisburg, Pennsylvania. Complications in the contract stalled us until early afternoon.
We thought we still had plenty of time. It was only a two-hour drive,
and we were leaving about four hours before candlelighting. Unfortunately, the major freeway between Baltimore and Pennsylvania was
closed in both directions due to a truck accident. The alternative route,
an old two-lane highway that meandered through the countryside, was
one giant traffic jam. We had no choice but to go on. As we neared
Harrisburg, I kept looking from the sun to my watch. Candlelighting
time. Still not there. The minutes took on a frightening significance.
I wondered what we would do if, God forbid, we did not arrive in
time. Thank God, we didn't need to find out. With at most a couple
of minutes to spare, we arrived at the Powers' home. At that moment,
I never wanted to travel on Friday afternoon again.

We needed the relaxing *Shabbos* we got in Harrisburg, where Orthodox life seemed a lot less "intense" than what we had experienced
in Baltimore. Or maybe it was just that we were spending it with
friends, whom I didn't need to explain anything to or hide anything
from. After the week we had just experienced, and with all the exhausting preparation for moving that lay ahead of us, this *Shabbos*
brought an especially welcome and well-needed rest.

Upon returning to Baltimore, we started packing in earnest. When
I was knee-deep in boxes, I received an unexpected call from Gloria,
one of the women who had been in my adult Hebrew class at the
Reform temple. She told me that she and a few other women were
having a group bat mitzvah, and that, since my class had been an important part of inspiring her to learn, she wanted me to come. Gloria
was a very special woman and I was touched that she cared enough

to ask. I didn't give her a definite yes, but said that I would certainly try to come. The truth is, I wasn't sure whether it was permissible for me to go.

I asked Rabbi Field. He considered all the issues and said that, in my particular case, he would advise me to go, even though the bat mitzvah was on a *Shabbos* morning and, of course, held in a Reform synagogue.

DK: When and how to participate in so-called 'life events" of friends and family that aren't celebrated according to Jewish law is always a sensitive subject, and one of the most difficult and painful for *baalei teshuvah* and converts. There's no easy solution, though patience and tolerance from all involved helps. After all, Rabbi Field might not have said the same thing *after* your conversion.

If our principles—the principles of *halacha*—are to mean anything, then we must abide by them most strongly precisely when they are challenged emotionally by those we love. Of course, whenever possible, accommodations should be made by both sides. (Can kosher meals be ordered for an otherwise non-kosher affair?) There may be times, however, when arrangements can't be made. The non-observant should recognize that living according to *halacha* isn't easy and can, in fact, be emotionally difficult. The hurt goes both ways. But if something's the right thing to do, even if loved ones don't agree, all that can be done is to find a way around the pain.

SZ: When the day came, I *davened* early, left Joe home with David and Julie, and walked over to the synagogue. On the way, I mused that it had been about a year since I had last been at the synagogue. In the meantime, the only synagogues we had been to were Orthodox—and there we had spent all the holidays and many a *Shabbos*. I wondered whether the services at the Reform synagogue would be as I remembered them.

I didn't remember very well, I guess, because the whole thing really shook me up. The video camera in the aisle, the organ and guitar and female cantor, the microphones, so many bare heads. So much had changed, but not at the synagogue. It had changed in me. I couldn't see this place as a synagogue anymore.

I watched as Gloria and the other women took turns reading from the Torah. I felt a little sad. I knew that physically they stood very close to the Torah, but in terms of really understanding it and living it, they stood very far away. I also realized that, had some minor events not triggered what they had in my life, I might easily have been a participant in this *Shabbos* affair rather than a spectator. I was happy though, that they were at least reaching out, in the best way they knew how, to make their Jewishness a real and important part of their lives. Sometimes, that is the only opening God needs to bring us back to Him.

DK: As long as the "leaders" don't put obstacles in our way.

SZ: Yet, if we are determined enough, we'll climb over them—or find true leaders. Anyway, I congratulated the women who were celebrating that day, then quietly left before the kiddush in the social hall.

DK: And you went back to completing your move, preparing for a celebration of your own.

SZ: As we were boxing everything for the move, we had to make some decisions about the stuff in the kitchen. Once the conversion was done—which we all expected would happen as soon as we moved—we would have to kasher everything that was kasherable, and dispose of everything that wasn't.

DK: Wasn't your old house already kosher?

SZ: I had learned a lot more about *kashrus* over the last year. I'd been making a lot of mistakes, like thinking that a "K" meant that something was necessarily kosher, or believing that cheese didn't need kosher supervision, or misusing the dishwasher. Adding to that were those questions of responsibility that we talked about before. We really did have to start over in this department.

Since I saw no reason to pay for moving dishes that I couldn't use anyway, I gave almost all of them to a gentile friend whom I knew could use them. We ate off paper the week before we moved. I started looking for new dishes and storage containers and utensils. I wondered whether most folks realized how expensive a conversion can be.

Camp Shoresh began on June 27. Although it was a day camp, the bus left from Baltimore. To make life easier for us, Joe Bondar (our realtor) and his wife, Helaine, had volunteered to let Julie stay with them for the week, and the Fields had offered to take David. We gratefully accepted. Our children left the house that Monday morning for the last time. The next time they came "home," it would be in Baltimore.

June 30 was the long-awaited moving day. It was raining. The movers arrived late in an undersized truck. By now, the glitches seemed normal; it was when things went right that we were surprised.

The movers finished at 2 A.M. on Friday, July 1. The next day, we unpacked the timers and whatever else we needed to get through *Shabbos*. We had invitations for both *Shabbos* meals, so I didn't need to worry about cooking.

` We had a special surprise early Friday afternoon. Norm Friedman, with whom I had corresponded many times on the Internet, knocked on our door to welcome us. He also brought a complete *Shabbos* dinner that he and his wife, Etta, had prepared for us. To say that we were touched is an understatement. Norm was always trying to cheer me up and reassure me that everything would work out; now I know why. He knew that there were folks like him and Etta out there who help *make* the happy endings.

It was a wonderful way to begin our life in Baltimore.

21
Jewish at Last

DK: At long last, everything seemed in place. You'd completed the required study; you were no longer just practicing the *mitzvos*—you were observing and living them; finally, you moved to Baltimore. The conversion must have seemed overdue.

SZ: Indeed. Now that we had moved to Baltimore, I was anxious to get the conversion finalized. Every passing day was difficult. Somehow I had expected to move on Friday and do the conversion on Monday.

DK: After what you'd been through, the feeling certainly seems justified.

SZ: Reality sometimes moves more slowly than our desires. At the beginning of the first full week in July, I spoke with Rabbi Field, who told me that, as far as he was concerned, I was now ready. He asked me to call Rabbi Feldman, the *Av Bais Din*. I met briefly with Rabbi Feldman that Thursday, but he wanted to meet with Joe and me together. We scheduled another appointment on Monday, July 11.

DK: How did you feel?

SZ: I suppose one would expect that at this point I would be ecstatic with the anticipation of finally coming home, but that was not how I felt.

DK: It's hard to say what one should expect in such a situation. I imagine that there would be a number of conflicting emotions: a suppressed ecstasy, certainly, but also a fatigued relief; some insecurity, doubts, and second thoughts; maybe even anger and jealousy on occasion. I suspect that all your emotions would participate. The closer we get to a goal, the harder it is to wait for it, or to believe that it will actually arrive. Ironically, we're often more certain of a far-off objective than one about to be realized.

SZ: You've described it well. Even though there was hope, light at the end of the tunnel, I was not home yet. I wrote about my feelings in my journal that afternoon:

I am in a raging river, unable to reach the other side without help. My teacher stands on the other shore, holding the rope to which I cling. I wait for someone to declare it safe for me to come up there. The bank has been too steep—we must move upstream, further and further. It is so difficult to pretend that everything is OK. The waters churn.

My children wait on the shore from which I came. They cannot cross until I do. Then, I will try to find a quiet current for them, and help hold the rope—but in the end they must cross themselves. They cannot see that I have entered the water. They think that we are all already on the other side, that I crossed already long ago. They do not know of the cold and deep darkness that envelops me. They do not know of my fears, of my tears, which swell this river. I feel like I have deceived them. The waters rise.

My husband waits with the children. He can cross to the other side whenever he chooses. His bridge was built at birth. He knows that I am in the water, but thinking me a strong swimmer, and not knowing the strength of the currents, he does not know how afraid and how tired I am. But he allows me to challenge the water. He sacrificed much to bring me to its shore. This is not water through which he will pass, but I pray that he will join me on the other side. The waters surge.

There are no promises, only hopes. Only an unquenchable desire, need, to reach the other side. And why . . . why go there, from the land of ease and abandon from whence I came, why go to the other side? Why? Why risk everything—sometimes it seems like life itself—just to cross this river?

And in my heart I know there is only one answer: Because that is where the mountain is.

DK: I remember reading this. By the way, have you ever noticed how much images of nature serve as analogies for your feelings?

SZ: Yes, I've always found nature to be a mirror reflecting God's power and awesomeness. To me, the whole universe—with the beat of its pulsing, and motion and power, and the orchestration of the "voices" of beauty and majesty—sings a song that every moment praises God. The important thing is to notice it, to "hear" it.

Nature allows me to express my inner feelings in tangible, physical ways. I try to borrow a little bit of that music of the universe and set my "song" to it.

DK: That's probably the romantic in you. Anyway, what happened when you and Joe met with Rabbi Feldman?

SZ: When we met, Rabbi Feldman again asked about our commitment to observe the *mitzvos* and to see that our children received a Jewish education. He also asked me whether I had received any instruction in the laws of family purity. I told him that Rabbi Field had gone over some of the general concepts and had me read a few books on the subject. Rabbi Feldman didn't seem entirely satisfied with that, and said that it would be important for me to learn with a woman who was knowledgeable in *taharas mishpacha*.

DK: Did you? And did you learn something the books didn't teach you?

SZ: I did. First I turned to a close friend, Belle Libber, and told her that I would be going to the *mikvah* and needed to know some things. Belle gave me as much guidance as she could, and also introduced me to Malka Kaganoff. Malka, the rebbetzin at a nearby *shul*, is the author of *Dear Kallah*, one of the books that Rabbi Field had given me to read. Malka and I got together once a week to learn about *taharas mishpacha* and, later, other topics. I also attended a review class at Etz Chaim. Of course, I learned more than what the books teach. Books are wonderful, but they will never replace learning with a teacher. Teachers answer the student's questions; books answer only the author's questions. Learning with a teacher also reinforces the importance of the *mitzvah* and personalizes it.

DK: I agree with your last statement. Sometimes, though, especially with well-written books, the author's questions and the student's questions coincide.

Was *mikvah* the only part of your preparation Rabbi Feldman wasn't completely satisfied with?

SZ: Rabbi Feldman told us that he normally expects a prospective convert to live in the community for a year before he completes the conversion. When he said that, my heart dropped into my shoes. Fortunately he added that, in our case, he would waive that requirement, since he knew that we had the children in Hebrew school in Baltimore, that I was learning here three times a week, and that we had been spending the *yomim tovim* with families in the community. In a sense, we had moved to Baltimore socially and religiously a long time ago.

DK: Psychologically, too.

SZ: Rabbi Feldman said that he would like to arrange the *mikvah* and David's *bris hatafas dam* quite soon, as he would be leaving for Australia to visit his son soon after Tisha B'Av, which fell on the coming Sunday. He would arrange for the *Bais Din*, and we would try to do everything on Friday, July 15.

I was very excited, and called Rabbi Field right away. Then I sent you this message:

Hi, David!

It has been a long time since we've heard from each other. I thought I'd drop a note to you to let you know how things were going. We moved to Baltimore just over a week ago. We are living on the north edge of the Eruv, about ¾ of a mile from the shul we will be attending.

I met with Rabbi Feldman, who is the head of the Bais Din here, last week. After that he asked that Joe and I come together to meet with him. He said that he would be willing to proceed with the conversion, and wanted to make it before he left for Australia (next week some time). So, if all goes well, and with God's help, I may yet get across this chasm.

Rabbi Field has continued to be wonderfully supportive. He is now not only my teacher, but also my son's tutor. David will, God willing, be entering the Chofetz Chaim Talmudical Academy in the fall, and needless to say, needed some assistance in the Hebrew studies. I think he is doing quite well, given the limited time he has. Both kids are attending day camp in Frederick, MD, at R' Field's suggestion. It is run by frum staff, but the campers are from across the spectrum of observance.

David has begun to wear tzitzis, at his request—though he complains that the tallis koton is sort of scratchy and gets twisted around on him. I'm afraid I can't offer much help in that arena. ;-)

Both kids have prepared a *dvar Torah* for camp (I think it's all part of the color wars). David is passing along a story that Rabbi Field told at a *Shabbos* we spent with them, and Julie is talking about Miriam.

And they both have started to make friends in the neighborhood.

Neither of them knows about the conversion situation yet. I worry about what needs to be said. I asked R' Field for help. He said he hadn't deserted us yet. Still, it will be a difficult step—for all of us.

So, I guess it is a mixture of good news and waiting . . . but you know, it gets no easier. The pain does not ease nor does one become numb. The need to come home, I think, only becomes more intense as one draws nearer to it. The journey continues. After crossing the river, I know I will be faced with the mountain.

I was happy to hear from you. You wrote:

Sue, it was _very_ good to hear from you. You and your family have been on my mind a lot—more so recently. I've been wondering how you're doing, how the conversion has been going, etc. (Needless to say, my life, too, has been somewhat complicated.)

I don't have time to go into a full reply or give you more details right now—hopefully later today. But I did want to just send a short note.

I'm happy that you were able to move and look forward to hearing the good news. I guess this means that _this_ Tisha B'Av you (and your children) will be able to celebrate and join the rest of your fellow Jews in Yerushalayim with Moshiach.

DK: I remember the exchange. I also remember being a little surprised, because I'd thought you'd moved to Baltimore several months before. I hadn't heard from you in a while and didn't know how, or if, your journey had ended.

SZ: "D-Day" had finally come. Joe and I needed to talk to the children now. I had asked Rabbi Field's advice on how we should approach David and Julie. He suggested that we try to keep it "light," that we were dealing not with a disaster, but with a technicality, albeit a very important one. Wednesday, July 13, we waited for the kids to return from camp and called a "family meeting" in our living room.

We don't have family meetings very often, so David and Julie suspected that something was up. I began the discussion.

"You both know that I'm a convert, right? Well, about a year ago I found out that there were some serious problems with the way that conversion was done. In fact, the conversion wasn't kosher, and, halachically, I'm not Jewish. The only way to fix that is to have a kosher conversion. That's why I've been studying with Rabbi Field all this time."

David's first reaction was to laugh. He thought it very funny that I wasn't Jewish. A bit of elaboration on our part silenced the laughter, as he realized this meant that he and Julie would also have to have a conversion. They wanted to know what that was going to mean. We explained that they would need to go to the *mikvah* and be willing to be Jewish. The "being Jewish" part wasn't so difficult; they had never thought of themselves as anything else. Of course, they wanted to know what the *mikvah* was all about. I did the best I could to explain it, having never been to one myself.

David, being his usual self, made some cracks about having given up bacon needlessly, but neither he nor Julie seemed traumatized by the news. We told Julie she could leave, but motioned to David to stay.

"In your case, there's one other thing . . ." Joe began.

"This doesn't have anything to do with circumcision, does it?" David ventured, obviously not thrilled with the prospect.

We explained that he didn't need to go through a real circumcision again, but that the *mohel* would just draw a drop of blood from the area where he was already circumcised. I told him that I had it on good authority (actually, from someone on the Internet) that it was almost painless. David was skeptical, to say the least. He is also a businessman at heart, and immediately decided to sweeten the deal.

"Okay, but you're going to owe me for this one, Mom!" "How much?" "Ten bucks and a trip to the arcade."

We agreed.

The next day I wrote to you again:

We spoke to our children tonight. We tried to keep the discussion from becoming too heavy. We had spoken with R' Field this evening and he gave us some guidance on how to approach things. I think that they took the news pretty well. The conversion is scheduled for Friday afternoon, so, God willing, we will observe this *Shabbos* as Jews. I guess that brings up an interesting question—if I bake challah on Thursday, would I be able to eat it on *Shabbos*? I think a bakery is a simpler answer (it just won't taste as good!).

You mentioned that your life had become complicated. Given recent events, that is certainly understandable. The passing of the Rebbe was a great loss to all Jews, especially, and to the world as a whole. In the rough times that are following, I only hope that everyone would remember that honor comes to our teachers and leaders, not when they fulfill our expectations of them, but when we fulfill their expectations of us. There is still much to do.

Please keep in touch. I see that it has been already over a year since we first started "talking." You have often been a source of encouragement. Thanks.

You were busy, but you got back to me right away:

DK: Mazel tov! (Why don't you ask a Rav about the challah?)

I will point out that you will become Jewish on *Shabbos* Chazon—Parshas Devarim—as Moshe prepares the Jewish people to enter Israel. Motzei *Shabbos* is Tisha B'Av—that this year, God willing, will be a day of rejoicing and celebration. From Tisha B'Av (as the Rebbe says in a sicha) we go directly to the tenth (indicating kedushah) and the eleventh (eleven days from Sinai to Israel), which in turn leads to the fifteenth—a day of great rejoicing, of making marriages—as it says about the rebuilding of the Temple and the coming of Moshiach, that there will be heard the sound of rejoicing and happiness, of groom and bride. Of course, the greatest "marriage" is that between the Jewish people and God—the first part of which occurred at Sinai when the Jews _became_ a people and the consummation of which will take place when Moshiach comes—and Tisha B'Av is appropriate to Moshiach.

On three occasions, all sins are completely forgiven and the person is as a newborn: two of these are at the time of conversion and at the time of marriage.

Why Moshiach had to wait no one can say. But that your conversion is taking place erev *Shabbos* erev Tisha B'Av, when this year we will, God willing, already be in Yerushalayim with Moshiach—is no coincidence, but Divine Providence. (As you know, all Jewish neshamos [souls] must fulfill their Divine mission before Moshiach can come.) Welcome, welcome home.

Mazel tov, mazel tov, mazel tov!

It was nice to be able to share my thoughts with you. Joe had been very quiet throughout this whole process. My sense was that he had been putting up with the entire process of conversion for my sake, not because he particularly thought it was necessary. I knew that I had his love; I wanted his emotional support, I wanted him to show a little excitement. I wanted him to seem happy that it was finally going to happen. But those are not the kinds of things a person can ask for. Either they come, or they don't. I was afraid even to suggest a small celebration for the event. No matter. If I felt that Joe wasn't celebrating with me, then it wouldn't be much of a celebration. A quiet resignation hovered over my anticipation.

Part of the problem might have been that Joe was left out. The rabbis were giving you and the children a lot of attention, but who looked after his feelings or needs? However much your questionable status devastated you, it must also have had an effect on him. You at least could act, could do something to channel your feelings. You had a direction that gave you focus and impetus—a way to deal with it all.

But Joe had nothing to do other than to wrestle with some powerful contradictions. If you weren't Jewish when you two got married, then an important part of the relationship had been based on a false premise. Your move toward observance probably forced him to examine your joint lifestyle, to confront some assumptions and habits (of thought and practice), not to mention to move out of his comfort zone. That's a lot to cope with for the sake of someone else; however willingly he accepted the changes, he was making adjustments for your needs, not his. I would think that, in some ways, that would make it even harder.

And what did he have to celebrate? That his wife had a problem? That his marriage hadn't been kosher? That his children weren't Jewish? That he had to rethink his approach to things and change his lifestyle?

You asked a lot of questions and got a lot of support. Whom could he turn to? Certainly not the same rabbis who were teaching you; how could he ask *his* questions, voice his doubts to them? And, if not them, then whom? In a sense, you were the star of the show, and he didn't even have a walk-on part. He had to wait offstage. He could be there for you, but he couldn't share your experience. That's got to be frustrating.

What was an exciting culmination for you was a disturbing confirmation for him.

SZ: I guess it wasn't easy for either of us. I've realized since then that my situation is not unusual, and a lack of excitement isn't the only difficulty we face. When one partner in a marriage suddenly becomes more religious, the couple may not move at the same pace or even with the same goals. It is easy for us, the religiously motivated spouses, to verbally or mentally criticize our partners, even blame them for not meeting our new expectations. That isn't fair and it isn't right. There has to be a constant recognition that each person is responsible for, and has a right to make, his or her own choices. This is especially true in an area as personal as commitment to God and Torah. What is the biggest mistake made by the religious spouse? Telling one's partner what he or she ought to be doing, rather than letting him decide for himself or herself—particularly in personal matters that do not affect the family.

DK: I agree. What's particularly ironic is that the "religious" spouse would never, it is to be hoped, think of approaching another non-observant Jew with such an attitude. Yet with the one they're closest to, the one they need the most, their spouse . . . .

SZ: On the other hand, practical family issues can be tough. Sometimes it is a fine line between competing values, even in practical things like choosing a school or what constitutes appropriate family entertainment.

DK: And that's where compromise, communication, and an experienced, sympathetic rabbi or *mashpia* become necessary.

SZ: Unfortunately, there isn't much guidance available for couples in this situation. Maybe if there had been, I wouldn't have had to learn so much from my mistakes.

DK: Even if there had been, you'd still have to learn from your mistakes. We all do. But maybe someone should write a book about getting along when there are different levels of observance in the family. The problem applies to parents and children, as well.
But we digress. . . .

SZ: Yes, we were still trying to get to the *mikvah*.
Friday, July 15, 1994. David and Julie stayed home from camp, and we spent a good part of the morning bathing and preparing for the *mikvah*. We were supposed to go at around 11 A.M.
The phone rang. It was Rabbi Feldman. He told me that the *mikvah* was broken. It was being repaired, but it would not be possible to have the conversion as planned. I was crushed, and fought back tears. I asked if there was any possibility that it would be fixed in time, or if there was another *mikvah* we could use. No. It would have to be rescheduled. Sunday was Tisha B'Av. We would try again on Monday. He would call to let me know the time. We had no choice but to wait.
I had hoped to celebrate that *Shabbos* as a Jew. I didn't.

DK: I'm glad I didn't find out until after the fact. The broken *mikvah* was like a final test and a final preparation. "When Av enters, reduce *simcha*," the rabbis tell us. But that's only true until Tisha B'Av.

SZ: Sunday was Tisha B'Av. I joined the congregation at our *shul* for *kinos*. Rabbi Weinreb guided us through a shattering but deeply meaningful service. When I returned home in the afternoon, I wrote the following in my journal:

It is Tisha b'Av, 5754. This may, with Hashem's help and permission, be my last day as a gentile.

It is a day of fasting, of lamenting, a day of tears. Though a wall still divides me from this congregation, as thin as a veil, as transparent as glass, today I sense that my tears seep under that wall. Today I sense that my tears and theirs are joined.

How deep is the pain spoken of in the kinos. How deep the flood of tears. The pain of my own life compared to their pain, like the hunger of this fast compared to their hunger, is a scratch, a pinprick.

Kinos. . . . We recall the tragedies. We recall the horrible deaths of so many without fathomable cause or purpose.

These were the Tzaddikim, these were the righteous. These were the infants who had done no one wrong. These were not Your enemies.

I will never understand, not really.

A cloud blocks our voices from You: We cannot cry out. The Bais Hamikdash is destroyed: We cannot serve nor sacrifice.

If You are angry why do You destroy those who can teach us Your ways?

Only so we should say "Perhaps we should have listened"?

I will never understand, not really.

You promised Avraham Avinu that his progeny would be as numerous as the stars—why did You rip the children from the arms of their parents only to die by the hands of strangers?

I will never understand, not really.

But we will return to You. It cannot be otherwise. Because our love for You exceeds the understanding of circumstance.

But this is the most painful thing of all—to see that our love for You is not returned. If You turn away from us, there is nothing worth living for.

If we cannot hope in You then there is no hope at all.

It is enough. For Your Name's sake, please, please, let us be children in Your arms once again.

Only bring us back to You, Hashem, and we shall return.

DK: It was a hard Tisha B'Av in many ways.

SZ: Monday, the children again stayed home from camp. Again we bathed and prepared. This time I waited for the phone to ring. And waited. . . .

I finally became very concerned. I called Rabbi Feldman and asked whether the conversion was still going to take place that day. He was very surprised. "No one called you? Yes, they're expecting you right now at the *mikvah*!"

We went into emergency mode, grabbed our stuff, and sped over to the *mikvah*, where the attendant was waiting for us. The rabbis on the *Bais Din* had not yet arrived, and we had plenty of time to finish our preparations. Julie and I shared one prep room; David went to another.

I was called in to meet with the *Bais Din* wearing only a robe, a snood, and the paper slippers that the *mikvah* provides. It was a little embarrassing. I didn't know until this point who would be sitting on the *Bais Din* besides Rabbi Mendel Feldman. I was introduced to Rabbi Moshe Rappaport, who also served as the *mohel* for David's *bris hatafas dam* [the ritual drawing of blood], and to the third *dayan*, Rabbi Benjamin Dinovitz, whose shul we had attended on a few occasions during Sukkos and Pesach.

The *dayanim* asked me a number of questions covering my knowledge of both basic Jewish concepts and practical *halacha*, as well as probing my commitment to continue living as an observant Jew. One *dayan* asked me to tell them some of Rambam's thirteen Principles of Faith. If they'd asked me the day before, I probably could have recited them in Hebrew. That day, I had trouble remembering some of them in English. Nerves.

DK: It's to be expected. In my experience, if an individual makes it that far, the *Bais Din* is usually gentle and sympathetic (as well as firm and meticulous).

SZ: I don't want to portray this as a horrible encounter. Quite the opposite. All three rabbis were respectful, kind, and compassionate. My nervousness was not necessary; we all had the same goals.

Afterward, the rabbis called the attendant, who took me down the hall to the *mikvah* room. A translucent sheet floated over the top of most of the *mikvah* to provide modesty. After I was in the water and concealed by the translucent sheet (except for my head), the *Bais Din* would briefly glance in to see me immersed.

I stepped into the water, and a sea split before me. I plunged beneath the surface, rising up to say the most important *brocha* I had ever said in my life. Twice more under, finally standing to *Shehechiyanu*. As I physically ascended the steps out of the water, spiritually I was stepping foot on the other shore of the sea. The waters raged no more. I looked for the mountain. The attendant congratulated me, "*Mazel tov!*"

DK: I've seen the look on the face of a convert. It must be a reflection of what the Jewish people looked like at Mount Sinai. Seeing someone so transformed is like watching him or her being born, but spiritually. Even the observer is transformed, elevated.

SZ: My children went in separately; neither was traumatized in the least. David told me that the *bris* didn't hurt very much, and that he thought the *mikvah* was "cool"—he'd be ready to come back every week!

DK: I've never met him, but I like his attitude.

SZ: Rabbi Feldman filled out the document attesting to our conversion. We all kept the same Hebrew names that we had adopted before. The other rabbis signed.
We were done.

DK: Again, *mazel tov*. The long-shorter way led you home.
Don't you wish you could have held on to that feeling, maintained that moment of transformation?

SZ: Yes, but it fades all too quickly. It is a gift of the moment, to be cherished and remembered, but never relived in quite the same way.
We left the *mikvah* and returned home to an empty house.

DK: Not an empty house. The home of a Jew is never empty, for the presence of God resides there.

SZ: True. God's Presence was home; Joe was still at work. I called Rabbi Field and Mark and Melody to tell them the news. They were all very happy for me. When Joe came home, I told him that we had all gone to the *mikvah* and that David had done fine with the *bris*. We didn't celebrate, though.

DK: Some passages celebrate themselves. Sometimes, a celebration detracts from the significance of an event. At the time, the right response may indeed be silence, a silence that unites, although there's still an impulse toward festivity. Rather than celebrate, perhaps the more appropriate response was, in fact, simply to appreciate and acknowledge.

SZ: Maybe. I waited until the next day to write to several of my friends on the Internet who had come along with me on so much of this journey.

Here is what I wrote to you:

Hi, David! I just wanted to send you a note to let you know that I have finally "come home"!

Yesterday (7/18), on the afternoon of the 10th of Av I appeared before a beis din, my son had a "mini" bris and we all did mikvah. My Hebrew name is Shoshanah.

I have crossed the river. Ahead is the mountain.

At first the rabbi had planned to do the conversion on Friday. We were all ready, but just an hour or two before the time, he called to say that the mikvah was being repaired (and drained) so he was very sorry, but it would have to wait. Tishah b'Av I cried as a gentile. I approach the 15th of Av, in hope, as a Jew.

I have had a lot of friends help along the way. Sometimes people ask what it was that caused me to begin this process, and I tell them, quite honestly, that much of it began because of my conversations over the net, and from the deeply honest (Torah based), and caring answers I received from friends that I have known, really, only over the net.

You and the other folks on the net are very much a part of the community who helped bring me home. Thank you for all you have taught me, for the support you have given me, for letting me be, at last, a part of your family.

May we all merit redemption, *bimheirah b'yameinu.*

—Shoshanah

You wrote back:

Welcome home! I am very, very happy for you. I have been a witness at a number of conversions, but there's something special about this one I was not at. I can imagine how you, Joe and the children feel.

There is much to discuss now—many things I want to ask you. But let it wait.

Shabbos Nachamu—the *Shabbos* of Comfort

Ki b'simcha taytzayun—with joy you shall go forth.

More soon—but mazel tov and siman tov!

Now that I was Jewish, I needed to kasher the kitchen right away. We ate out for a day or two; then Mark and Melody came over with a blowtorch, cans of oven cleaner, and lots of steel wool, and we all set about scrubbing and kashering every last accessible surface and screw in the kitchen. They had both been *mashgichim* [one who supervises the *kashrus* of a company or restaurant] for a *kashrus* organization before, and Mark had once been a kosher caterer. They knew kashering. What we didn't finish that afternoon, I did the next day.

I spent the better part of the following afternoon at the *mikvah kelim* (*mikvah* for dishes) dunking my pots and pans and dishes and trays and silverware and glasses. It was hard and tedious—and I loved every minute. This was a time when every *mitzvah* had a heightened meaning.

Other emotions were heightened, too. Once the intense activity of moving, converting, and kashering settled down to a more normal level of daily life, I began to struggle with deeper feelings that seemed to be rising up from deep within me. I pulled out my journal and wrote.

I've wanted to stop and write down my feelings and finally seem to be getting the chance to do so. It's been almost a month since I became

Jewish. My lack of journal notes isn't because of lack of importance of the event or the feelings around it so much as just not getting around to doing it.

It is said that a person gets a new soul when they convert. Perhaps it was just the influence of knowing that, or perhaps something more: There was a point—I think it was when I first addressed the deficiency of my earlier conversion with an orthodox rabbi and became committed to having a kosher conversion—that I began to be aware of what seemed like a presence, which I perceived as the Jewish soul that I was to bring home. In fact, this "soul" needed me and I needed it. Neither it nor I could perform mitzvot alone. The soul needed embodiment and I needed to be Jewish—to have a Jewish soul. I think that there was a shared pain, a shared frustration, a shared desire to accomplish the task. I felt that the soul was always at hand, hovering as it were, watching me perform the actions that comprise the mitzvot, wanting, but unable, to participate. And, because I was doing them as a non-Jew, the actions were devoid of sanctity, and we both knew it. At the mikvah we were joined. There was a sense of wholeness and completion that enveloped me. "We" had come home. We/I could truly fulfill mitzvot. Happiness and awe come to mind, but the event was really beyond words.

I guess that all sounds very strange, yet it is, in fact, how I perceived the experience. I wonder if that perception is shared by others. . . .

Another feeling I had—still have, to be honest—is a real need to talk about the experience. I felt like I just had the most important event in my life. I needed, if not to celebrate it, at least to talk about it. There were, of course, a few kind "mazel tov's" and some sighs of relief that it finally happened. Still, my husband barely seemed to acknowledge the event, and I never really had a chance to just talk it out with anyone. I guess I feel a little guilty that I haven't been able to take the attitude of "It's done—now it doesn't matter anymore." The fact is, that it does matter to me. I really want to talk out what just happened, maybe just to come to grips with what seems like the enormity of it. Intellectually I understood what I was committing to before I faced the Beis Din, but no amount of learning could prepare me for the emotional impact of conversion. I want so badly to "talk it out." Time—at least a month of it—does not seem to be causing that need to abate. Maybe writing it down will help. . . .

Shortly before I converted, I wrote in this journal how I felt like I was crossing a raging river, that I needed to get to the mountain on the other side. I have crossed that river, and find myself now standing on this most amazing mountain. The objective does not seem to be to reach the top of the mountain—indeed I am not sure there even is one—but ascending it seems to be the important thing. The higher one goes, I think, the further one "sees," the better the perspective on life, on existence, on the meaning of holiness which provides the landscape around and beyond the mountain. I also notice that, like any mountain, it always seems easier to go downhill than to exercise ones potential and climb to new heights. Even standing still is not reasonable, for without new vistas, one wastes away.

So I am on the mountain. I want very much to climb it, but although my learning provided me the knowledge to cross the river, I feel greatly unprepared to climb the mountain. I gaze out from the heights and feel afraid—of falling, perhaps, or maybe just afraid that I have not learned enough to be able to really follow the path markers which will lead me up, and not astray.

So, what am I really saying? I feel like I have so many questions that pop up—some just random questions about things I read in Torah, some practical problems of living, some involving personal/family relationships that are affected, some halachic, some involving perspective and emotions. I don't know who to ask, or whether it is fair or reasonable to impose on anyone to spend their limited time helping me deal with some of those questions. I feel uncomfortable asking those who have already invested so much in getting me across the river, to help me climb the mountain, and the process of reaching out, trusting, has always been a difficult one for me. My response is simply to withdraw, to not ask anything, to pretend, as it were, that I know the path, when, in fact, at times I feel quite lost.

Maybe it is because I felt compelled to move quickly into a religious lifestyle. Conversion seemed to demand it—I did not sense that I had the luxury of time to move more slowly, as most BT's are encouraged to do—and I have no regrets for having done so. Still, I feel at times that I want to shout out to anyone who will hear "Help! I'm still new here and trying to learn my way. Don't leave me alone!" Community is desperately important to me. Sometimes I wonder, in such a big shul as we joined, if newcomers don't have a harder time getting situated.

Even trying to reach out has its limitations.

We've started inviting folks over for *Shabbos*. I had enough of being alone in our old neighborhood where there was no (religious) Jewish community. Here, since we weren't invited out, I have had the opportunity to invite others to us, and our Shabbatot have certainly been the better for it. So what's the problem? Well, we seem to be part of a very mixed congregation, some very religious, some more "modern." I think it is important to reach out for friends who will influence us in the direction of more Yiddishkeit. I'd really like to be able to get to know some of the more religious families, even have them over for *Shabbos*, but am afraid to pursue the idea because as "neophytes" we aren't really able to "do *Shabbos*" as ideally as some—with *zemiros* and *dvar Torah* and all. We still feel kind of awkward and new at this. I worry that this fact would end up taking away from our guests' *Shabbos* rather than enhancing it. I wish I could count on them understanding the situation and knowing that we would welcome guests bringing their traditions into our home. My worry is that most folks would likely not "interfere" with the hosts—put up with remaining on our "level" and end up losing more than they would gain by being our guests. I wouldn't want to spoil anyone's *Shabbos*.

Of course that assumes the first step, that I can manage to get to know more frum folks. I sympathize with the difficulties our children will have making new friends at school. It's hard for us adults, too.

My thoughts wander. . . . I was imagining earlier today how I felt.

Once I was a small creature who knew that the ability to fly must be a wonderful thing. When one rabbi taught me to ride on the wings of airplanes, I really thought I could fly. It was effortless, and I thought I had the view and perspective. No one questioned me when I told them I could fly. Then I saw that some flew without riding on the wings of airplanes. At first I objected that such flight was a terrible idea—look how hard they had to work just to fly. Then I began to sense my own loss of freedom in flight. I could not go wherever I wanted. I could not soar to new heights even if I wanted to. I wondered whether "I" could really fly. So, I went to another, more learned, rabbi and told him my story.

"No," he said, "you cannot fly. Your soul has no wings."

And I knew then that, more than anything, I wanted a soul with wings. I was willing to trade the ease of false flight for the effort and freedom of true flight. I asked the rabbi to help me get a soul with wings. And he taught me what I would need to know to be able to fly, and when I finally emerged from the mikvah, I had a new soul with wings. And I took to flight, and thrilled in the joyous freedom.

But, now that my soul has wings, I need to understand where it is that I am supposed to fly. . . . How do I use these wings to serve Hashem?

DK: A powerful outpouring of feelings. I'd like to let it stand on its own, and take up the issues later. I will point out, though, that the confusion and ecstasy are both precious and normal. After a victory, after investing all—including one's essence—to win, there's a natural letdown, an obvious what-do-I-do-now sensation.

SZ: There was still one more matter with which we needed to deal: *chuppah*. Joe and I were required to physically separate for 90 days and then have a kosher marriage. The long wait has to do with eliminating doubt as to the status of any child that might be born after the conversion.

DK: It does. There's also the technicality that a Jewish marriage can take place only between Jews. Now that you were a Jew, you couldn't very well be observant and live with someone without being married.

SZ: This took us through all the High Holidays. We went to services at Shomrei Emunah, which we had joined soon after my conversion. I had already met with Rabbi Weinreb to meet him and to apprise him of our situation. It presented no problems.

We put up our own *sukkah* for the first time that year. Joe's folks came down to be with us. It was a very special season.

When the prescribed separation was over, Rabbi Weinreb arranged for us to have a small *chuppah* at the *shul*. He said he would take care of everything, including making sure that there was a *minyan*.

As it turned out, he had called a couple of very special people to be part of the *minyan*: Rabbi Field and Rabbi Porter. I was very happy to have them there. Rabbi Field was one of the witnesses; the other was Rabbi Larry Ziffer—in "real life" our sons were in the same carpool. We already knew most of the other folks there, but a few we met that night. Julie brought a bouquet of flowers—she'd always wanted to be a flower girl. David just took it all in. The ceremony went quickly. I basically did whatever the rabbi said. Joe gave me a ring. The men sang something while we were under the *chuppah*. Afterward, Joe and I spent some time in private in the *shul* office before coming out and sharing cake and whiskey with our "guests."

My life was now back together, as much as it could be, and I could go on living it.

22
Questions and Afterthoughts

DK: We've spent a lot of time talking about your past—your thoughts and feelings and experiences. Discussing and analyzing (maybe sometimes overanalyzing) your journey home has, as the saying goes, been a pleasure and a privilege.

But becoming a Jew is only the start. In a sense, converting is the easy part. Torah and *mitzvos* are known quantities, so to speak: What to do and how to do it are clearly laid out in *halacha*. If we don't know the answer or can't find it in the *Shulchan Aruch*, well, that's what rabbis are for—to answer the what and how questions.

Your history, while singular, isn't unique; you're not the first to travel from another religion's fundamentalism to a life of Jewish observance. It's a natural progression, for the impulse that got you started—an irresistible spiritual demand from some inner self—almost automatically led you to a life of Torah and *mitzvos*. As we've discussed, the Torah is God's wisdom, and *mitzvos* are the garments of the soul; thus, our Godly soul expresses itself through Torah and *mitzvos*.

Being observant, though, doesn't mean that the questions, the doubts, and the searching end. Too often, *baalei teshuvah*, converts, and even the "*frum*-from-birth" think that. You'd found truth; but that's intellectual and theological. What of *simcha*—joy?

SZ: Serving God with joy is still a goal for me, something that I have yet to fully achieve. Is this where I should be saying, ". . . and she lived happily ever after"?

DK: Stories end with "and they lived happily ever after" because there's no more story. The wedding closes the plot. But lives go on; there's always another story. The "happily" comes from the hard work— "serving God with joy." Let's just talk about the "ever after."

SZ: Okay, but you should know that talking about "ever after" isn't always easy. Over the last couple of years, I've had many opportunities to talk or correspond by e-mail with many other converts and *baalei teshuvah*. Conversing amongst ourselves, we—the "newly observant"—often share thoughts, fears, and experiences that aren't normally discussed openly, because we are either embarrassed to have such thoughts, or are uncomfortable relating them. I'd like to talk about some of them, but please bear in mind that I'm presenting them not as valid difficulties (they often result from misperceptions on the part of the newly observant), but as typical areas of struggle. Certainly not every newly religious Jew experiences all of these challenges, but they are real, and not uncommon.

DK: Before we get into the details, I want to make a few comments on what you've said already. First, as we both know, e-mail provides a means of "communication without embarrassment" previously unavailable. That's an important observation, because it has allowed you and other newly observant to talk "amongst yourselves." I've found that one of the biggest—if not *the* biggest—barriers to spiritual growth is embarrassment. (It's not a new thought; it's found in *Pirkei Avos*.)

Second, what's a "valid difficulty" if not an "area of struggle"? But I think you mean that the insecurities and self-consciousness that accompany adjustment and growth don't excuse one from observance—and that the "newly observant" with those feelings continue to observe even as they struggle with feelings and thoughts. Of course, so do the "oldly" observant. It's the fate of the "average Jew" who doesn't qualify as a *tzaddik*.

Third, I want to emphasize something I tell my students: If you've got a question, at least two others have the same one, and three more don't even realize that the question was bothering them. So ask. It's important to realize that while the *experience* of thoughts, fears, and so on is unique, the thoughts and fears themselves probably aren't. Even the "*frum*-from-birth" aren't immune to the *yetzer hara*.

This is a good place to discuss some of the unexpected difficulties and controversies that are part of living "(happily) ever after."

Okay, on to the challenges.

SZ: To begin with, there is a sort of childish belief that "since I've tried to do everything right, God should give me a break: Life should go on without a hitch, and I should get some kind of reward for being so 'good.'" Ah, but life isn't perfect, and then we feel a little betrayed. Part of this feeling stems from an innocent, though perhaps uninformed, belief that because God will reward those who follow His *mitzvos* and punish those who don't, *teshuvah* should bring not only forgiveness, but also its own little "Garden of Eden." Obviously, it isn't so. We have to acknowledge the tarnish on our pristine and naive image of what being Jewish is all about.

DK: I don't know that the image is tarnished. God does reward those who observe the *mitzvos* and punish those who don't (assuming that their lack of observance comes from willful disobedience rather than ignorance); that's a fundamental principle of Jewish faith. *Teshuvah* does bring its own little "Garden of Eden." However, neither concept automatically leads to an end of our struggles. Unless one is a *tzaddik*, there's still a *yetzer hara* to contend with. As the Alter Rebbe explains in *Tanya*, that's the critical difference between a *tzaddik* and a *benoni* [an "average" Jew]: They both "do the right thing," but the *benoni* still has to struggle with his *yetzer hara*.

More than this, there's a transformative value to the struggle. Conquering one obstacle, elevating one aspect of one's corner of the world, still leaves another spot that needs to be prepared, transformed into a dwelling place for Godliness.

The realization that "getting there" actually means more struggle, albeit of a different, more satisfying or meaningful nature, can be a bit overwhelming. Observing the *mitzvos* doesn't make life easier, just more significant.

But I think what you mean by "God should give me a break" is that trying hard should count just as much as doing it. I used to tell my students—actually, I still do—that while I appreciate the effort they put into an essay, for example, and while I'm willing to help them as much as possible during the process of writing it, I can grade them only on the final result. After all, people have different talents and skills; one person can do in an hour what another requires ten to accomplish (if the other can do it at all).

Of course, God can grade effort, but he didn't put souls in bodies and create a physical environment to "grade" us on effort. If the world itself is truly to be a dwelling place for Godliness, the job has to get done. You don't get paid for trying to build a house; the house has to be built in a literal, physical sense. The same is true of a *mitzvah*, following *halacha*, living as a Jew according to Torah: It's got to be done, and done right.

SZ: I see what you're saying. Becoming observant gives us the skills and the tools to do the job that God sets before us. It doesn't release us from the responsibility to do the work; if anything, it strips us of our excuses. It is like that in our work world, too. When the boss promotes you for doing a good job, it is so that you can take on a position of even more responsibility, not so that you can sit back and do nothing.

Some *baalei teshuvah* think that once one grasps Torah, there should be an unambiguous right-or-wrong answer to every question that life raises. Then we encounter what seems like three answers for every question, and wonder. . . .

DK: Objectively—that is, from God's perspective—there *is* an unambiguous right-or-wrong answer. We tend to forget that often the questions themselves are life-specific, that is, particular to an individual's environment, background, feelings, intellectual ability, and the like. Thus, if the same question seems to have two different answers, it's really not the same question. Of course, the questions may be in the same category (an issue of *kashrus*, for example), but there's enough circumstantial variation to require a different halachic response.

This "phenomenon" is quite common in law, which is why law codes and records of judicial decisions are so thick; often enough, a legal or evidentiary difference requires a new or at least modified ruling.

Let me give you an example. Can you eat rice on Pesach? As you probably know, that depends. If you're Ashkenazi (your family came from Europe), no; if you're Sephardi (your family came from North Africa or the Middle East), yes. It's a contradiction, but only an apparent one: The answer depends on the bread-making process and the use of grains (which, in turn, speaks to the issue of *chametz*). So the question whether you can eat rice on Pesach isn't really a question—or, at least, a complete question. It should be something like: Can an Ashkenazi eat rice on Pesach, and, if not, what is the source of the *minhag* [custom]?

Sometimes we expect a hard-and-fast rule for every situation. True, there are some: Don't start a fire on *Shabbos*, except to save a life. (As you can see, even the hard-and-fast rule has a not-so-hard-and-fast exception.)

SZ: And the answer also depends on which rabbi one asks (even the same person and the same situation). That is especially disconcerting, I think. We've been nurtured along, been told how critical Oral Torah is to our understanding of the smallest of details, then find that this rabbi says, for instance, *cholov Yisroel* is mandatory, while a respected *kashrus* organization certifies non-*cholov-Yisroel* products. Suddenly, the "small details" begin to seem quite arbitrary.

DK: It helps, I think, that *halacha*, as a system of ethics, law, and behavior, defines a relationship—that between the Jewish people and God—and that a relationship, by its nature, is dynamic and therefore a little "ambiguous"—not in the sense of unclear, disordered, or confused, but in the sense of being unlimited and boundless, vigorous, energetic: alive. So *halacha* sets borders within which our love and fear of God can be experienced and their infinite possibilities expressed.

Halacha suffers from two misperceptions (sometimes officially sponsored): one, that it is something dead, unresponsive, regressive, and repressive; two, that it is no more than legal acrobatics and can—or should—be twisted to fit the times or at least pushed to the limits of what people want (a leniency for every cause, as someone I knew often said, only half-joking). Both misperceptions lead one to think that *halacha* is indeed arbitrary.

However, *halacha* is simply the practical expression of the relationship between God and the Jewish people. As I said before, a relationship has vitality *and* rules (rituals). In a dynamic relationship, the
same rules sometimes will result in variations, depending on the circumstances to which they must be applied.

SZ: Finding our place within those borders takes a while. There can be
a bit of trial and error before we get "settled in." Community plays a
big role in the adjustment. Then, too, as a person settles in with a given
rabbi or two of whom he or she asks questions, the confusion abates.
Of course, there are also limits to questions.

It came almost as a surprise to me that I could not take *any* question to my local *Rav* and find a clear and definite answer to it. I thought
that Torah had all the answers and that my rabbi ought to be able to
plumb its depths to find them. What I found was that even "technical" questions ("Can I kasher this fork?") often had shades of differences, and the tougher questions, like "How do I inspire my children
to love Torah?" may have resulted in guidance, but seldom brought
concrete answers, specific steps, and an agenda straight from Torah.

There were, and are, times that I just give up, figuring, "Why ask?"
particularly with questions that require more than just a technical
answer.

DK: Rather than just give up, why not just put them on hold? Not every question requires an immediate answer, nor do we immediately
comprehend every answer. You might even change your question
from "Why ask?" to "Why ask now?"

Also, the Torah isn't meant to do your job for you. Inspiring your
children to love Torah, for instance, is your task. Torah does provide
the guidelines, but the concrete answers, the specific steps, depend
on the individuals involved—and are your responsibility.

SZ: It's part of *my* job, not the rabbi's, right?

DK: Obviously (though we sometimes don't see—or want to see—the
obvious).

SZ: Sometimes I worry about asking too many questions. While I may
know that I don't have the answers I need in certain circumstances, I

seldom feel that my question is important enough to justify imposing on the rabbi's time. I look to our congregational rabbi to be my
posek [halachic decisor]. Of course, so do a few hundred other families . . . and he has a lot of communal obligations, and classes to teach,
and so on. So, unless my question is really a "crisis question" or can
be answered in twenty-five words or less, then I just assume that I
shouldn't be asking it. I feel like I'm being a bother. Even if I do meet
with the rabbi, I'm so hesitant to take up his time that I seldom ven-
ture to go into depth on anything, and consequently the questions that
I needed and intended to ask are neither asked nor answered.

DK: And that's why there are friends, counselors, and so on. I can't
give you one of those hard-and-fast rules here. (I don't think you really want one, anyway.) Part of the solution may be recognizing our
limits. Not every question we have needs to be asked; if we ask it, it
may not need an answer.

SZ: Which questions should be asked? The *baal teshuvah* is also fighting a lack of practical knowledge, and does not have a "feel" for things
that others might take for granted.

DK: The practical questions you have to ask. The philosophical-
theoretical ones can wait until there's a *farbrengen*, a *melave malka*,
or a spare half-hour. And these don't necessarily require the rabbi.

SZ: And the numerous "quickie questions"? I had questions literally
every day, but how could I bother the rabbi every day?

DK: In my experience, it's only a bother when it's the same question
over and over. A competent rabbi isn't bothered even when the question seems to be of the you-should-know-the-answer type, if in fact
the questioner honestly doesn't know.

   As a friend says, in order to be a rabbi, one is tested in four sections of the *Shulchan Aruch*. There's a fifth section one should know,
however, namely, the rules of common sense. A major portion of those
deal with patience.

   Having decided to convert or become observant means learning
as you go. That's true of any commitment. Of course, the difficulties, obstacles, and questions can be frustrating, but they're part of

"growing up." You're describing the experience of, "According to the effort is the reward."

The quote is from *Pirkei Avos*. Actually, it's "According to the pain (or painstaking effort) is the reward." The now-cliched "No pain, no gain" actually matches the Hebrew rhythm pretty well (*l'fum tzara agra*).

SZ: It's odd how sometimes I've thought I was asking a simple, unimportant question and the answer turned out to be quite complex. Other times I was sure my question was of shattering significance and it turned out to be almost nothing when viewed from a slightly different perspective. Sometimes casual conversations with observant friends lead me to re-evaluate whether or not a question needs to be asked. They try to look out for me.

DK: I know what you're talking about. We all experience it, as both children and adults; we just don't always expect it as adults. Still, the observant community has a responsibility to give reassurance and continued support to *baalei teshuvah* (but not to be a "welfare state"). It's also hard for others to "guess" how much you know and where you need help. After a while, those "already there" may assume that you're there, too, unless you ask. Those who helped get you there— or wherever you currently are—may think that you don't, or shouldn't, need as much support as you feel you ought to have. Sometimes we want nurturing; sometimes we desire it but don't need it.

SZ: Another fear I've encountered among a few *baalei teshuvah* is that, after reaching a certain point, they will be abandoned.

There is a sort of excitement and enthusiasm that accompanies a *kiruv* effort. Everyone seems eager to get a Jew to the point where he or she accepts observant Judaism, but afterwards the relationship can drop off dramatically. Sometimes this is because the *kiruv* worker makes the "uncommitted" his or her priority, and lacks the time or resources to continue relationships with those who have already "arrived." Sometimes it is simply because the *baal teshuvah*'s questions become more infrequent and she doesn't feel that she has a "reason" to make demands on the other person's time. Either way, there is a real risk here.

In the process of becoming religiously committed, the person has probably worked very closely with one or two teachers (who may or may not be rabbis) and developed a relationship of tremendous trust. Part of that trust is based on a belief that the teacher really cares about her. If, now that she has "arrived," the relationship suddenly disappears, then there is a temptation to wonder whether she was just another "feather" in the teacher's "*kiruv* cap," and to wonder why the *kiruv* worker *really* was concerned; to wonder whether she was important as a person or only as a statistic.

Remember that piece where I described the raging river? What I'm saying here is that once the guide has pulled his charge out of the river, he cannot assume that everything will be all right. He needs to make sure that he has some help climbing that mountain. It probably doesn't need to be much: just a plan to meet occasionally to check up on progress and to deal with any unasked questions or unresolved difficulties. Not only does it encourage the student, but it keeps that relationship of trust intact.

DK: I agree that the contact has to be maintained. Of course, the extent depends on the individuals and the circumstances. If the person moves (to be in a bigger Jewish community, for a job, because of graduation), it's harder to keep in touch, but it can and should be done. Then, too, the need, at least for a certain type of reassurance, sometimes diminishes.

You've touched on a real problem, one that is really a philosophical divide in the frum community. For many *kiruv* workers, as you've pointed out, the newly observant is just a brownie point or statistic. In this regard, the term *kiruv* bothers me (and many others who are professional "lamplighters"). The word *kiruv* means "close," and implies that Jews who aren't observant need to be brought close to God and Torah, implying that they aren't close already. That's simply not true, and the attitude behind it can become condescending and the opposite of *Ahavas Yisroel*. ("I'm at the center and bringing you close.") No Jew is far from Torah or from God.

(The term "outreach" seems preferable, if only because it implies that the lamplighter must do the reaching, that it's the job of the teacher to seek out and light the soul of the student. The Lubavitcher Rebbe has emphasized the dictum that, "every Jew is as full of *mitzvos* as a pomegranate is full of seeds." If so, how can a Jew be far? Such an approach fosters an appreciation of the responsibility that comes with helping and educating another.)

It also seems to me that if the relationship is genuine, that if the student is more than just another point to be scored, then the continued contact will happen rather automatically. We consider those who have spent Friday night with us as friends, even family. But the exigencies of life often dictate the frequency (and content) of communication over the years.

Certainly, given the depth and intensity of the relationship, becoming Jewishly independent, so to speak, can generate the same kind of separation anxiety that any maturation brings. That's different, though, than being abandoned.

SZ: I think that many *baalei teshuvah* see their mentors as spiritual parents. It's crucial that the communication between us and our teachers remain open. I remember that in December 1994, several months after we had moved and the conversion had been completed, I was struggling and needed the insights of a teacher and mentor. I addressed the following note to Rabbi Field, knowing that he always kept the door open for me to come to him. I wrote:

I know I was going to call you this evening, but instead, I hope you'll have a chance to read this. Then, hopefully we will be able to talk at some point when it works out. The issues aren't urgent, but they are emotionally intense. It isn't something I can deal with on the phone, especially with other ears possibly listening in. I think you'll understand why.

. . .

So here I am again. More concerns, more questions. Some new things, some old. I hope you will understand if I need to go back to settle some things that we've already talked about, but still, for whatever reason, I have not been able to really resolve. I deeply appreciate—I hope you realize how much—the fact that I can come to you with thoughts like these.

I remember back to when we spent the afternoon talking in front of your house, when you patiently talked with me, getting me to pull down the wall of pretense that I had built and be honest with you with who I was— and was not.

I remember when you said you'd sponsor my conversion, and said that I would need to trust you. I resolved at that point that I would, and have never regretted doing so.

I remember when you, on a couple of occasions, gently pushed and pulled at the walls I put up to protect my emotions, until they were broken down, and we were able to get to the heart of the matter. I remember the box of tissues you brought out.

I need your help again.

I don't know if I could manage to say what needs to be said if I just come at this cold and in person. I am afraid that I would build walls again and not get to the point. The reason I wanted to write this letter was to keep that from happening—or at least to make it obvious to both of us if I try.

These are hard thoughts, emotions—I don't really know what to call them—to deal with. When they surface I feel sadness and fear and guilt and confusion and helplessness. I don't know how to overcome them to make peace with them or even to understand them, so I just shove them back down and try to ignore them. Like a balloon submerged under water, though, the deeper I try to bury them, the greater the force with which they suddenly emerge when I momentarily lose my grip on them.

Somehow I need to face these issues, deal with them, and learn to live with them.

[Deep breath]

OK. We spoke the other day about making a shiva call. I really wanted to go. I called our shul to try to find out where they were sitting shiva, but they didn't know. I called a couple of friends but they weren't home. Maybe it was the delay.

I lost control of the balloon.

I found myself crying. First I figured that I was just empathizing with the loss that the family felt—imagining that it had been my mother and husband involved in the accident. And that was certainly part of it. But there was more. . . . I couldn't get a grasp on it. . . . The balloon was rising. . . .

I began to understand that there were more selfish feelings involved in these tears.

There are tears in my eyes as I write this, because I am angry at myself, and ashamed of these feelings, and I want to put up a wall and deny them—but I can't.

I realized that, at some level, I envied this woman, because she *could* sit shiva for her mother. Not, of course for the tragic loss, but for the fact that she had, in such a desperately difficult time, a way to know the support of her friends and community.

Had it been *me* and *my* mother . . . or, God forbid, even one of my children . . . because I am a convert. . . .

. . . and I began to think about it, and then found myself facing the deeper feelings: The balloon had surfaced.

I have to tell you that everything inside of me seems to be fighting saying what I know I have to say. I don't want to write it out. I don't want to admit it to anyone, even you, even me. Please forgive me if I struggle with the words—I am struggling with the emotions. I have to sacrifice finesse for honesty.

I feel resentful:
  —toward the rabbi who did the earlier "conversion," as much as I have tried to forgive him, I evidently have not succeeded in doing so. . . .
  —toward what seems to be the harshness of halacha in forcing me to deny the ties of family, of parents and sibling and even children, that are still part of my life. I am confused by the division that halacha puts between us and the love that binds us.
  —toward myself, for having not listened 20 years ago when there were hints that something was not quite right. I have never told you or anyone else this before, but I want to get it out. Two things happened: One, the rabbi told me that the swim suit I was wearing was "too much"(he didn't go into detail) and that it would be a good idea for me to get in touch with the rabbi in Seattle (he was Chabad, I think) who had visited our synagogue recently with some of his bachurim, and re-do the mikvah. In the end, I was too shy to do it. The second "hint," a girlfriend told me about a novel she was reading where it described a woman getting ready for a mikvah, with washing and combing all over etc. She asked me if that was how I had to do it. Rather than ask about it, I just assured her that that wasn't what the rabbi had had us do. Maybe the mikvah wouldn't have made the difference, but it likely would have put me in contact with someone who *would* have told me what I was getting into. *Why was I so stupid?*

I feel guilty:
  —for (*I don't want to say this* . . . *God help me*) having made the decision to become frum. *How can I feel that something was absolutely the right thing to do, and still feel guilty about it?* I keep thinking—even

though I know it's not right—that if I'd just been content to be a nice quiet member of the conservative synagogue that none of these conflicts would have come up. Everybody'd always have been Jewish (for all we knew) and I wouldn't have to feel guilty—

—for the fact that even my husband is affected by what I have done, or failed to do in the past. Not only have my mistakes caused me to lose a very precious connection to my children, they have caused him to lose it also. Sometimes I feel like what I have done is like murder. I have caused a great wrong that I cannot, no one can, rectify. I cannot pay back or put back nor replace. Joe and I have never talked about this. I am afraid to talk to him. And that makes me feel guilty . . .

—because I can't talk to him about it . . . but you and I have been through the communication issue before (and I feel guilty that I haven't succeeded in dealing with that either—I feel like I've let you down somehow, too, for my failure there).

I feel guilty:

—because I have also caused my children to lose that connection. I hope it won't be for a great many years, but how will they feel when, having lost a parent, they cannot sit shiva?

—because I let my emotions overpower me and keep me from making a shiva call that I wanted to make—because I knew that I would end up in tears—being a burden rather than a strength for the bereaved—and in that I feel guilty—

—because I realize that this is only self-pity and I am wrong to even be having any of these feelings. But I do, and I don't know how to get them to go away.

I find myself wondering: "Are all of these things punishment for my failure 20 years ago?—or just facts of life, the way it is, too bad, so sad."

I don't know what to make of these feelings. Maybe there are even more, deeper ones I've hidden. I just know that I needed to bring them up. I need to confront them. I need to find healing.

I'm scared.

I no longer really know for sure where questions of religion end, and emotions begin.

That's why I needed a friend I could trust on both a personal and religious level.

Thank you for being there.

I sent a copy of the letter to you, too. I needed a lot of help just then. I needed to reach out to those whom I'd grown to trust.

DK: I remember the letter. It had a strong effect, then as now. I'd like to expand on the reply I sent you.

Deep emotions, "hard feelings," by their nature seem too chaotic for words. The very force of what we want to express makes us inarticulate, fearful, and helpless. A lot of preliminary rambling, hemming-and-hawing, and stage-setting is really just a way of focusing ourselves, so we can communicate and deal with feelings that seem overwhelming and inexpressible.

Your long introduction (until the parenthetical "deep breath") strikes me as just that sort of energy-gathering chatter. Perhaps, I should say, energy-releasing, for I get the impression that you had too much; you had to get rid of that excess emotional energy before you could confront, concentrate on, or even identify, the real issues.

Earlier I told the story in which the Alter Rebbe declared that we should never be too busy to hear the cry of a child. We need to remember that every Jew is in some way a child. However, the *baal teshuva* and the convert have a special cry, for while they are adults in many ways (and need to act as such), they still need to be comforted as if they were children.

As to the content of the letter, I remember remonstrating with you about the *shiva* issue, because there are ways a convert should mourn a parent. (I may have even recommended that you look at Lamm's *The Jewish Way in Death and Mourning*, which discusses this issue.) You talked about *chumras* (stringencies) earlier. It seems to me that precisely in an area such as this, the newly observant or newly Jewish need to understand—or be taught—that while there are certain formal restrictions, it's not only acceptable, but proper, that they also mourn.

Your reaction to the request to make a *shiva* call—an imaginative hurricane—came from your situation as much as anything else. As a new member of the community (both spiritually and physically), you didn't yet have that support system. So you imagined yourself in the same position, but without the support. It was your newness more than your "status" that affected you.

Now, how do we deal with your resentments and guilt? Although quite natural, they reveal a basic misconception we have toward any transformative experience. I refer to what someone has surely called the "happily-ever-after" syndrome. By that I mean the tendency to project a utopic vision into the "afterward." After I get married, after I get that job, even after I become observant or Jewish, things will be perfect.

But we can't just walk away from our past, who we were (unless we're *tzaddikim* or prophets). Nor do the external problems or difficulties disappear. What changes is our perspective and their importance. But they still have to be dealt with; the bills have to get paid, so to speak. Our inner transformation, though, should—among other things—prioritize our thoughts, feelings, and actions: Not only what we put ourselves into, but how we do it, should be different.

Does this mean it's wrong to have conflicts, to be confused (or, as in your case, to be resentful and guilty)? I don't see how feelings in and of themselves can be wrong. They spring from our "natural soul"; it's like saying it's wrong not to like chocolate ice cream. The word doesn't fit. Maybe it's better to say that feelings can be inappropriate. A feeling can be disproportionate to its stimulus; it can disorient us; it can dislocate our thoughts and disconnect us from others. In these and a myriad ways, a feeling can be inappropriate. But we deal with the inappropriate differently than we deal with what's wrong. If something's wrong, it needs to be fixed. Something inappropriate needs to be moved.

In this case, I don't think your resentment is wrong in the sense that it needed to be denied or destroyed. It was simply misplaced: What did you do with the resentment (or guilt)? Did you allow the feeling to overwhelm you? Did you indulge it? Did the resentment control you? Or did it become a tool for self-improvement, for increasing your observance, for reaching out to others?

We can say I resent this and will hold the resentment dear; I feel guilty and am therefore paralyzed. Or we can say, I resent this and will learn from it and prevent it from happening again; I feel guilty and will do *teshuvah*.

In other words, what can be wrong is how we respond to the feeling. There's a simple test: Is the feeling in charge? Have we exchanged responsibilities for whims? Are we indulging our animal soul when we should be reining it in, redirecting it?

Having said all that, I want to look more closely at each of your "I feel resentful toward . . ." and "I feel guilty for (because) . . ." statements.

You said, "I feel resentful toward the rabbi who did the earlier 'conversion,' as much as I have tried to forgive him, I evidently have not succeeded in doing so. . . ." It's hard to argue with such resentment. It would seem that you have a right to feel he should have at least told you about all the options, informed you of the different "standards" for and responses to conversion.

Certainly, anyone who accepts a position of leadership must also accept the responsibility for any guidance—or misguidance—given. Yet did he know he was doing anything wrong? That has some bearing on whether you should forgive him—and whether you *can* forgive him. He may have been uneasy about something, because he did tell you to go to the *mikvah* in Seattle as a precaution.

Still, we can always play the "what if" game: What if he had presented the options, shared his misgivings? Would you have responded "appropriately"? Or would you have taken what you could get at the time? These questions bring me back to the issue of *hashgocha pratis*—Divine Providence—and something we've discussed before. If, as Chassidus teaches, the soul of a convert is a Jewish soul that got lost, then in a sense you had to make your journey home the way you did.

I suspect that your resentment toward that rabbi is really just an expression of the resentment toward yourself "for having not listened 20 years ago when there were hints that something was not quite right." You remark that, despite two significant hints (one from the rabbi, the other from a friend who was reading a novel), you were "stupid." But in our discussions, you've defended your "younger self," excusing decisions because they were made with the best knowledge available at the time. You've constantly asked me, how one knows whom to trust and what to do without the proper kosher environment.

I've pointed out that, in fact, without the proper education and environment, a person is like a "kidnapped child." That doesn't excuse mistakes and other wrongdoings; it does, however, obviate the "what if" game. Should you have taken the hints? Probably. Were you emotionally ready to do so? Obviously not.

Let me put it another way: Had you not lived your life, undergone all the experiences you had, you would not be able to do what you're doing now, helping others as you do, observing *mitzvos*, and so on.

There's a big difference between regret, which is part of *teshuvah*, and resentment, which precedes revenge.

This brings me to your final "resentment," toward "what seems to be the harshness of *halacha* in forcing me to deny the ties of family, of parents and sibling and even children, that are still part of my life. I am confused by the division that *halacha* puts between us and the love that binds us." We've talked about this type of issue before, as well. Essentially, it's a selfish response to denial. Why can't I have what I want? Of course, the standard protest is that wanting to have a relationship with family members is hardly selfish, and why should that relationship be altered just because of a difference in belief?

First, *halacha* doesn't force you to deny the "ties of family." In fact, it states quite clearly that a convert still has obligations to his or her biological parents. What occurs with conversion, however, is not just a change of belief, in the way that one changes clothes. Rather, there is a fundamental transformation. The convert gains a Jewish soul and becomes a different person. Spiritually, his biological parents are no longer his spiritual parents. (I'm not sure if the analogy to adoption is helpful here, but at least it points out the idea of a change in status: The adopted child's parents are no longer his or her biological parents.)

Halacha doesn't tell you to stop loving biological family members. If nothing else, you still have a responsibility to teach them the seven Noachide commandments, a corollary of which is honoring your parents. And one always must recognize the innate Godliness in all creation. More than this, though, *halacha* doesn't limit affection. What *halacha* does demand, however, is a change in action: Certain celebrations are off-limits, certain activities one can't attend, and so on. But these limitations exist "naturally": How many family events are missed because of distance or work? Further, nothing prevents the others from accommodating you as much as possible.

The deeper, harder issue, of course, occurs in a situation like yours, where the conversion affects children as well as parents. Even though everyone in the family is now Jewish, the children aren't obligated to sit *shiva*, nor do they inherit; all of the obligations (and privileges) that *halacha* demands of the Jewish child (or parent), it denies to these Jewish children (and their parent) because they and their mother converted after they were born.

Practically, of course, the effect is minimal: You're still responsible for raising them, educating them, making sure that they grow to a life of Torah, *chuppah*, and good deeds.

Undeniably, though, something isn't there. (It's hard to say that something's been lost if it was never really there to begin with.) There's nothing I or anyone can say to diminish the pain or its reality. That truth is sometimes painful makes it no less true; nor does its truth diminish the pain.

Just as a lost Jewish soul needed a home—you, so two other lost Jewish souls needed homes—David and Julie. One way or another, those souls had to be invested in a Jewish body. Think of the pain, struggle, and turmoil you and your Jewish soul went through to be reunited. If nothing else (and it's not a small thing, spiritually), you've made the journey home easier for them.

There's another point to be made here. Earlier we referred to the last Mishna of *Pirkei Avos*, "According to the painstaking effort is the reward." A more literal translation is, "According to the pain (itself) is the reward." This Mishna, which concludes and thus summarizes *Pirkei Avos*, is attributed to a man called Ben–Hey–Hey, who our sages tell us was a convert. ("Ben–Hey–Hey" wasn't his real name, but a nickname, indicating that he was a ben Abraham and a ben Sarah—both of whom had the letter "hey" added to their names.)

The Rebbe, in an interesting and intricate *sicha* [public discourse], discusses this Mishna. He points out that normally one is rewarded for the effort, the product, or the profit produced. What the Mishna is telling us, however, is that in certain cases there is a reward for the pain (or trouble) itself. This occurs when one accepts upon himself or herself some aspect of Torah or *mitzvos* for which there is no obligation. But since a Jew exists "only to serve God," at some level a Jew is always obligated to observe and increase in observance.

However, a non-Jew who converts (and at the time of the giving of the Torah, all Jews were converts) can so obligate himself or herself. Furthermore, because we will inevitably fail to observe the *halacha* in all its details, conversion also inevitably involves a degree of pain, both to the convert (as punishment) and to God, so to speak (since His will was not fulfilled exactly). Nevertheless, because the convert willingly accepts the obligation to learn Torah and observe *mitzvos*, the very pain involved itself generates a reward.

And this lesson—that a convert teaches and exemplifies more than any other—applies not only to every Jew, but is the essence and purpose of *Pirkei Avos*, the talmudic tractate of *chesed* [kindness].

I'm paraphrasing this *sicha* at length to tell you that while your pain is real, that very pain is part of your relationship with God—and the reward that comes from that relationship.

To return to the general tone of the letter: The feelings must be acknowledged and accepted; they cannot be allowed to control. (That itself isn't easy, and may be painful.) It's a question of priorities (as always): Are my *transient* feelings more important than acting according to the system and principles of Torah? That's what it comes down to, really—feelings versus principles.

And where does all this resentment lead you? To misplaced guilt. You feel guilty for having decided to become *frum*, because it makes demands and puts a strain on others; you feel guilty for having affected your husband by your actions; you feel guilty because your actions have affected your children; you feel guilty because you didn't feel up to making a *shiva* call; you even feel guilty about feeling guilty.

Where does this lead? To inaction, to the success of the *yetzer hara*. Everything you feel guilty about is something beyond your ability to change. Everything you feel guilty about prevents you from acting. Everything you feel guilty about denies fundamental principles of Judaism, particularly Divine Providence.

Does this mean that you shouldn't feel sad? Does this mean that you shouldn't regret mistakes, lost connections? Of course not. Sadness, or, more properly, bitterness, is important for self-evaluation and spiritual growth. Regret, as I mentioned, is an all-important first step of *teshuvah*.

But if you dwell on the feelings in the letters, then you're refusing to have lived your life, to accept God's rulership and to do the *mitzvos* you were given a Jewish soul to perform.

Having made a perhaps too lengthy response, I want to say that, obviously, you weren't paralyzed. Writing such letters is often cathartic; sometimes we just need a friend to listen, or a *mashpia* [counselor] who will let us cry.

Becoming Jewish, practicing the *mitzvos*, moving to a new city—all are traumatic events. It's understandable and normal to have conflicting feelings, to emotionally "backslide" on occasion, to just feel like an overwhelmed child.

But then, it's time to move on. And you did. Still, I'm sure that there were other difficulties, practical (as opposed to emotional) problems.

SZ: Yes, there were many practical difficulties; little things, mostly. For instance, when I first needed to use the *mikvah*, I had to ask a friend to explain the practical details: How do I pay? How do I get in? What if it is *Shabbos*? What do I need to take with me?

DK: I know that when you're first starting out, little things can seem huge. But these are, again, normal adjustments to a new experience. With practice, do they still seem so terrifying and overwhelming?

SZ: With practical issues, just asking about them and getting a few answers makes them seem far less threatening. Social issues sometimes have to resolve themselves. Entering into already-established circles of friends is hard, both for our children in school and for us in the community at large. I remember how hurt David was when he was the only boy in his class not invited to one classmate's *bobayom* [birthday party for a bar mitzvah boy]. And I remember feeling awfully left out when one person whom we had gotten to know—had even invited for *Shabbos* a couple of times—overlooked inviting us to a special *siyyum*. I'm not sure there is an easy solution. Everybody can't be invited to everything. Mostly I just try to keep reaching out, and keep hopeful that, as time goes on, friendships will grow.

DK: You're right—there isn't an easy solution. It's one of the hazards of being the "new kid on the block." The friendliness and acceptance of a community is not a function of its "frumkeit." You're probably right that the observant community needs to be more aware of the special needs of converts and the newly observant, more sensitive of their ignorance and social awkwardness. But then, for many, the influx of *baalei teshuvah* is a new phenomenon as well.

SZ: Sometimes questions revolve around community customs: Do the men wear a *kittel* on Rosh Hashanah or Yom Kippur? Do women come to *shul* on Friday night? While it's true that any of these can be resolved with a simple question, there is always some embarrassment at having to ask, especially when one is doing one's best to "fit in" and not be seen as a struggling *baal teshuvah*. It is a common worry: "If I ask too many questions, will I be branded as 'not *frum* enough' and find, for instance, that people won't feel comfortable eating with me?"

DK: Not in my experience. If the questions are of the honest "I-don't-know" variety, I don't see how that would present a problem. I still ask relatively simple "that-should-be-obvious" questions myself.

I understand the embarrassment and the need to fit in. I see it all the time in my classes. Frequently, students will ask me privately questions that I know others in the class would also like to ask. How does *Pirkei Avos* put it? "A bashful person can't learn."

Differentiate between questions of fact and practice on the one hand, and feelings and relations on the other, and I think that you would get rather the opposite reaction: Here's someone very concerned with observance and getting things right. Even though I know the answers to some of her questions, she might be "frummer" than me, because she's so particular about everything.

SZ: Nevertheless, the *"frum* enough" worry is a big one. It isn't just meals; we also see what goes on when people are trying to make a *shidduch* [find a marriage partner for someone]. Suddenly the operative word is *"yichus."* Is the person's family and ancestry religiously "correct"? This is probably one of the most painful aspects of Orthodoxy for me, because I know that it is an arena for which no *teshuvah*, no amount of learning, no amount of effort on my part, can ever atone. In some ways we can never be good enough.

DK: I know that some people make a social distinction between "FFB" (*frum*-from-birth) and "BT" (*baal teshuvah*), but *yichus* goes beyond a "religious correctness" (RC) issue.

I'm not belittling the problem, though I suspect it's as much a "networking" issue as it is a social one. And anyone who thinks that you can never be good enough obviously doesn't think that Onkelos, Rabbi Akiva, even King David, is good enough. Anyone who thinks that a convert, or a convert's child, can never be good enough, also thinks that he or she is better than Torah and *halacha*.

(Of course, parents have a responsibility to investigate a child's prospective partner, and that partner's family. Many factors determine compatibility, present and future; I would hope that "status issues" such as conversion, wealth, learning, and the like are examined from the perspective of goals and compatibility, not socially stigmatized into "good-enough" categories.)

I guess I have a different attitude toward the anxieties of fitting in.

Leaders, those who take responsibility for helping others become more observant (a responsibility incumbent upon every Jew), also have a responsibility to be there after someone has become observant. At some point, of course, the hand-holding stops (you have to rely on your own judgment about what you do in your own kitchen); but the connection, the relationship remains. So I figure that my being 'good enough' is also a reflection on my teacher; it's his or her responsibility as well.

SZ: Maybe all I'm asking is that we and our children be judged on the merits of who we are, not on who we are not. We are not all alike, but we are all family.

DK: Often people look at observant Jews as a monolith. They're not. There's a shared commitment to the truth of Torah (Revelation at Mount Sinai to Moses) and therefore to living according to *halacha* (broadly speaking, the Oral Torah, the application of Torah principles to daily life). Beyond that, there's a wide variety. And the essence of *Ahavas Yisroel* is respecting that variety (and, needless to say, the Jewish soul within the non-observant, as well).

SZ: By the way, I want to emphasize that the two incidents I mentioned earlier were isolated events occurring within a community whose members (including those involved in the incidents) are extremely warm, welcoming, and exemplary of just such *Ahavas Yisroel*. It has been a pleasure to live here; it is a wonderful place to which to "come home."

23
The Future

DK: We've had an interesting discussion about your journey. Even though this part of your story is over, as we've already mentioned, another story is just beginning. That's appropriate, since while Judaism finds verification in history, its purpose is in the future. I'm reminded of the famous *midrash* concerning the giving of the Torah. When God asked the Jewish people for guarantors, He did not accept the Patriarchs or even Moses and Aaron, the leaders of the time. He accepted the children.

The Torah is always cognizant of the significance of children. Regarding the Exodus, we are told to tell them its story (which we do at the Pesach seder). The *Shema*, the fundamental declaration of faith, contains within it the commands to love God and to teach Torah to one's children. Many stories of the sages emphasize their interest in and efforts to educate children. In Russia, under both the czars and the Communists, the battle was for the minds, hearts, and souls of the children.

As you said so poignantly, you didn't journey alone. You brought your children with you. Maybe we should conclude by talking about them. How did they adjust to the move, to their new status—to all

319

the changes that occurred just as they were preparing for a transformation of their own—to young adulthood?

SZ: David and Julie had been in their new schools now for a couple of months. They were adjusting quite well, despite the need to catch up with their classmates in Hebrew studies, and having longer school days.

Do you remember my experience with covering my hair? When I moved to Baltimore, it was so nice to see the other women covering their hair; I felt like I fit in. I'm sure it was that way for my children. Socially, they fit in. All those demands that had set them apart before now allowed them to join fully with their peer group.

In late November, David entered an essay contest sponsored by Etz Chaim. He wrote about a boy named Yaakov, but it was really his own story—from how it felt to be Jewish in a non-Jewish environment to how it felt to become *frum*. I'd like to share it with you.

TRUE FAITH

Very few people knew what happened to him in his everyday life. Everyone thought he was that weirdo who would never do anything fun. His life had been torn into five with false accusations that he didn't believe in God. He had very few understanding friends.

Yaakov was his name. Oh, everyone called him Jake, but he knew in his heart that his real name was Yaakov Moshe ben Aaron. He was a Jew, but sadly, not an observant one. He believed with perfect faith that Hashem was God. Fortunately, he would return to observant Judaism before his life was over.

One fateful day, his mother told him, "Jake, I've made a decision. This family will not buy stuff on *Shabbos* anymore." And it seemingly got worse, "No more driving. Shomer *Shabbos* (Observe Shabbat). No breaking the spirit of *Shabbos*."

At first, this seemed to be possibly one of the worst things that could happen to Jake. "Why can't you come over anymore on Saturdays?" asked his friends. Two words, "Religious reasons." Oddly enough, it made him feel better, that he was closer to Hashem, when he observed the *Shabbos* laws. He ignored the constant mockery of his classmates.

His family had started coming up to Baltimore a month or two after they had become shomer *Shabbos*. Yaakov didn't know it at the time, but he would know his classmates before he even thought about going to TA [Talmudical Academy]. He realized that if he was going to be frum, TA would be the only place for him to go. He would never complain whenever his family would take him on these Yom Tov (holiday) outings.

Back home, things seemed to be at their worst. Classmates would tease him for not going to Friday night and Saturday events. A few of his friends remained steadfast in friendship. He still thanks them today for their support. He went on a few overnights which were supposedly fun, but were not for Yaakov. "Why do you bring your own food?" had been a common question to him. "Why can't you eat a hamburger (unkosher) with us?" He responded by ordering a salad with a friend.

Yaakov would constantly go on NCSY [National Conference of Synagogue Youth] Shabbatons and he realized that fellow Jews together did not share the common air of distrust as he had been used to. They would lend, share, give and be friendly to each other all the time. Yaakov felt great at these Shabbatons and loved them.

All these events paved the way for him to become an observant Jew. He went to Camp Shoresh, got tutoring for TA, and moved up to Baltimore County. He entered TA and is still having a great time there. Does he like being Frum?

"Yes! By far the best thing to ever happen to me!"

DK: That's a beautiful essay. You and Joe must have been quite proud of him. And you, I know, breathed a sigh of relief.

SZ: I certainly did. David won second prize in the contest, but the story was a grand-prize-winner for me. At many points I had worried whether I was asking my family to pay too high a price for my "selfishness" in wanting to be Jewish; was my happiness costing them their own? This essay was a gift, an answer—not only to my questions, but also to my prayers.

DK: We'd discussed your children's responses a lot over the Internet while you were making your decision, then going through the learning process. I remember telling you to have faith in them; of course, there would be rough spots, but if presented with love and understanding, they'd accept the necessary enthusiastically.

SZ: You were right, too.

Not unexpectedly, the school calendar began to run our lives. It was nice not to have to juggle class schedules to accommodate Jewish holidays. School vacations now coincided with them. The kids even got a couple of days off at Chanukah.

Our celebration of Chanukah wasn't much different than it ever had been. We lit our menorahs, shared a few gifts, and ate homemade jelly doughnuts. Chanukah did, though, take on a different meaning than it had in the past. When we lived in Bowie, Chanukah was always treated like "what Jews celebrate instead of Christmas." In Baltimore, it was what the whole community was celebrating. Even the local shopping center celebrated only Chanukah. Again, it felt very good not to be isolated.

DK: I've seen that kind of "coming together," that sense of community without defensiveness, at the Chabad Chanukah celebrations. It's not just a public display of one's Jewishness, though that would be enough. Rather, it's a declaration of *Ahavas Yisroel*, a unity that breaks through the barriers of economics, philosophies and movements, and social strata.

While your children—and you!—were adjusting to life at a Jewish day school, I'm sure you found other outlets of Jewish activity.

SZ: Of course. I still had my Internet connections. By now, I was both asking questions and answering them. I had kept in contact with Y. Y. Kazen (of the Chabad Internet site), and he had begun to use me as a resource for those who wrote to him and either were prospective converts or were in situations that paralleled my own. I wondered whether I was really far enough along to be acting as a guide for others. I've learned since that "when one knows *aleph*, one teaches *aleph*."

DK: The Rebbe has emphasized that concept; we've talked about it. It's the premise behind being a lamplighter: The issue isn't my own level of knowledge or observance, but what I can do to help another Jew increase his or her level. More importantly, how can I help another Jew *b'gashmiyus* (materially) as well as *b'ruchniyus* (spiritually).

SZ: I don't always hear the end of the story. Sometimes, I was just a person at a crossroad, sharing what I knew about the paths that intersected there. Other times, I was a shoulder to cry on, someone who would listen. I remember how important that was for me along the way, and I wanted to try to give a little back. Often I would send copies of my responses back to Y.Y., mostly so that if I were to get seriously off-track in any of my responses, he could jump in and set me straight. Actually, that never happened, but a few of my responses did end up in the archives on conversion at the Chabad site.

DK: One of the strange things about the Internet is how things get circulated. I've gotten e-mail from people who have read something I posted and forgot about, but that someone else circulated. Anyway, your involvement is rather fitting. You've asked so many questions, you've got to know a few answers. And since you've asked the questions so well. . . .

SZ: I shared the story of my journey with many people on the Internet. Doing so forced me to look back and assess what had been lost or gained. Had I done the right thing? Was I "happy" now? What decisions did I make right—or wrong?

DK: So what are the answers? We've done this kind of assessment before—the "how would you answer them now" analysis. We may as well do it again, at the "end" of the story.

SZ: All the questions can be summed into one: Am I now traveling the path of truth, *emes*, for which I sought so long? When one follows the path of *emes*, one is happy, has done the right thing, and has immeasurably gained. Somehow, almost thirty years ago, I knew that there was a road of truth when I wrote in my journal:

> Pure Truth is a road not a man has trod.
> It is near and far and always great beyond him.
> It is the essence of the immanence of God.

I was close, but I was wrong. Truth is the road upon which we are obligated to travel, the path that is as near to us as every choice we make. It is what reveals Godliness in this world. It is what brings us close to God.

DK: Truth is also the attribute of Jacob (as kindness is the attribute of Abraham, and discipline is the attribute of Isaac). As such, it is the middle path, combining the other two. In Jewish mysticism, truth is related to, and sometimes synonymous with, beauty or harmony. Love and fear combine to provide a path, to connect what's below with what's Above.

We could write a book on this subject, but when the sages say, *"Torah Emes"* [Torah is Truth], one thing they mean is that "what reveals Godliness in this world [and] what brings us close to God" [to quote you] can occur only through Torah—and Torah in the broad sense of the Oral Torah, *halacha*, Chassidism, and the like.

SZ: And without that truth? Never was I so unhappy, so despondent, as when I did not know who God was and what was my relationship to Him. Never have I been so happy, in the deepest sense of the word, than now, as I walk along this road of Torah. It is both home and the way home. I am no longer looking for new paths—only to traverse this one as best I can.

Once you told me that what we want most for those we love is not happiness, but meaning. I think that, ultimately, they are one and the same.

DK: Ultimately, yes, because true happiness is not the satiation of desire, but the sense of meaningfulness that comes from doing beyond oneself, literally doing things for God's sake. In hasidic terms, it is making this physical world a dwelling place for Godliness.

If we knew that an honored and distinguished guest was coming, would we not see to every detail, no matter how mundane or otherwise beneath us? All the more so if we were preparing our homes for our parents, or a king, to live in. Then, the most menial cleaning task would be joyful, significant, and, yes, meaningful.

SZ: For me, unhappiness was being alone in the universe, of having no purpose or meaning. As a Jew, I know that God, the Creator of the billions of stars and the tiniest subnuclear particles, has said to me, "You have a task and responsibilities. I have chosen you, and I have given you meaningful choice. Now, choose life. Choose Me, choose My ways, choose Torah."

Am I happy? Yes. Am I always full of joy, of *simcha*? No—but, as I said, I'm working on it (it's just up the road). Do I miss some of the things I left behind? Sometimes. Would I trade them for what I have now? Would I take a very different path if I "knew then what I know now"? Not in a million lifetimes.

Have I made mistakes along the way, even after finding this path? Plenty, but even from those I have learned. If the "me" of now could advise the "me" of the past few years, I think I'd tell myself to worry less and to trust God more. I'd tell myself to be more concerned with the steps I am taking *now*, and less concerned with how I'd stumbled in the past or what obstacles I might chance upon in the future.

For all its turns and dips, inclines and embankments, this *is* the road by which God has brought me to where I am, taught me what I know, given me what I have. And I have so much. Materially: family, home, community . . . so much. And spiritually, even more: a connection to the Infinite; and, through Torah, a way to comprehend it and live it.

DK: What more do we have to discuss? You have taken us to Chanukah 1994—an appropriate holiday, since it's about rededication, education, and conquering the forces of assimilation. You and your children have been Jewish—truly Jewish—for about six months.

There was one more milestone that brought closure to your journey.

SZ: Yes. With the beginning of 1995, we were quickly approaching just that milestone: David would become bar mitzvah in May of that year.

DK: Do you remember writing about yourself as being a member of the family who suddenly was asked to leave? What better event than your son's bar mitzvah to confirm in your own mind that, indeed, you were completely and irrevocably welcomed home?

SZ: It seemed so. There was a real sense of completion. At the same time we looked forward to the event, though, we also worried about it, wondering how much David could reasonably take on and what were the social protocols in the community. We turned to those who should know—Rabbi Weinreb, the *Rav* of our shul, and Rabbi and Mrs. Field, who, with their many sons, had some practical experience in such things. Both told us that we could do whatever was comfort-able for David and for us, from a quiet Monday-morning *aliyah* to a catered affair.

David wanted to read Haftorah, so he began studying with a tutor every week. We began making the other plans: A *Shabbos* kiddush in *shul* so that we could share our simcha with the congregation; a *bobayom*, a meal with his friends and rebbe, at home; and, finally, a reception in New York to accommodate the many relatives who still live there. We kept each as simple as possible. Celebrations are im-portant, but I felt strongly that they should not overshadow the mean-ingfulness of the event.

DK: I agree. I don't think that the size of the celebration has anything to do with its meaningfulness. Rather, the critical point is whether the celebration marks a beginning as well as an end, whether it's an achievement as well as a show.

SZ: The *bobayom* was first. David's Hebrew birthday conveniently fell on a Sunday (Mother's Day). With rented tables and chairs, we man-aged to fit over forty people in the room. Most were David's class-mates, all dressed in dark suits and many sporting black hats, as well-behaved as they were dressed. We were truly impressed. Rabbi Weinreb came, as did David's rebbe from school. During the meal, each shared some words of Torah with the boys, and David and his father also spoke. I remember David's speech the best: He explained that now that he was personally responsible for doing the *mitzvos*, they were much more meaningful to him, just as fruit tastes much sweeter to the person who has planted and watered and cared for it. A famil-iar lesson: "According to the effort is the reward." It is a lesson that I hope he carries with him throughout life.

DK: A lesson that, from what we discussed a little while ago, should also be particularly significant to him.

SZ: Yes, both he and Julie had persevered through a painstaking pe-riod to get where they were. I think that David was expressing, in his own way, the value of the challenges, that, as you paraphrased from the Rebbe's *sicha*, "the obligation to learn Torah and observe *mitzvos*, the very pain involved itself generates a reward."

David was called for an *aliyah* and read *maftir* and Haftorah at Shomrei Emunah on the *Shabbos* of *parsha* [weekly Torah reading] Bechukosai. We had few relatives there—just Joe's parents and two distant cousins who live in Baltimore. The Fields walked two miles to join us. That day, the community congregation was also our family, and being with them brought its own special *simcha*.

DK: Indeed. That *parsha*, it seems to me, was also particularly appropriate, given the circumstances surrounding the bar mitzvah. It starts with, "If you follow [literally, 'go in'] my statutes," which refers specifically to the laws of the Torah beyond human logic or societal conventions. These are the commands that can be only "because God said so" laws. And isn't that the path of Abraham and Sarah?

SZ: Yes. And it is the path of those who become their children, as every convert does.

Early in the service, there was a power outage, leaving the only light in the auditorium-sized room coming from some narrow windows in the back of the women's section, which made it difficult to read the *siddurim* [prayerbooks], let alone the Torah. The *baal kria* [person reading the Torah] *layened* [read] beautifully, despite the environment. The *aliyos* went well. David was called for *maftir*. We held our breath.

We needn't have. David read, darkness and all, more beautifully than we had ever heard in his many evenings of practice at home. To say that we were proud is an understatement.

Julie had done an admirable job of handing out little bags of candy to all the women. After the final blessing of the Haftorah, we all rained our "wishes" for a sweet life on David.

The rabbi spoke briefly about David and our family and gave him, as he does each boy who becomes bar mitzvah, a siddur, a blessing, and an assignment for study. Yet it was what happened next that was the most memorable part of the *drasha*.

Baltimore had recently lost a most special and beloved Rabbi. Rabbi Yehuda Naftoli Mandelbaum, *olav hashalom*, had been a devoted rebbe to children, and a counselor to many in the community. He had had a special sensitivity to the needs of those who turned to him for guidance, whether they were students looking for guidance on a yeshiva or adults looking to reconcile a family difficulty. One rabbi who knew him well compared him to a star, which goes on shining even during the day, when no one notices. Rabbi Mendelbaum had a quiet, but major, effect on many lives in ways both great and small.

Acknowledging that *Shabbos* was not a time for a *hesped* [eulogy], Rabbi Weinreb did share with us lessons from the greatness of Rabbi Mandelbaum's life. What happened that morning was no coincidence. At the first mention of Rabbi Mandelbaum's name, the lights began to flicker back on. First the *ner tamid* [eternal light] above the ark lit up; then the whole room filled with light. Somehow I sensed that this *tzaddik*, whom I had never met, had also come to my son's bar mitzvah. It was a special day in many ways.

DK: I understand exactly what you mean.

SZ: If we lacked for relatives at the *shul*, we did not lack them at the reception in New York. We saw many family members whom we had not seen in years, a number of whom had attended Joe's bar mitzvah almost three decades before. The affair was modest. We had a photographer and a keyboardist. David had asked us to see that there was no mixed dancing, a restriction that had never been the rule in previous family gatherings. We agreed, but had no idea how to pull it off without offending someone. Ah, but God sometimes sends angels. In our case, it was our favorite "almost-relatives," Susan and Ira Schwartz. Susan and Ira, also observant, are no strangers to such situations. Susan told me that she'd take care of it—and she did. She coached the keyboardist on a few carefully chosen words, and, the next thing I knew, we were all dancing away, men over there, women over here.

We had a great time.

DK: I've found that, if handled with respect and tact, most people are willing to accept the conditions and follow the rules. Insisting on *halacha* can sometimes create tension. But by being courteous and polite, many socially awkward situations can become a vehicle for learning and the strengthening of relationships. (Of course, there are times, unfortunately, when the tension simply has to be accepted; at those times, we have to find other ways to reach out.)

SZ: We had another visitor to the reception. Y.Y. Kazen stopped by to meet us. It was one of those wonderful opportunities to meet someone with whom I'd corresponded so many times over the Internet.

The events were almost over. David, now bar mitzvah, had accepted for himself the privilege and obligations of being a Jew, affirming the actions that the *Bais Din* had taken on his behalf almost a year before. He shared with all gathered the same words he had shared at the *bobayom*. His grandfather, obviously proud of both grandchildren, spoke next, welcoming family and offering David words of encouragement.

Joe followed. He had seen how far David had come in such a short time, with the stresses of moving, re-establishing his whole social structure, and needing to learn so much. Yet, David had done it; he had accomplished his goal. Now Joe counseled David that, although he needed to recognize his limitations, he should never set his aspirations too low.

Then it was my turn.

Words are never quite sufficient, even words that fill a book. And I had only words for a few minutes, but they were words forged in the fire of my heart.

As I spoke, I was keenly aware that this time was both a beginning and an end, a first chapter and a last:

David,

I thought a lot of what to say to you today. Mothers are like that, I guess. We see our son becoming a man and our thoughts rush back to the past. I remember when you were only a baby—so tiny—the crib dwarfed you. With your birth I remember thinking that I had fulfilled my destiny in life, my reason for being: To bring forth a new life, a new soul to continue the chain of Jewish life of which I found myself a part. But I was wrong.

You see, David, it is not we, your parents, who give life and give a soul, but God, Who does. We are only privileged to be His partners in the process. Birth was not the end of the task, but the beginning. Childhood was a time for growing, for becoming, for learning with the openness and imagination that children have in so much abundance. What you have gained from childhood you now take with you as you become a man, accepting upon yourself all the new demands of life and Torah that are given to you today.

It is said that the word "Ivri," Hebrew, means "from the other side." I've often thought about that phrase, and in my mind have always pictured a scene of two great, green pastures separated by a mighty river. On one side is Judaism, Yiddishkeit, and on the other side—everyone and everything else.

Now, some can cross the river to Yiddishkeit over bridges that their parents built. They have only, it seems, to choose to walk across. Others must challenge the water, plunging to its depths and emerging on the other side.

But it is not enough merely to cross the river, to stand on this side, to be a Jew. There is more than just a green field over here—there is the Mountain—the Mountain of Holiness. Every mitzvah you observe is a step up the mountain, and it is your task, our task, as Jews, to climb it.

But how? How do you scale this mountain whose loftiness is beyond mortal comprehension? This mountain will challenge you. As you climb you will encounter new, beautiful, awesome and breathtaking sights, yet at times the ascent will be painfully difficult, exhausting, seemingly impossible. You can never climb this mountain alone, so, David, I want to tell you how you can climb it.

First, you must know that you are not the first to climb the mountain. Others have gone before. Others have built paths. Above you on the mountain are the Sages and Tzaddikim. With their teachings they have left you ropes onto which you can seize. Hold fast to them, pull yourself up with them. Around you is community, rebbeim, teachers. Reach out to them for balance, for perspective. They can often help you find the handhold which is within your reach, but which you cannot from your current viewpoint, see. As your family, we are going to be behind you, pushing you onward when no one else will.

But there is one other thing, without which you can never climb this mountain, not even take the first step. It is Torah. Torah is your strength and your life. Hold it fast, for more than you carry it up the mountain, it will carry you.

In your backpack I have placed what little a mother can: Love, and hope and what blessing I might be permitted to give:

As you go from child to man, may you go from strength to strength, from simcha to simcha. May you and your children climb high on the mountain, and carve paths and give help to others who make the journey after you. And may Hashem guard you every step of the way.

Index

About the Authors

Susan (Shoshana) Zakar, a native of Spokane, Washington, lives in Baltimore with her husband and two children. A graduate of Western Washington State College, she worked with the Department of Defense as a linguist and computer systems scientist for thirteen years. Subsequently she has been an active volunteer in both the community and synagogue. Susan Zakar is a familiar presence on the Internet, maintaining the world wide web pages for Jews for Judaism, Havienu L'Shalom, a "Virtual Shul," and local Jewish organizations. She is frequently called upon to offer online support and guidance to others who are in the process of converting or becoming more observant. She and her husband now run a web-design business.

Dovid Y. B. Kaufmann is the director of campus activities for Chabad Lubavitch of Louisiana, and spends much of his time tutoring and counseling students. He received a Ph.D. in English literature from Tulane University, where he is also an adjunct professor of Jewish Studies. His other publications include *The Silent Witness*, a novel, *Besuros HaGeulo*, translated and edited with Rabbi Heschel Greenberg, and articles in *Philosophical Quarterly*, *Studies in the Novel*, and *Religion and Literature*. Dovid Kaufmann also scripts audio lessons on Moshiach and Redemption, and is a regular contributor to *Beis Moshiach* magazine. He resides in New Orleans with his wife, Nechama, and six children.

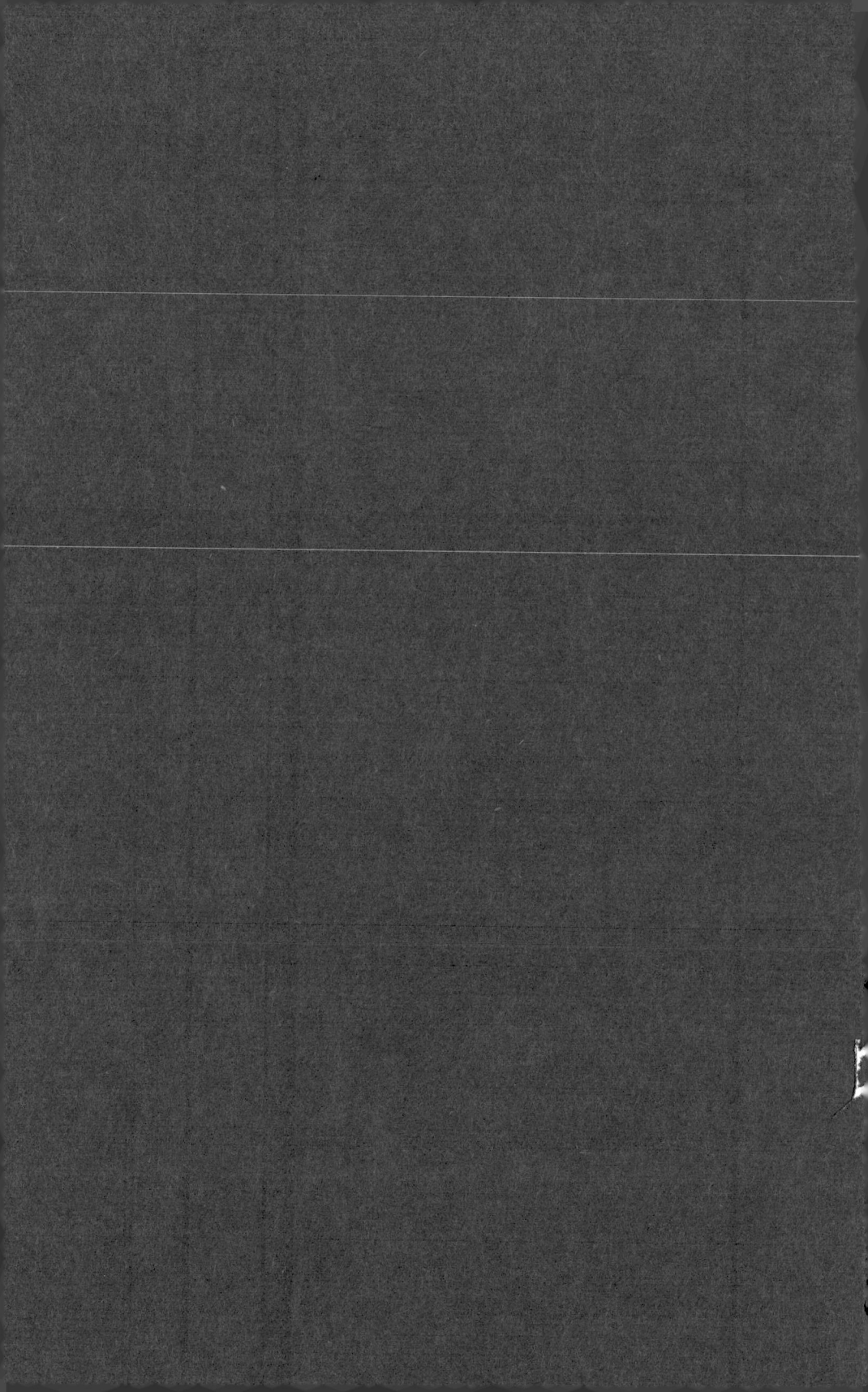